The Vegetarian Silver Spoon

The Vegetarian Silver Spoon

Classic &
Contemporary
Italian Recipes

6 Introduction
9 Legend

10

Snacks & Small Plates

48

Breads & Pizzas

174

Pasta, Dumplings, & Crêpes

228

Vegetable Tarts & Pastries

84

Salads
&
Vegetable
Sides

138

Soups
&
Stews

268

Grains,
Gratins,
&
Stuffed
Vegetables

318

Sweets
&
Desserts

354 Recipe Lists
366 Index

Introduction

What does it mean to cook vegetarian Italian food? Italian cuisine has a rich tradition of vegetable dishes, notably *primi* and *contorni*, the salads, soups, and side dishes of a classic Italian meal. There is also the beloved *cucina povera*, a rustic style of cooking that celebrates resourcefulness, and ingredients that are repurposed or already in the home kitchen. While a celebratory meal might focus on meat for the main course, the Italian diet has never centered on meat. Italian home-style cooking more often revolves around substantial vegetarian dishes like gratins or stews.

Italians have traditionally focused on grains, legumes, tubers, and nuts in various forms—reflecting the diversity of regional Italian agriculture. Familiar ingredients such as pasta, tomatoes, and herbs are all naturally present when defining Italian cooking, vegetarian or otherwise. Additionally, there is a vast array of staples that have deep historical roots and are perhaps even more beloved by locals than dishes that have made Italy famous around the world. In northeast Italy, for example, there are *canederli* (bread dumplings) or polenta, rather than pasta, while in the southwest you'll find potatoes and peppers are considered the most central items on any table.

The Vegetarian Silver Spoon features more than 200 vegetarian recipes, both classics from the Italian culinary canon and dishes featuring contemporary ingredients. They are all meat-free dishes that can stand alone as a meal or be combined into multiple courses for a more formal occasion. You could start a meal with an *aperitivo* of Tomato Rice Fritters (page 35), then move into a Fennel and Artichoke Salad (page 92), then a Quinoa Torte (page 288). Or you could have a simple but substantial meal of *infarinata*, a dish of polenta with kale and beans (see page 304). Dessert might be Chestnut Pudding (page 345), or Seeded Spice Cake (page 328).

In the coming chapters there are recipes that celebrate vegetarian eating through through the intersection of tradition and contemporary influences. Beyond an introduction to the vegetarian and vegan dishes that are part of the Italian canon, there are also ideas for integrating new ingredients into classic formulas—using tofu in place of cheese, for example, or adding seitan or avocado to turn a side dish into a more filling main course. These recipes are beloved favorites, but updated, and many of them make special use of ingredients from around the world that are becoming more common in contemporary Italian home cooking. Whole grain flours, including spelt, buckwheat, and even chickpea, are used in pastas, crepes, and tarts to make them more nutritionally complete when served as a single course. Salads and breads feature sprouted legumes, nuts, and seeds.

This collection truly represents the best of both classic and contemporary Italian vegetarian food. Italian culinary tradition, where fresh vegetables and grains are the stars of a meal, anchors all of these ingredients and recipes. Regional identity and seasonality are emphasized, and meals have a progression from delicate to more substantial flavors. Chapters are organized by dish, moving from lighter to heavier, and recipe notes offer suggestions for how to make recipes as main courses, or pare something down to serve as an *aperitivo*. Additionally, each recipe features a set of icons that easily identify whether a recipe is vegan, gluten-free, fast and easy, or based on few ingredients. There are also markers indicating "contemporary tastes."

The best vegetarian food celebrates seasonality, bounty, flavor, and variety—all hallmarks of Italian cuisine. These recipes are satisfying and exciting for any home cook interested in exploring Italian food and creating simple, but elevated vegetable dishes.

Legend

(DF)   Dairy-Free

(GF)   Gluten-Free

(VG)   Vegan

(CT)   Contemporary Tastes

(30)   30 minutes or less

(5)   5 ingredients or fewer

Snacks & Small Plates

The appetizer—*antipasto* in Italian—was introduced by the ancient Romans as the first course for sumptuous banquets. Its role was to stimulate the palate and prepare the guest for subsequent courses. It also has a playful function, associated with the colors and varieties of the ingredients used. And if it is prepared in a balanced way, it can find its rightful place among the courses of a vegetarian meal.

Something to whet your appetite

A traditional Italian meal always begins with a small appetizer or snack, followed by an additional two or three courses of increasing size. Hot or cold, appetizers must be attractive and have a distinctive flavor—without, however, overwhelming the flavors of subsequent courses. They must be delicious, but never heavy.

A matter of portions

Some appetizers were born as such. Many others dishes of various types, however, can be adapted into excellent vegetarian starters by simply reducing their portion sizes. Some examples? Quiches, flans, and savory tarts, but also salads, soups, omelets, and raw vegetable preparations.

From a small taste to a strong dish

In vegetarian cooking, an appetizer may simply be raw vegetables dressed with extra virgin olive oil and vinegar or lemon juice. More elaborate dishes may feature grains, legumes, eggs, cheese, and other protein-rich foods such as tofu, tempeh, and seitan; in these cases, the appetizer dish can replace a first or second course, if desired.

Start slow

It is good to eat starters slowly and to wait for ten minutes or so before moving on to the next course, so the sensation of satiety can be sent by the stomach to the brain. This helps us arrive at the main course with a reduced sense of hunger. Vegetable-based appetizers—like crudités served with a tasty yogurt–based sauce—are especially good for this, as vegetables are rich in fiber, which has high satiating power.

Lots of great ideas for the table

The classic crudité platter never goes out of fashion. Alongside this, however, local traditions and the imaginations of chefs have provided an abundance of other vegetarian starters.

Dips

Ubiquitous on party tables and at happy hour, dips are prepared by blending vegetables and cheeses with oil, salt and pepper (or other spices such as curry or cumin), and aromatic herbs and served with crudités, crackers, breadsticks, or tortilla chips (crisps).

Mousses and pâtés

Sweet mousses are perhaps better known than their savory counterparts, but vegetable, legume, or cheese versions are just as tasty. The ingredients are puréed until airy (mousse means "foam" in French), then refrigerated until set, and are usually served cold. Pâtés, on the other hand, are normally made with chopped ingredients mixed with butter (or nondairy cream) and spices, and refrigerated until set.

Aspics and terrines

The essential ingredient in aspic is broth mixed with a thickener, such as agar-agar (a plant-based thickener derived from algae). The broth mixture is poured into a loaf pan or other mold over chopped ingredients, and the whole preparation is then refrigerated until the broth has gelled and holds its form when unmolded. Terrines take their name from the container in which they are prepared. The ingredients are coarsely chopped and layered in a terrine, which is then set in a roasting pan partially filled with water (a setup called a bain-marie) and baked.

Bruschetta and canapés

Bruschetta are small slices of homemade bread that have been toasted, rubbed with garlic, and drizzled with oil, seasoned with salt and pepper, then topped with other ingredients. Canapés, known in Italy as *tartine*, are slices of bread, cut into various shapes, on which other ingredients, such as sauces, pâtés, cheese, or vegetables, are spread or layered.

Salads and flans

Starting a meal with a mixed salad pleases the palate and offers nutritional benefits: fiber helps you feel full, while vegetables and fruit, eaten raw, activate the metabolism, helping the body better process fats. Flans and savory custards—*sformato* in Italian—are prepared with various ingredients (vegetables, béchamel sauce, breadcrumbs, eggs), placed in a ramekin or other baking dish, and baked or cooked in a bain-marie.

The ingredients to always have on hand

Much better than the predictable bowls of olives and chips (crisps), there is a great variety of ingredients that, on their own, make great snacks for a vegetarian cocktail hour.

Tofu

Tofu is a versatile ingredient because it can absorb the flavors of the ingredients with which it is mixed. It comes in a variety of firmnesses. The softest variety, called silken tofu, can be puréed in a blender with basil, oregano, mint, or thyme to make an aromatic herbed spread, which can be served on toasted bread or with crudités for dipping.

Nuts

Walnuts, hazelnuts, almonds, pistachios, and peanuts—nuts are an important source of protein, minerals, and "good" unsaturated fats, which help fight cholesterol. Oily seeds, rich in fiber, antioxidants, fats, and trace elements, are just as beneficial. Pumpkin seeds and sunflower seeds are excellent as a snack on their own, while other seeds (sesame, flaxseed/linseed, fennel) impart their flavor to crackers, breadsticks, and other snacks.

Chips (crisps)

Root vegetable chips (crisps) are ideal to lighten and give color to an appetizer spread. Beets (beetroot), celeriac, parsnips, sunchokes (Jerusalem artichokes), daikon, carrots—almost all root vegetables can be baked and transformed into this crunchy snack.

Edamame and seaweed

A typical ingredient in Japanese cuisine, edamame are young soybeans, usually boiled or steamed for a few minutes and served lightly salted. As well as being crunchy and tasty, they contain lots of magnesium, potassium, and other minerals and vitamins, and are especially high in protein (1 cup/155 g provides an incredible 17 g of protein). Dried sheets of nori seaweed, marinated in soy sauce or drizzled with wasabi, are another delightful snack, and energizing, too, as nori contains abundant calcium, iron, phosphorus, magnesium, and amino acids.

Marinated Eggplant

Melanzane marinate

- 1 lb 5 oz (600 g) eggplant (aubergines), cut into ¼-inch-thick (0.5 cm) slices
- ¾ cup (175 ml) olive oil
- 1 chile, seeded and chopped
- 3 cloves garlic, finely chopped
- 1 tablespoon capers, drained, rinsed, and chopped
- 10 mint leaves, chopped
- Salt and pepper

Preparation Time: 45 minutes plus 6 hours marinating
Cooking Time: 25 minutes
Serves: 4

Put the eggplant (aubergine) slices in a colander, sprinkle with salt, and let drain for about 30 minutes.

Heat a heavy-bottomed nonstick frying pan over high heat. Rinse the eggplant slices, pat dry, and brush with some of the olive oil. Working in batches if necessary, add the eggplant to the frying pan and cook until golden brown on both sides.

In a small bowl, mix together the chile, garlic, capers, and mint and season with salt and pepper.

Make a layer of eggplant slices in a salad bowl, sprinkle with 1 tablespoon of the chile mixture, and continue making layers until all the ingredients have been used. Pour over the remaining oil and let marinate in a cool place for at least 6 hours before serving with some of the olive oil.

Trio of Dips: Eggplant, Pea, and Robiola Cheese

Tre creme di melanzane, piselli e robiola all'arancia

- 2 round eggplants (aubergines)
- 8 Taggiasca or Niçoise olives, pitted
- 1 tablespoon salt-cured capers, rinsed
- 1 clove garlic
- Handful of basil leaves
- 2 cups (300 g) shelled fresh peas
- 5 tablespoons (75 ml) extra virgin olive oil
- 1 heaping tablespoon tahini
- Leaves from 3 sprigs mint
- Pinch of ground cumin
- 7 oz (200 g) robiola cheese
- Grated zest of ½ orange, plus a few strips of zest for garnish
- ¾ oz (20 g) Pecorino Romano cheese, grated
- ¼ cup (10 g) chopped chives
- Whole-grain crackers, toast, crudités, and/or small breadsticks, for serving
- Salt and black pepper

Preparation Time: 15 minutes plus resting time
Cooking Time: 45 minutes
Serves: 4

Preheat the oven to 350°F (180°C).

Prick the eggplants (aubergines) with a toothpick, place them on a sheet pan, and bake for about 30 minutes, or until they have collapsed and their flesh is soft. Remove from the oven and let cool.

Halve the eggplants and scoop the flesh into a strainer set over a bowl. Press the flesh with a spatula to squeeze out any water, then transfer the flesh to a blender. Add the olives, capers, garlic, and basil and blend until smooth. Transfer the eggplant dip to a serving bowl and set aside. Clean the blender jar.

Bring a small pot of salted water to a boil. Add the peas and cook for 10 to 15 minutes, until tender, then drain them and let cool.

Transfer the peas to the blender and add 2 tablespoons of the olive oil, the tahini, mint, cumin, and a pinch of salt. Blend until smooth. Transfer the pea dip to a serving bowl and set aside. Clean the blender jar.

In the blender, combine the robiola, the remaining 3 table-spoons oil, the grated orange zest, pecorino, and a pinch of salt. Blend briefly to combine. Add the chives and blend until well combined and smooth. Transfer the robiola dip to a serving bowl. Sprinkle with some pepper and the strips of orange zest.

Serve the trio of dips with crackers, toast, crudités, and/or small breadsticks.

Sprouted Chickpea Hummus

Hummus di ceci germogliati

- 1½ cups (200 g) sprouted chickpeas (see note below)
- Grated zest of ½ lemon
- Juice of 1 lemon, strained
- 4 to 5 tablespoons (60 to 75 ml) extra virgin olive oil, plus more as needed
- 2 tablespoons tahini
- Pinch of salt
- 1 hot red chile, seeded and very finely chopped
- 1 clove garlic, coarsely grated

Preparation Time: 20 minutes
Cooking Time: 5 minutes
Serves: 4

Bring a large pot of water to a boil. Add the chickpeas and blanch for 1 minute. Drain and let cool, then transfer them to a food processor.

Add the lemon zest, lemon juice, olive oil, tahini, and salt and process until well combined and smooth. Add the chile and garlic and process to incorporate.

Transfer the hummus to a serving bowl and drizzle with oil. Serve.

To sprout the chickpeas, place them in a bowl, add cold water to cover, and let soak for 24 hours. Drain and rinse them in a colander, then set the colander over a bowl and cover the top with a plate. Set aside at room temperature, out of direct sunlight, until they begin to sprout, at least 48 hours; dampen them twice a day.

Cannellini and Black Bean Hummus

Hummus di cannellini e fagioli neri

- 1 spring onion
- 8¾ oz (250 g) beets (beetroot), steamed, peeled, and chopped
- ⅔ cup (100 g) canned cannellini beans, drained and rinsed
- 3½ tablespoons full-fat Greek yogurt
- Juice of 1 lemon
- 1 teaspoon brown rice miso paste
- 1 (14 oz/400 g) can black beans, drained and rinsed
- 3 tablespoons extra virgin olive oil
- Leaves from 1 small bunch cilantro (fresh coriander)
- Vegetable crudités, for serving
- Salt

Preparation Time: 15 minutes
Cooking Time: 5 minutes
Serves: 4

Bring a medium pot of salted water to a boil. Add the spring onion and cook for 5 minutes, then drain and let it dry on paper towels.

In a food processor, combine the beets (beetroot), cannellini beans, yogurt, half the lemon juice, the miso, and a pinch of salt. Process until smooth and well combined. Transfer the cannellini bean dip to a serving bowl and set aside. Wash the food processor bowl.

Coarsely chop the spring onion and put it in the food processor. Add the black beans, the remaining lemon juice, the olive oil, a few cilantro (fresh coriander) leaves, and a pinch of salt. Process until smooth and well combined. Transfer the black bean dip to a serving bowl.

Garnish the bean dips with cilantro and serve with vegetable crudités alongside.

To make miso, soybeans are fermented with salt, a fungus called *koji*, and sometimes grains such as rice, barley, or rye, then ground into a paste. Miso is rich in vitamins, protein, and minerals, and it must always be added to recipes at the end of the cooking time, as heat can alter its nutritional qualities.

Trio of Dips: Red Lentil, Fava Bean, and Chickpea

Creme di lenticchie, fave fresche e ceci

- 1 cup (200 g) dried split red lentils, rinsed
- 1 (¾-inch/2 cm) piece fresh ginger, peeled and grated
- 1 clove garlic, smashed, peeled, and halved
- Zest and juice of 1 orange
- 1 tablespoon tahini
- 5 tablespoons (75 ml) extra virgin olive oil
- 1 heaping teaspoon sweet paprika
- 2 cups (300 g) shelled fresh fava (broad) beans
- 3½ tablespoons full-fat Greek yogurt
- 4 or 5 mint leaves, plus more for garnish
- 2 lemons
- Pinch of cayenne pepper
- 1 (14 oz/400 g) can chickpeas, drained and rinsed
- Pinch of ground cumin
- Handful of cilantro (fresh coriander) leaves
- Salt
- Whole wheat (wholemeal) bread, toasted, or whole-grain crackers, for serving

Preparation Time: 30 minutes
Cooking Time: 30 minutes
Serves: 4

Put the lentils in a medium saucepan, add 2 cups (500 ml) water, and bring to a boil. Cook for 15 minutes, then drain the lentils and let cool.

Transfer the lentils to a food processor and add the ginger, ½ garlic clove, orange zest, orange juice, tahini, 2 tablespoons of the olive oil, ½ teaspoon of the paprika, and a pinch of salt. Process until smooth and well combined, then pour the purée into a serving bowl and sprinkle with the remaining ½ teaspoon paprika. Set the red lentil dip aside.

Bring a large pot of water to a boil. Add the fava (broad) beans and cook for 5 to 6 minutes, then drain them and let cool. Remove the beans from their skins and put them in the food processor. Add the yogurt, mint, the juice of ½ lemon, the cayenne, and a pinch of salt and process until smooth and well combined. Transfer the fava (broad) bean dip to a serving bowl and set aside.

Place the chickpeas in a clean kitchen towel and rub gently to remove their skins; discard the skins and transfer the chickpeas to the food processor. Add the remaining garlic, remaining 3 tablespoons oil, the juice of the remaining 1½ lemons, the cumin, and a pinch of salt and process until smooth and well combined. Transfer the chickpea dip to a serving bowl.

Sprinkle the lentil dip with a few mint leaves and the chickpea dip with a handful of cilantro (fresh coriander) leaves. Serve the dips with toasted whole wheat (wholemeal) bread or whole-grain crackers.

For a vegan dish, replace the yogurt in the fava (broad) bean dip with the same quantity of silken tofu or natural soy yogurt. Split red lentils do not need to be soaked before cooking; they are low in fat and rich in iron and vegetable protein.

Bruschettas with Kale, Tomato, and White Beans

Bruschette con cavolo nero, pomodoro e fagioli

- 311 oz (300 g) Tuscan kale (cavolo nero), stemmed and cut into strips
- ⅔ cup (150 ml) extra virgin olive oil
- 4 ripe tomatoes on the vine
- Pinch of dried oregano
- 4 or 5 basil leaves, chopped
- 1⅓ cups (200 g) cooked cannellini beans
- 4 cloves garlic
- 4 sage leaves
- 6 slices Tuscan bread
- Salt and black pepper

Preparation Time: 25 minutes
Cooking Time: 20 minutes
Serves: 4

Bring a large pot of salted water to a boil. Add the kale leaves and cook for 5 to 6 minutes. Using tongs, transfer the kale to a colander to drain. Transfer to a bowl, sprinkle with a pinch of salt, and drizzle with ¼ cup (60 ml) of the olive oil. Cover to keep warm.

Return the water to a boil, add the tomatoes, and blanch for 30 seconds. Drain and let cool slightly. Peel and seed the tomatoes, then cut the flesh into cubes and transfer to a small bowl. Sprinkle with the oregano, basil, and a pinch of salt, then drizzle with 3 tablespoons of the oil. Set aside.

In a small saucepan, combine the beans, 1 garlic clove, the sage, the remaining 3 tablespoons oil, and a ladleful of water. Cook over low heat for 10 minutes. Discard the garlic and the sage, then sprinkle generously with pepper.

Toast the bread. Halve the remaining 3 garlic cloves and rub the cut sides over the bread, then halve each slice of bread.

Arrange the bread on a serving platter. Top four pieces with the kale, four with the tomatoes, and the final four with the beans.

For an alternative topping, in a medium frying pan, heat ¼ cup (60 ml) extra virgin olive oil over medium heat. Chop 3½ oz (100 g) seitan and add it to the pan, along with 1 clove garlic, 1 teaspoon chopped capers, a pinch of salt, and a drop of vin santo wine, then cook for 10 minutes.

Watercress Tartines

Tartine al crescione

- 4 hard-boiled eggs, peeled and chopped
- ¼ cup (60 ml) mayonnaise
- Juice of 1 lemon, strained
- 1 bunch watercress, coarsely chopped, plus more for garnish
- 4 to 8 slices white bread, crusts removed
- Salt and pepper

Preparation Time: 25 minutes
Serves: 4

In a large bowl, stir together the hard-boiled eggs, mayonnaise, and lemon juice. Season with salt and pepper and stir in the watercress. Cut the slices of bread in half and spread the mixture over them, dividing it evenly. Place the tartines on a platter, cover, and refrigerate until ready to serve. Just before serving, garnish with watercress sprigs.

Sunflower and Poppyseed Crackers

Sfogliatine croccanti con semi di papavero e girasole

- Scant 2½ cups (300 g) whole wheat (wholemeal) flour
- ⅓ cup (80 g) butter, cut into small cubes
- 2 tablespoons raw sugar
- 1 level teaspoon baking soda (bicarbonate of soda)
- ¾ cup (180 ml) milk
- 1 teaspoon apple cider vinegar
- 5 tablespoons (80 g) mixed seeds, including sunflower seeds, flaxseeds (linseeds), and poppy seeds
- Salt

Preparation Time: 20 minutes
plus resting time
Cooking Time: 15 minutes
Serves: 4

In a food processor, combine the flour, butter, sugar, baking soda (bicarbonate of soda), and a pinch of salt and process to combine.

In a measuring cup, combine the milk and vinegar. With the food processor running, add the milk mixture and process until the dough comes together and forms a ball. Wrap the dough in plastic wrap (cling film) and refrigerate for at least 2 hours.

Preheat the oven to 400°F (200°C).

Divide the dough in half. On a sheet of parchment paper, roll out one piece of the dough into a very thin sheet.

Sprinkle the sheet of dough with half the seeds and use your rolling pin to press them into the dough. Transfer the dough on the parchment to a sheet pan. Repeat with the remaining dough and seeds.

Bake the crackers for about 15 minutes, until golden brown and crisp. Remove from the oven and let cool, then break the cracker sheets into irregular pieces.

Serve the crackers in a basket as a snack with cocktails.

In order to act as a leavener, baking soda (bicarbonate of soda) must be activated with an acidic ingredient, such as vinegar or lemon juice, on their own or mixed with milk, or yogurt.

Seeded Crackers with Shallots

Gallette di semi allo scalogno

- 2 shallots
- Scant ⅔ cup (30 g) wild fennel or fennel fronds
- 1½ cups plus 1 tablespoon (200 g) whole wheat (wholemeal) flour, plus more for dusting
- ¾ cup (100 g) ground flaxseed (linseed)
- 2 teaspoons (8 g) instant yeast, sifted
- ¼ cup (60 ml) extra virgin olive oil
- 3 tablespoons whole flaxseeds (linseeds)
- 3 tablespoons white sesame seeds
- ¼ cup (30 g) black sesame seeds
- 3½ tablespoons sunflower seeds
- 5 tablespoons (40 g) pumpkin seeds
- 1 teaspoon salt

Preparation Time: 20 minutes
Cooking Time: 15 minutes
Serves: 4

Preheat the oven to 450°F (230°C). Line a sheet pan with parchment paper.

In a small food processor, combine the shallots and fennel and pulse until finely chopped.

In a large bowl, combine the flour, ground flaxseed (linseed), and yeast. Add the olive oil, a scant ½ cup (100 ml) water, the shallot mixture, whole flaxseeds (linseeds), sesame seeds, sunflower seeds, pumpkin seeds, and salt, then mix until well combined. As needed, add up to an additional ¼ cup (60 ml) water to bring the dough together.

Transfer the dough to a lightly floured surface and gently roll it into a very thin sheet. Cut it into irregular pieces and transfer them to the prepared pan.

Bake the crackers for around 15 minutes, until crisp and lightly browned. Remove from the oven and let cool before serving.

These crackers can also be made using all-purpose (plain) flour instead of the whole wheat (wholemeal) flour, and without yeast. Prepare the dough as directed, then cover it and let rest for 30 minutes. Shape and bake the crackers as directed.

Mini Semolina Custards

Margottini alla bergamasca

- 3½ tablespoons (50 g) butter
- Breadcrumbs, for coating
- 2 cups plus 2 tablespoons (500 ml) vegetable broth
- ¾ cup (130 g) semolina flour
- 3 tablespoons grated Parmesan cheese
- 2¾ oz (80 g) Gruyère cheese, coarsely grated
- 4 egg yolks
- Salt and black pepper
- Basil, for garnish
- 2 small tomatoes, halved, for garnish

Preparation Time: 20 minutes
Cooking Time: 30 minutes
Serves: 4

Preheat the oven to 350°F (180°C). Grease four small smooth-sided ramekins with the butter, then sprinkle them with breadcrumbs, turn them to coat evenly, and tap out any excess.

In a medium saucepan, heat the broth over high heat until just boiling. While whisking, pour in the semolina and whisk to combine, then season with salt. Reduce the heat to low and cook, stirring continuously, for 10 minutes. Remove from the heat, stir in the Parmesan, and season with pepper.

Divide half the semolina among the prepared ramekins and use a teaspoon to spread it over the bottoms and up the sides. Divide half the Gruyère among the ramekins, then gently place an egg yolk in each. Cover with the remaining Gruyère and top evenly with the remaining semolina. Bake for 12 to 15 minutes, until lightly golden.

Turn the custards out of the ramekins onto individual serving plates. Garnish with the basil and tomatoes and serve hot.

This dish is a classic of Bergamo, in Lombardy, in Northern Italy. The name refers to the mold traditionally used to prepare them—*margot*—which is the shape of a bucket. For a vegan version, the egg yolks can be replaced with a cube of vegan cheese and the Parmesan with grated vegan cheese.

Fava and Chia Pâté

Pâté di fave ai semi di chia

- 3⅓ cups (500 g) shelled fresh fava (broad) beans
- ½ cup (120 ml) extra virgin olive oil
- 1 white onion, very thinly sliced
- Leaves from 3 sprigs mint
- 1 teaspoon agar-agar
- 2 tablespoons chia seeds
- 3½ oz (100 g) tofu, cut into ¾-inch (1.5 cm) cubes
- Salt

Preparation Time: 25 minutes plus resting time
Cooking Time: 25 minutes
Serves: 4

Bring a large pot of water to a boil. Add the fava (broad) beans and blanch for 1 minute, then drain them and let cool. Remove the beans from their skins and set aside in a bowl.

In a large frying pan, heat ¼ cup (60 ml) of the olive oil over medium heat. Add the onion and cook for a minute or two. Add the beans and a scant 1 cup (200 ml) water, then season with salt. Cover and cook for 7 to 8 minutes, until the beans are tender.

Add two-thirds of the mint and the agar-agar. Using a hand blender, carefully purée the mixture directly in the pot. Cook for another 5 to 6 minutes, then remove from the heat.

Pour the purée into a 8 x 4-inch (20 x 8 cm) loaf pan, cover, and refrigerate for 6 hours.

Just before serving, in a medium nonstick frying pan, heat the remaining ¼ cup (60 ml) olive oil over medium-high heat. Place the chia seeds in a shallow dish. Sprinkle the tofu cubes with salt and roll them in the chia seeds to coat, then add them to the hot oil and fry until golden.

To serve, unmold the terrine onto a plate, surround it with the tofu cubes, and garnish it with the remaining mint.

Agar-agar is a vegan thickening agent derived from red algae and can be used in place of gelatin. It can be added to cool mixtures or during cooking, and dissolves at high temperatures.

Kale and Red Onion Flan

Sformato con cavolo nero e cipolla rossa

- 1 bunch Tuscan kale (cavolo nero), leaves stemmed
- ¼ cup (60 ml) extra virgin olive oil
- 1 red onion, cut into thin wedges
- 5¼ oz (150 g) tofu, cut into cubes
- ⅓ cup (20 g) wild fennel or fennel fronds
- Pinch of red pepper flakes
- 1 egg
- Scant ½ cup (100 ml) soy cream or other nondairy cream
- Salt

Preparation Time: 20 minutes plus resting time
Cooking Time: 55 minutes
Serves: 8

Preheat the oven to 350°F (180°C). Line a 7-inch (18 cm) round baking pan with parchment paper.

Bring a large pot of salted water to a boil. Add the kale leaves and cook for 5 minutes. Drain and let cool, then squeeze out any excess water and finely chop the kale.

In a nonstick frying pan, heat the olive oil over medium heat. Add the onion wedges, a pinch of salt, and ¼ cup (60 ml) water and cook for 10 minutes, or until the water has evaporated.

Transfer some of the onion to a small plate and set aside to use for garnish. Add the tofu, fennel, chile, and kale to the pan with the remaining onions and cook over medium-high heat for 5 minutes. Remove from the heat and let cool, then transfer the mixture to a food processor. Add the egg and the cream, season with salt, and process until well combined and smooth.

Pour the tofu mixture into the prepared pan and bake for about 35 minutes, until set. Remove from the oven and let cool in the pan for 5 minutes.

Invert the flan onto a serving plate and garnish with the reserved onion.

For a vegan version, omit the egg and divide the tofu mixture among four lightly oiled individual ramekins; bake for about 25 minutes, until set. Serve in the ramekins.

Tomato Tartlets

Tartelette di pomodorini

- 1½ cups plus 1 tablespoon (200 g) all-purpose (plain) flour
- 7 tablespoons (100 g) butter, cut into small cubes and chilled
- 12 cherry tomatoes
- 1 teaspoon sugar
- 2 cloves garlic, thinly sliced
- Leaves from 4 sprigs thyme, plus more for garnish
- Extra virgin olive oil, for drizzling
- 1 teaspoon old-style mustard
- 7 oz (200 g) crescenza (stracchino) cheese
- Salt

Preparation Time: 15 minutes
plus resting time
Cooking Time: 55 minutes
Serves: 4

In a food processor, combine the flour, butter, and a pinch of salt and pulse until the mixture is crumbly. With the motor running, drizzle in a scant ½ cup (100 ml) cold water and process until the dough comes together and forms a ball. Wrap the dough in plastic wrap (cling film) and refrigerate for 30 minutes.

Preheat the oven to 300°F (150°C) with a rack in the lower third. Line a sheet pan with parchment paper.

Put the tomatoes on the prepared pan. Sprinkle them with the sugar, garlic, and thyme. Drizzle a little olive oil over them and bake for about 35 minutes, until they have softened and collapsed. Remove from the oven and set aside; keep the oven on.

On a lightly floured surface, roll out the dough to a thickness of 2 mm. Cut out twelve 2-inch (5 cm) disks of dough and use them to line 1¼-inch (3 cm) tartlet pans, pressing the dough gently into the bottoms of the pans. Prick the dough all over with a fork and dab the bottoms with the mustard. Tear the crescenza cheese into 12 pieces and put one in each tartlet shell.

Bake in the lower third of the oven for 15 to 20 minutes. Remove from the oven and let cool. Place a tomato in each tartlet (discard the garlic), top with a little of the liquid from the pan and some fresh thyme and serve.

Baking the tartlets in the lower third of the oven means the bottoms get more heat from below, which ensures a more evenly cooked crust, and allows you to avoid blind baking altogether.

Fried Squash Blossoms with Tofu and Capers

Fiori di zucca fritti ripieni di tofu e capperi

- 10 salt-cured capers, rinsed
- 8 Gaeta or other black olives, pitted and coarsely chopped
- ¼ cup (40 g) pine nuts
- 5¼ oz (150 g) tofu
- Handful of basil leaves
- 2 eggs, separated
- Scant ½ cup (100 ml) lager/beer
- ⅔ cup (80 g) all-purpose (plain) flour
- Peanut (groundnut) oil, for frying
- 8 squash blossoms (courgette flowers), pistils removed
- Salt

Preparation Time: 25 minutes plus soaking time
Cooking Time: 5 minutes
Serves: 4

Put the capers in a small bowl, add warm water to cover, and set aside to soak for 15 minutes, then drain. Chop the capers and put them in a medium bowl. Add the olives and pine nuts and stir to combine.

In a blender, combine the tofu, basil, and a pinch of salt and purée until smooth. Pour the puréed tofu into the bowl with the caper mixture and stir to combine. Clean the blender jar.

In a large bowl, whisk together the egg yolks, beer, and a pinch of salt, then add the flour and whisk the batter to combine.

In a medium bowl using a whisk or handheld mixer, beat the egg whites until they hold soft peaks, then gently fold them into the batter.

Fill a high-sided frying pan with 2 inches (5 cm) of peanut (groundnut) oil and heat over medium-high heat. Line a sheet pan with paper towels.

Stuff the squash blossoms (courgette flowers) with the tofu mixture, setting them on a large plate as you go. Working in batches, dip the squash blossoms in the batter, letting any excess drip off, then immediately add them to the hot oil and fry for about 1 minute, until they are puffy and golden. Transfer to the paper towels to drain. Serve hot.

For a vegan version, prepare the batter with a scant ¾ cup (100 g) all-purpose (plain) flour, a pinch of salt, some black pepper, 1 level teaspoon ground turmeric, a pinch of vegan yeast for savory preparations, and a scant 1 cup (200 ml) beer.

Tomato Rice Fritters

Supplì di riso al forno

- 1¼ cups (100 g) textured soy protein
- ¼ cup (60 ml) extra virgin olive oil
- 1 shallot, finely chopped
- ¼ cup (60 ml) tomato paste (purée)
- 1 bay leaf
- 1½ cups (300 g) short-grain rice, such as Roma
- 4 eggs, beaten
- 6 tablespoons (40 g) grated Parmesan cheese
- 4½ oz (130 g) mozzarella cheese, cut into small cubes
- 1 cup (100 g) breadcrumbs
- Salt

Preparation Time: 25 minutes plus soaking time
Cooking Time: 1 hour
Serves: 4

Soak the soy protein in cold water for 20 minutes, then drain and squeeze out any excess water.

Preheat the oven to 350°F (180°C). Line two sheet pans with parchment paper.

In a large frying pan, heat the olive oil over medium-low heat. Add the shallot and cook for a minute or two, then add the soy protein, tomato paste (purée), and bay leaf and season with salt. Pour in a scant 1 cup (200 ml) hot water and cook the ragù for 30 minutes.

Meanwhile, bring a medium pot of water to a boil. Add the rice and cook for half the time indicated on the package, then drain and let cool.

Remove the bay leaf from the ragù and add the rice, half the eggs, the Parmesan, and a pinch of salt. Stir well to combine. Transfer the rice mixture onto one of the prepared pans, smooth it into a thin layer, and let cool.

Shape a heaping 2 tablespoons of the rice mixture into a ball. Make an indentation in the center and insert a cube of mozzarella, then re-form the rice mixture into a ball around the cheese. Repeat with the remaining rice mixture and mozzarella.

Place the remaining eggs in a small bowl and beat in a pinch of salt. Place the breadcrumbs in a separate bowl. One at a time, dip the rice balls in the egg, letting any excess drip off, then roll in the breadcrumbs to coat and place on the second prepared sheet pan. Bake the rice balls for about 30 minutes, until golden brown. Serve hot.

Textured soy protein is made with defatted soy flour. After being rehydrated, the granules can be used to make ragùs, meatballs, and meat loaves, or a filling for baked vegetables.

Fried Veggie Chips

Chips di verdure

- 3 small raw beets (beetroot), peeled
- 2 large carrots
- 1 daikon radish, peeled
- Peanut (groundnut) oil, for frying
- All-purpose (plain) flour, for coating
- Salt

Preparation Time: 25 minutes
Cooking Time: 5 minutes
Serves: 4

Very thinly slice the beets (beetroot) on a mandoline. Spread the slices over paper towels to dry. Very thinly slice the carrots and daikon on the mandoline, keeping them separate.

Fill a high-sided frying pan with about 2 inches (5 cm) of peanut (groundnut) oil and heat over medium-high heat. Line a sheet pan with paper towels.

Put some flour in a medium bowl. Toss the sliced beets in the flour to coat, then transfer them to a sieve and shake to remove any excess. Working in batches to avoid crowding the pan, carefully add the beets to the hot oil and fry until golden and crispy. Transfer the beet chips (crisps) to the paper towels and sprinkle with salt. Repeat to fry the carrots, then the daikon, coating them with flour before frying as you did the beets.

Serve the veggie chips (crisps) hot or at room temperature. Leftovers will keep in an airtight container at room temperature for 2 to 3 days.

Instead of frying the raw vegetables, you can bake them: spread the sliced vegetables in a single layer on a sheet pan, sprinkle them with salt, and bake in a preheated 425°F (220°C) oven for 10 to 20 minutes.

Medley of Fried Snacks

Cuoppo

- 3 medium potatoes
- 1¼ cups (300 ml) tomato purée (passata)
- 2 tablespoons extra virgin olive oil
- 1 egg
- 6 tablespoons (40 g) grated Parmesan cheese, plus more for serving
- Breadcrumbs, for coating
- All-purpose (plain) flour, for coating
- 1 large round eggplant (aubergine)
- 10½ oz (300 g) Basic Bread Dough (page 74)
- Peanut (groundnut) oil for frying
- Salt

Preparation Time: 25 minutes
Cooking Time: 1 hour 5 minutes
Serves: 4

Put the potatoes in a medium saucepan, add water to cover, and bring the water to a boil. Reduce the heat to maintain a simmer and cook for 40 minutes, or until tender.

Meanwhile, in a small saucepan, combine the tomato purée (passata), olive oil, and a pinch of salt. Bring to a simmer over medium-low heat, cover, and cook for about 20 minutes.

Preheat the oven to 200°F (95°C).

Drain the potatoes and let cool, then peel them, transfer the flesh to a medium bowl, and mash it with a fork. Add the egg, Parmesan, and a pinch of salt and stir well to combine.

Fill a shallow dish with breadcrumbs. Shape the potato mixture into small cylindrical croquettes and roll them in the breadcrumbs to coat, setting them on a sheet pan as you go.

Fill a shallow dish with flour. Slice the eggplant (aubergine) into rounds about ¼ inch (6 mm) thick, then cut them into ¼-inch-wide (6 mm) sticks. Toss them in the flour to coat, shake them to remove any excess, and set aside on the sheet pan with the potato croquettes.

Pull off 4 apricot-size pieces of bread dough and stretch them (not too thinly) into small rounds. Lightly flatten the middle of each round. Cut the rest of the dough into bite-size chunks and roll them into small balls.

Line a sheet pan with paper towels. Fill a high-sided frying pan with about 1 inch (2.5 cm) of peanut (groundnut) oil and heat over medium-high heat. Carefully add the dough rounds to the hot oil and fry until golden, 3 to 4 minutes. Transfer to the paper towels and place them in the oven to keep warm. Repeat to fry the dough balls, then the eggplant sticks, and finally the potato croquettes.

Spread the tomato sauce over the fried rounds of dough and top with Parmesan. Place them on a serving platter with the fried eggplant sticks, dough balls, and potato croquettes (or serve these in separate paper cones, if you like). Serve hot.

Traditionally, this fried mixture is served in paper cones, which give the dish its Italian name. You can garnish the mini pizzas with grated Parmesan and shredded basil, if you wish.

Rice Balls

Arancini

- 1½ cups (300 g) Vialone Nano or other medium-grain rice
- 2 tablespoons (30 g) butter
- 6 tablespoons (40 g) grated Parmesan cheese
- ¾ cup (100 g) shelled pistachios, finely chopped
- ⅓ cup (20 g) chopped wild fennel or fennel fronds
- 4 mint leaves, chopped
- 3 eggs
- 4¼ oz (120 g) scamorza cheese, cut into cubes
- Peanut (groundnut) oil, for frying
- All-purpose (plain) flour, for coating
- 1 cup (100 g) breadcrumbs
- Salt

Preparation Time: 20 minutes
Cooking Time: 20 minutes
Serves: 4

In a medium saucepan, bring 2 cups (500 ml) water to a boil over high heat. Salt the water, then add the rice. Stir, reduce the heat to low, and cook the rice, uncovered, for 15 minutes, until it has absorbed all the water.

Add the butter, Parmesan, pistachios, fennel, and mint. Remove from the heat and let the rice cool.

Beat 1 egg and stir it into the cooled rice. Shape the rice into balls the size of an orange. Make an indentation in the center of a rice ball and insert a cube of the scamorza, then re-form the rice into a ball around the cheese. Repeat with the remaining rice balls and scamorza.

Fill a heavy-bottomed large saucepan with 4 inches (10 cm) of peanut (groundnut) oil and heat the oil over medium-high heat.

Put some flour in a shallow bowl and the breadcrumbs in a separate shallow bowl. Beat the remaining 2 eggs with a pinch of salt in a medium bowl. Roll the rice balls in the flour to coat, then dip in the egg, letting any excess drip off, and finally roll them in the breadcrumbs to coat. Working in batches to avoid crowding the pan, carefully add the rice balls to the hot oil and fry for 5 minutes, until golden brown. Transfer them to paper towels to drain, and serve while still warm.

In traditional recipes, these rice balls are filled with meat ragù. For a vegetarian version, this ragù can be prepared with 10½ oz (300 g) seitan, finely chopped and cooked with 10½ oz (300 g) peas, 4 to 5 tablespoons (60 to 75 ml) tomato purée (passata), ¼ cup (60 ml) olive oil, and a pinch of salt.

Artichoke and Fennel Fritters

Carciofi e fionocchi in pastella fritti

- 2 fennel bulbs, cut into wedges
- Juice of ½ lemon, strained
- 4 globe artichokes
- 1 egg
- ¼ cup (60 ml) milk
- 6 tablespoons (50 g) all-purpose (plain) flour
- Olive oil, for frying
- Salt

Preparation Time: 15 minutes
Cooking Time: 10 to 20 minutes
Serves: 4

Bring a large pot of salted water to a boil. Add the fennel wedges and cook for 5 minutes, then drain.

Fill a large bowl with cool water and add the lemon juice. Trim the artichokes, cut them into wedges, and cut the fuzzy choke from the center, dropping the wedges into the bowl of lemon water as you go (this prevents them from browning).

In a medium bowl, mix together the egg and milk, then gradually beat in the flour and a pinch of salt and beat until smooth. Let the batter stand for 5 minutes.

Fill a high-sided frying pan with about 3 inches (7.5 cm) of olive oil and heat over medium-high heat to 350° to 375°F (180° to 190°C), or until a cube of day-old bread browns in 30 seconds.

Drain the artichokes and pat dry. Dip the artichokes and fennel into the batter, a few pieces at a time, and let any excess drip off. Carefully add the battered vegetables to the hot oil and fry for 5 to 8 minutes, until golden brown. Use a slotted spoon to transfer them to paper towels to absorb excess oil. Keep warm while you fry the remaining vegetables.

Pile the vegetables onto a serving dish, sprinkle with salt, and serve immediately.

Cauliflower Custard with Broccoli and Walnuts

Sformato di cavolfiore, broccoletti e noci

- 3 tablespoons all-purpose (plain) flour
- 14 oz (400 g) cauliflower, cut into florets
- 14 oz (400 g) broccoli, cut into florets
- ⅔ cup (80 g) walnuts
- 1½ oz (40 g) Parmesan cheese, coarsely chopped
- 1 oz (30 g) Pecorino Romano cheese, coarsely chopped
- 3 eggs
- Scant 1 cup (200 ml) nondairy cream
- Zest of ½ orange, removed with a vegetable peeler
- Handful of chopped parsley
- 2 teaspoons (10 g) butter
- Salt and black pepper

Preparation Time: 30 minutes
Cooking Time: 55 minutes
Serves: 4 to 6

Preheat the oven to 350°F (180°C). Butter a 9-inch (22 cm) loaf pan and dust it with the flour, tapping out any excess.

Bring a large pot of salted water to a boil. Add the cauliflower and cook for 4 to 5 minutes. Using a slotted spoon, transfer the cauliflower to a colander to drain, then spread it over a clean kitchen towel. Add the broccoli to the boiling water and blanch for 4 to 5 minutes, then drain and spread over a second kitchen towel.

In a food processor, combine the walnuts, Parmesan, and pecorino and pulse until evenly broken down into fine crumbs. Add the eggs, cream, a pinch of salt, and some pepper and process for a few seconds to combine. Pour the walnut mixture into a large bowl.

In a medium bowl, combine one-quarter of the cauliflower and one-quarter of the broccoli and purée with a hand blender, then add the purée to the walnut mixture and stir well to combine.

Place the remaining cauliflower and broccoli florets in the prepared pan. Pour the walnut mixture over the vegetables in the Bundt pan and gently tap the pan on the counter to distribute it evenly. Place the Bundt pan in a roasting pan and put the pan in the oven, then carefully pour enough boiling water into the roasting pan to come two-thirds up the sides of the Bundt pan.

Bake for about 40 minutes, until firm. Remove from the oven and let cool in the pan for 10 minutes.

Meanwhile, finely chop the orange zest and mix it with the parsley.

Invert the custard onto a serving plate and garnish with the orange zest–parsley mixture.

The recipe is rich in protein because of the eggs and walnuts. Walnuts are also a good addition to vegetarian and vegan diets because they contain copper and zinc, nutrients otherwise obtained from meat, as well as phosphorus, magnesium, iron, and potassium.

Zucchini and Goat Cheese Frittata

Frittata di zucchini al caprino

- 3 tablespoons olive oil
- 1 lb 5 oz (600 g) zucchini (courgettes), thinly sliced into rounds
- 1 sprig thyme
- 8 eggs
- Pinch of curry powder
- 7 oz (200 g) goat cheese, crumbled
- 3½ oz (100 g) Parmesan cheese, grated
- 3 tablespoons chopped flat-leaf parsley
- 1 tablespoon snipped chives
- 1 tablespoon chopped chervil
- 3 oz (80 g) black olives, pitted and halved
- Milk, if needed
- Salt and pepper

Preparation Time: 40 to 50 minutes (including cooling)
Cooking Time: 20 minutes
Serves: 6

In a large frying pan, heat the olive oil over medium heat. Add the zucchini (courgettes) and thyme and cook, stirring and turning occasionally, until the zucchini (courgettes) have softened and any moisture they release has evaporated. Remove from the heat and season with salt and pepper. Remove and discard the thyme.

In a medium bowl, beat the eggs, curry powder, and some salt and pepper, then stir in the goat cheese, Parmesan, parsley, chives, chervil, and olives. If the mixture is too thick, thin it with a little milk. Pour the egg mixture into the pan over the zucchini (courgettes) and cook over medium heat for about 5 minutes, until the eggs have set.

Remove the pan from the heat, loosen the frittata with a spatula, and slide it onto a serving dish. Let cool to room temperature, then cut into slices and serve.

Vegetable and Quinoa Tartare

Tartare di verdure e quinoa

- 4 tablespoons (60 ml) olive oil
- Scant ⅔ cup (100 g) red quinoa, rinsed and drained
- 1 stalk celery, finely diced
- 2 small zucchini, finely diced
- 2 tomatoes, finely chopped
- 1 carrot, finely diced
- Juice of ½ lemon
- 1 spring onion, sliced
- 1 tablespoon capers
- 8 Kalamata olives, pitted and sliced
- Salt and pepper

Preparation Time: 20 minutes
Cooking Time: 25 minutes
Serves: 4

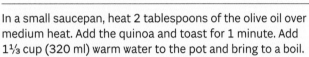

In a small saucepan, heat 2 tablespoons of the olive oil over medium heat. Add the quinoa and toast for 1 minute. Add 1⅓ cup (320 ml) warm water to the pot and bring to a boil. Add a pinch of salt, then cover and simmer for 20 minutes. Let cool, then fluff the grains.

In a large bowl, combine the quinoa, celery, zucchini, tomatoes, and carrot. Add the remaining 2 tablespoons oil and the lemon juice and season with salt. Pack the mixture into four 3-inch (8 cm) ramekins, then invert each onto an individual serving plate.

Garnish with the spring onion, capers, and olives and drizzle with olive oil. Sprinkle with pepper, then serve.

Quinoa must always be rinsed thoroughly before cooking to remove saponin, a naturally occurring substance with a bitter taste. Toasting amplifies the flavor of the quinoa.

Onion Bundt Cake

Ciambella con cipolle caramellate

- 3 tablespoons (40 g) butter, plus more for greasing
- 1 lb 2 oz (500 g) red onions, thinly sliced
- Pinch of salt
- All-purpose (plain) flour, for dusting
- 10½ oz (300 g) Basic Bread Dough (page 74)
- 1 tablespoon raw sugar

Preparation Time: 25 minutes plus resting time
Cooking Time: 1 hour 10 minutes
Serves: 4

In a large nonstick frying pan, melt the butter over low heat. Add the onions and salt and stir. Cover and cook, stirring occasionally, for about 40 minutes, until the onions are deeply browned and caramelized. Remove from the heat and let cool completely.

Butter a tube pan with a removable bottom and dust it with flour, tapping out any excess.

Punch down the dough slightly and, using your hands, roll it into a log about 16 inches (40 cm) long. Join the ends to form a ring and transfer the ring to the prepared pan. Distribute the caramelized onions over the top. Sprinkle with the sugar. Set aside in a warm place to rise for about 30 minutes.

Preheat the oven to 350°F (180°C).

Bake for about 30 minutes, until the cake is golden brown. Remove from the oven and let cool in the pan for 15 minutes. Remove from the pan, slice, and serve.

For the onions to cook evenly, they must be cut into even slices, so use a mandoline to slice them, if you have one.

Breads & Pizzas

Flour, water, yeast: With these limited and simple ingredients, bread has been an essential component of human diets since ancient times. From the same base, enriched with a variety of sauces and fillings, it is possible to make an incredible variety of pizzas and focaccias, great classic dishes of Italian cuisine, beloved all over the world by vegetarians and omnivores alike.

From a simple accompaniment to a complete dish

Considering bread's nutritional values, the World Health Organization recommends the consumption of at least 8 oz (250 g) of bread per day.

A precious source of carbohydrates

Bread is rich in carbohydrates, which, in a balanced diet, should provide 50 to 55 percent of total daily calories. It also contains protein, B vitamins, and minerals such as phosphorus, potassium, and magnesium. The same nutrients can also be found in pizza crusts, and the pizzas themselves can help you incorporate vegetables (starting with the traditional tomato), cheeses, and extra virgin olive oil—a precious source of unsaturated fats and antioxidants—into your diet.

Not just wheat

The nutritional value of bread, pizzas, and focaccias relies strongly on the type of flour used to make their dough. The most commonly used is soft wheat flour, but many others, when added to the dough in the right proportion, are also suitable for bread-making. Cornmeal, farro, rye, and Kamut flours provide not only varied flavor but also different nutritional content. Whole-grain flours are even better; because the grains are not refined, more nutrients are retained, including vitamins, minerals, and insoluble fiber, which aids digestion.

Main course or snack

Pizzas and focaccias are versatile preparations, which can easily be consumed at different stages in a meal, depending on the size of the portion and the ingredients used. Enriched with significant portions of vegetables and protein-rich ingredients, such as dairy products, tofu, or seitan, they can be consumed as a main course or even a complete meal, to be accompanied perhaps by a side salad or fruit. In smaller sizes, or cut into squares, they are also very popular as starters or appetizers with aperitifs.

Sourdough starter, an everlasting yeast

For those who love the taste of tradition or who prefer a natural leavener: sourdough starter is made with a dough of flour, water, and sugars (honey, yogurt or fruit). Periodically refreshed with flour and water to keep alive the microorganisms that compose it, it has a practically eternal life. It also makes for more easily digestible and tasty breads and pizzas.

Commercial yeasts, including fresh yeast, may contain stabilizing agents (such as E470a) and other elements of animal origin. A fully vegan alternative is cream of tartar, a natural leavening agent. It needs to be supplemented with baking soda (bicarbonate of soda), but it is possible to purchase sachets containing the two products already mixed together. Vegans can also use a sourdough starter prepared by fermenting only flour and water, without any yogurt and honey.

Lots of great ideas for the table

The starting point is the same for all varieties: the dough. From there, through specific cooking styles and with the addition of various ingredients, it is possible to make a wide range of baked products.

Bread
Dating back to ancient Egypt, bread is made with a dough of flour, yeast, and water. The dough almost always includes salt; some varieties, such as Tuscan bread, exclude it. Some breads, like matzo, are unleavened. Common additions to bread, whether incorporated into the dough or used as toppings, include oil, milk, whole grains, and sesame seeds.

Pizza and calzone
Bread dough made with olive oil forms the base of pizza and calzone crusts. It is stretched and topped with vegetables, dairy products, and other ingredients, spaced evenly to ensure even cooking. A calzone is made when the dough is folded over the filling to form a half-moon, enclosing the filling.

Focaccia
The word focaccia derives from the Latin word *focus*, the hearth on which it was originally cooked. Compared to pizza, focaccia dough has a higher oil content and, once stretched over the pan, is pressed with the fingertips to form the bread's classic dimples.

Breadsticks and crackers
The creation of breadsticks is attributed to bakers in Turin in the seventeenth century. The Italian word for bread-sticks, *grissini*, derives from *ghersa*, an elongated Turinese bread. Spices and often also fats are added to the dough, giving breadsticks a higher caloric content. Their longer cooking time, however, makes them easier to digest. The same characteristics apply to crackers. Cracker dough must be pricked with a fork before baking to prevent air pockets from forming.

The ingredients to always have on hand

Soft wheat flour is the most commonly used flour in the preparation of bread and baked products. There are, however, plenty of alternatives, and these are often richer from a nutritional point of view.

Wheat

Common varieties include all-purpose (plain) flour, bread flour (strong white flour), pastry flour, and whole wheat (wholemeal) flour. The protein content varies for each type. In Italy, soft wheat flour is classified, depending on its degree of refining. Durum wheat flour is used mainly for the preparation of pasta, but also in some types of bread.

"2" flour, a winning choice

Generally speaking, using whole-grain flour is an excellent idea. But a good compromise is type "2" flour. It is partially made with whole-grain flour, which retains a good portion of the grain's nutrients. It can be used without mixing it with other flours and releases an unmistakable aroma during baking.

Corn and rice

The best cornmeal for breadmaking is the fine-grained variety. Cornmeal has a slightly sweet taste and is gluten-free, so it can be used by people with celiac disease or gluten intolerance. It shares this quality with rice flour, which is very white and fine, and has a delicate flavor.

Rye and farro

Widely used in Northern Europe for the production of black bread, rye flour is normally mixed with wheat flour, which compensates for its limited gluten content. Rich in fiber and minerals, farro (emmer) flour has a good capacity for developing gluten; for this reason, up to 50 percent can be used to make bread dough.

Buckwheat, Kamut, and quinoa

Gray-blue in color and with a flavor reminiscent of walnuts, buckwheat flour is an excellent choice for gluten-intolerant people. Obtained from Khorasan wheat, a red grain originally from Iran, Kamut flour contains more proteins, vitamins, and minerals than common wheat flour. Quinoa (a pseudograin of Andean origin) has a high nutrient content, especially amino acids and minerals.

Potato Flatbread with Salad

Pinza di patate con insalata

- Extra virgin olive oil
- 1 lb 5 oz (600 g) potatoes
- 3 eggs
- 2 tablespoons all-purpose (plain) flour
- 1 (5¼ oz/150 g) head radicchio, leaves separated
- Salt and black pepper

Preparation Time: 20 minutes
Cooking Time: 1 hour
Serves: 4

Preheat the oven to 400°F (200°C). Generously brush a 9- to 12-inch (23 to 30 cm) round pizza pan with oil.

Put the potatoes in a large saucepan, add cold water to cover, and bring the water to a boil. Cook for 30 minutes, then drain the potatoes and let cool.

Peel the potatoes, transfer the flesh to a large bowl, and mash with a potato masher. Add the eggs, flour, a pinch of salt, and some pepper and mix quickly to combine.

Press the potato mixture over the prepared pan and bake for about 30 minutes. Remove from the oven and let cool for 10 minutes.

Put the radicchio in a medium bowl, drizzle it with olive oil, and sprinkle with salt, then toss to coat.

Turn the flatbread out onto a serving dish and top with the radicchio. Serve warm.

For a vegan version, leave out the eggs and add 1 cup plus 2 tablespoons (100 g) sifted chickpea flour to the potato mixture.

Sourdough Farro Bread

Pane di farro con lievito madre

- 5¼ oz (150 g) sourdough starter (see note below)
- Scant 2 cups (250 g) farro (emmer) flour
- Scant 2 cups (250 g) whole-grain farro (emmer) flour
- 2 tablespoons extra virgin olive oil
- 1 teaspoon salt

Preparation Time: 20 minutes plus resting time
Cooking Time: 30 minutes
Serves: 4

Place the sourdough starter in a bowl and dilute it with ¾ cup (180 ml) warm water. Add the two types of flour, the olive oil, and the salt and stir to combine. Knead the dough for at least 10 minutes. Shape the dough into a ball, cover it, and let rise in a warm place for about 4 hours.

Line a sheet pan with parchment paper. Punch down the dough and knead it thoroughly, then shape it into a long loaf and place it on the prepared pan. Let rise for another 3 to 4 hours.

Preheat the oven to 400°F (200°C).

Bake the bread for about 30 minutes, or until it sounds hollow when you tap the bottom of the loaf. Transfer it to a wire rack to cool before slicing and serving.

To make sourdough starter, in a medium bowl, stir together a scant ¾ cup (100 g) all-purpose (plain) flour, ¼ cup (60 g) plain yogurt (be sure it has active cultures), and a scant ½ cup (100 ml) water. Set it aside to ferment at room temperature for 1 week, then move to the refrigerator. After 1 week, the starter is ready to use. To maintain your starter, every 48 hours, weigh the starter and feed it by stirring in an equal weight of flour and half its weight in water. For a vegan version, ferment 1½ cups (200 g) bread flour (strong white flour) with a scant ½ cup (100 ml) warm water.

Soda Bread with Seeds and Raisins

Pane senza lievito ai semi e uvetta

- ⅓ cup (50 g) raisins
- 4 cups (500 g) whole wheat (wholemeal) flour
- 1½ teaspoons baking soda (bicarbonate of soda)
- Scant 2 cups (450 ml) milk
- 1 teaspoon apple cider vinegar
- 1 teaspoon salt
- 1¾ oz (50 g) mixed seeds

Preparation Time: 20 minutes plus resting time
Cooking Time: 40 minutes
Serves: 4

Preheat the oven to 350°F (180°C). Line a 9 x 5-inch (22 x 12 cm) loaf pan with parchment paper.

Put the raisins in a small bowl, add warm water to cover, and set aside to soak for 10 minutes, then drain.

Sift the flour and the baking soda (bicarbonate of soda) directly onto your work surface, form it into a mound, and make a well in the center. In a small bowl, stir together the milk and the vinegar. Add the milk mixture and the salt to the well in the flour and use a fork to gradually incorporate them into the flour until the dough comes together. Knead the dough for a few minutes. Add the seeds and the raisins, then knead for another 5 to 6 minutes.

Shape the dough into a loaf and place it in the prepared pan. Cut a cross in the top of the dough with a sharp paring knife.

Bake the bread for about 35 minutes, until golden brown. Let cool in the pan before slicing and serving.

This bread can also be made with all-purpose (plain) flour mixed with farro flour or barley flour. Serve with vegan cheese, jam, or vegetables. Soda bread is traditionally prepared with buttermilk; If you'd like to go that route, replace the milk with an equal amount of buttermilk and omit the vinegar.

Cornmeal-Millet Rolls

Panini di mais e miglio con fiori di sambuco

- ½ oz (15 g) fresh yeast, crumbled, or 1¾ teaspoons active dry yeast
- 2½ cups (300 g) millet flour
- Scant ½ cup (100 g) fine cornmeal
- 1 tablespoon rice malt
- 3 tablespoons extra virgin olive oil
- 1 teaspoon salt
- 2 tablespoons fresh elderberry flowers

Preparation Time: 20 minutes plus resting time
Cooking Time: 25 minutes
Serves: 4

In a large bowl, combine the yeast and ⅔ cup (150 ml) warm water and stir until the yeast has dissolved. Add the millet flour, cornmeal, rice malt, and olive oil and stir for 1 minute to combine. Add the salt, then knead for 10 minutes. Cover the dough and let it rise in a warm place for 2 hours.

Preheat the oven to 350°F (180°C). Line a sheet pan with parchment paper.

Lightly punch down the dough, then divide it into chunks of around 1 oz (30 g) each. On a lightly floured surface, roll each piece of dough into a ball, placing them on the prepared pan as you go. Invert a large bowl over the rolls and let rise for 30 minutes.

Use a pair of kitchen scissors to cut a cross into the top of each roll. Sprinkle with the elderberry flowers and bake for 20 to 25 minutes, until golden brown.

Another use for fresh elderberry flowers is an infused syrup. In a large saucepan, heat 4¼ cups (1 l) water and 5 cups (1 kg) sugar over medium heat, stirring, until the sugar has dissolved. Remove the syrup from the heat and let cool. Pour the syrup into a large jar and stir in a scant ½ cup (100 ml) apple cider vinegar, 8 elderberry flowers, and 2 lemons (washed and cut into wedges). Leave to infuse for 3 days. Strain the syrup, discarding the solids, and pour it into jars or bottles.

Walnut, Fig, and Raisin Rolls

Panini multicereali con noci, fichi e uvetta

- Scant 3¼ cups (400 g) mixed-grain flour
- Scant 1 cup (200 ml) milk, warmed
- ⅓ oz (10 g) fresh yeast, crumbled, or ½ (¼ oz/7 g) packet active dry yeast (1⅛ teaspoons)
- 2½ teaspoons (10 g) sugar
- 1 teaspoon salt
- 3 tablespoons (40 g) butter, at room temperature
- ⅓ cup (50 g) raisins
- 6 dried figs, coarsely chopped
- 1 cup (100 g) coarsely chopped walnuts

Preparation Time: 20 minutes
plus resting time
Cooking Time: 25 minutes
Serves: 4

Put the flour in a large bowl. In a small bowl, combine the warm milk, yeast, and sugar and stir until the yeast has dissolved, then pour the mixture over the flour and begin to knead the ingredients together. Add the salt and the butter and knead for at least 10 minutes more. Cover the dough and let it rise in a warm place for 2 hours.

Put the raisins in a small bowl, add warm water to cover, and set aside to soak for 10 minutes, then drain.

Punch down the dough and divide it into three equal portions. Knead the raisins into one portion, the figs into the second, and the walnuts into the third.

Line a sheet pan with foil. Shape the dough into apricot-size balls and place them on the prepared pan. Let rise for 30 minutes.

Preheat the oven to 350°F (180°C).

Bake the rolls for about 20 minutes, until golden brown. Serve with butter.

To make the rolls shiny, in a small bowl, whisk together 1 egg yolk and 1 teaspoon milk and brush it over the rolls just before baking.

Raisin and Rosemary Rolls

Panini al ramerino

- ⅓ cup (50 g) raisins
- Leaves from 2 sprigs rosemary, coarsely chopped
- 3 tablespoons extra virgin olive oil
- ⅓ oz (10 g) fresh yeast, crumbled, or ½ (¼ oz/7 g) packet active dry yeast (1⅛ teaspoons)
- Scant 3¼ cups (400 g) all-purpose (plain) flour
- 1 teaspoon sugar
- Black pepper
- 1 teaspoon salt

Preparation Time: 20 minutes plus resting time
Cooking Time: 25 minutes
Serves: 4

Put the raisins in a small bowl, add warm water to cover, and set aside to soak for 10 minutes. Drain, pat dry with paper towels, and set aside.

In a small saucepan, combine the rosemary and olive oil and heat gently over low heat for about 5 minutes, until fragrant. Let cool completely, then strain the oil through a fine-mesh sieve set over a bowl; discard the rosemary and let cool.

In a large bowl, combine the yeast and a scant 1 cup (200 ml) warm water and stir until the yeast has dissolved. Add the flour, sugar, rosemary oil, and a generous sprinkle of pepper and mix for 1 minute to combine. Add the salt and the raisins, then knead the dough for 10 minutes. Cover the dough and let it rise in a warm place for 2 hours.

Preheat the oven to 400°F (200°C).

Lightly punch down the dough and divide it into chunks of around 1¾ oz (50 g) each. Using your hands, roll each chunk into a ball and place them on a sheet pan. Cover and let rise for 30 minutes.

Bake the rolls for about 20 minutes, until golden.

These rolls can also be made with half all-purpose (plain) flour and half whole-grain farro (emmer) flour. When you leave the rolls to rise, tent them with foil, being sure the foil does not come into contact with the dough.

Whole-Grain Olive Focaccia

Focaccia multicereali con olive

- Scant ¾ cup (100 g) all-purpose (plain) flour
- Scant ¾ cup (100 g) whole-grain farro (emmer) flour
- ¾ cup (100 g) barley flour
- 6 tablespoons (50 g) ground flaxseed (linseed)
- ⅓ cup (50 g) oat bran
- 6 tablespoons (50 g) wheat germ
- 1 tablespoon- flaxseeds (linseeds)
- 1 tablespoon sunflower seeds
- ⅓ oz (10 g) fresh yeast, crumbled, or ½ (1/4 oz/7 g) packet active dry yeast (1⅛ teaspoons)
- 1 teaspoon acacia honey
- 5 tablespoons (75 ml) extra virgin olive oil, plus more for greasing
- 4 teaspoons (10 g) salt
- Leaves from 2 sprigs thyme, chopped
- ¾ cup (100 g) pitted Taggiasca or Niçoise olives

Preparation Time: 20 minutes plus resting time
Cooking Time: 25 minutes
Serves: 4

In a large bowl, combine the all-purpose (plain) flour, farro (emmer) flour, barley flour, ground flaxseed (linseed), oat bran, wheat germ, whole flaxseeds (linseeds), and sunflower seeds. Add the yeast, honey, 2 tablespoons of the olive oil, and 1 cup plus 2 tablespoons (270 ml) warm water and knead the dough for a few minutes. Add the salt and thyme and knead the dough for at least 10 minutes. Just before you are done kneading, add the olives and gently fold them into the dough. Cover the dough and let it rise in a warm place for 2 hours.

Oil a pizza pan. Punch down the dough slightly, transfer it to the oiled pan, and use your hands to stretch it to the edges of the pan. Cover and let rise for 30 minutes more.

Preheat the oven to 400°F (200°C).

Press your fingertips into the dough, creating lots of dimples. In a small bowl, whisk together the remaining 3 tablespoons oil and 3 tablespoons water and quickly brush it over the dough.

Bake the focaccia for about 25 minutes, until golden brown, then serve.

For a vegan version, replace the honey with 1 tablespoon barley malt or rice malt.

Ferrara Breadsticks

Coppia ferrarese

- 4 cups (500 g) all-purpose (plain) flour
- Scant ½ ounce (12 g) fresh yeast, crumbled, or 1¼ teaspoons active dry yeast
- 1 teaspoon sugar
- 3½ tablespoons (50 g) butter, at room temperature
- 2 tablespoons extra virgin olive oil
- 4 teaspoons salt

Preparation Time: 20 minutes plus resting time
Cooking Time: 20 minutes
Serves: 4

Put the flour in a large bowl. In a small bowl, combine the yeast, sugar, and a scant 1 cup (220 ml) warm water and stir until the yeast has dissolved, then pour the mixture over the flour. Add the butter, olive oil, and salt and stir to combine. Knead the dough for 10 minutes. Shape the dough into a ball, cover it, and let rise in a warm place for 2 hours.

Preheat the oven to 425°F (220°C). Line a sheet pan with parchment paper.

Lightly punch down the dough. Divide the dough into 3 equal portions. Working with one portion at a time, divide it in half and stretch each half into a triangle with two sides of the same length. Roll up each triangle from the long side toward the peak. Stack the two pieces of rolled-up dough perpendicular to each other, press them together at the center with your fingertips, and gently twist them around each other to form an "X" shape. Place it on the prepared pan and repeat with the remaining dough. Let rise for 30 minutes.

Bake the breadsticks for about 20 minutes, until golden brown.

For a more traditional take, prepare these breadsticks with 1¾ oz (50 g) sourdough starter (see page 56) in place of the yeast.

Hemp Sandwich Bread with Thyme and Pumpkin Seeds

Pane con farina di canapa, timo e semi di zucca

- Scant ½ oz (12 g) fresh yeast, crumbled, or 1¼ teaspoons active dry yeast
- Scant 3¼ cups (400 g) whole wheat (wholemeal) flour
- 6 tablespoons (50 g) hemp flour
- 2 tablespoons extra virgin olive oil
- 1 teaspoon honey
- Black pepper
- 1 teaspoon salt
- Leaves from 2 sprigs thyme, chopped
- 6 tablespoons (50 g) pumpkin seeds, toasted and coarsely ground

Preparation Time: 25 minutes plus resting time
Cooking Time: 30 minutes
Serves: 4

In a large bowl, combine the yeast and a scant 1 cup (200 ml) warm water and stir until the yeast has dissolved. Add whole wheat (wholemeal) flour, hemp flour, olive oil, honey, and a generous sprinkle of pepper and stir for 1 minute to combine. Add the salt, thyme, and pumpkin seeds and knead the dough for 10 minutes. Cover the dough and let it rise in a warm place for 1 hour 30 minutes.

Preheat the oven to 350°F (180°C). Line an 8 x 4-inch (22 x 8 cm) loaf pan with parchment paper.

Lightly punch down the dough and transfer it to the prepared pan. Cover and let rise for another 30 minutes.

Use a sharp paring knife to make a slash down the center of the dough, then bake for about 30 minutes.

The hemp flour gives this bread a distinctive flavor and a particular firmness when baked. To improve the cooking of the bread, fill a small oven-safe saucepan with boiling water and place it at the bottom of the oven; this creates steam as the bread bakes.

Easter Cheese Bread

Torta di Pasqua con formaggio

- ⅔ oz (20 g) fresh yeast, crumbled, or 1 (¼ oz/7 g) packet active dry yeast (2¼ teaspoons)
- 1 teaspoon sugar
- 4 cups (500 g) all-purpose (plain) flour, divided
- Scant ½ cup (100 ml) milk
- Scant ½ cup (100 ml) extra virgin olive oil
- 1 cup (100 g) grated Pecorino Romano cheese
- 1 cup (100 g) grated Parmesan cheese
- 2¾ oz (80 g) fresh pecorino cheese, cut into cubes
- 5 eggs, beaten
- Salt and black pepper
- Wild radicchio and cheese or vegan charcuterie, for serving

Preparation Time: 30 minutes
plus resting time
Cooking Time: 30 minutes
Serves: 8

Line a deep 7-inch (18 cm) round baking pan with parchment paper.

In a large bowl, combine the yeast, sugar, and 3½ table-spoons (50 ml) warm water. Add 6 tablespoons (50 g) of the flour and stir to combine. Cover the bowl and let stand for 30 minutes to activate the yeast.

Mound the remaining flour on your work surface and make a well in the center. Add the yeast mixture, olive oil, milk, eggs, grated pecorino, Parmesan, a pinch of salt, and some pepper to the well and use a fork to gradually incorporate them into the flour to form a dough. Knead the dough for 5 minutes.

Add the fresh pecorino and knead for another 5 minutes, slamming the dough against your work surface. Form the dough into a ball and place it in the prepared pan. Tent the dough with foil and let it rise in a warm place for 2 hours.

Preheat the oven to 350°F (180°C).

Uncover the dough and bake for about 30 minutes, until a wooden skewer inserted into the center comes out clean. Remove from the oven and let cool. Serve with wild radicchio and cheese or vegan charcuterie.

For a vegan version of this recipe, leave out the eggs and replace the cheeses with vegan cheeses (use a hard vegan cheese for grating and a softer one to replace the fresh pecorino). For additional flavor, add a pinch of saffron (one 0.4 g sachet) or 1 teaspoon ground turmeric to the dough.

Onion Focaccia

Focaccia di cipolle

- 1 cup (250 ml) warm milk
- 1 teaspoon sugar
- 2 teaspoons active dry yeast
- 2 cups (250 g) all-purpose (plain) flour
- 1 egg
- 3½ tablespoons (50 g) butter, plus more for greasing
- 2 large onions, finely chopped
- 2 sprigs parsley, finely chopped
- Olive oil
- Salt

Preparation Time: 20 minutes
plus 2 hours rising time
Cooking Time: 30 minutes
Serves: 4

Pour half the milk into a bowl and stir in the sugar. Sprinkle the yeast over the surface and let stand for 10 to 15 minutes, until frothy. Stir well to make a smooth paste.

Mix the yeast with sufficient flour to make a small ball of soft dough about the size of a bread roll. Cover and let rise at warm room temperature for about 1 hour.

Sift the remaining flour and a pinch of salt directly onto your work surface and form it into a mound. Make a well in the center of the mound. Break the egg into the well, add the dough, and stir with a fork to combine them with the flour, adding enough milk to form a soft dough. Shape into a ball, cover, and let rise for 1 hour.

Preheat the oven to 350°F (180°C). Grease the bottom of an 8-inch (20 cm) shallow cake pan with butter.

In a medium frying pan, melt the butter over low heat. Add the onions and cook, stirring occasionally, for 8 to 10 minutes, until very soft but not colored. Season with salt, stir in the parsley, and remove the pan from the heat.

Reserve a few spoonfuls of the onion mixture and add the remainder to the dough, working it in briefly by hand. Shape the dough into a round and put it into the prepared pan. Spread the remaining onion mixture over the top, cover with foil, and bake for 30 minutes. Remove from the oven, turn out onto a serving plate, and serve hot.

Herb-Stuffed Bread

Erbazzone

- Scant 2½ cups (300 g) all-purpose (plain) flour
- ½ cup (120 ml) plus 1 tablespoon extra virgin olive
  - oil
- 4 spring onions, sliced
- 1 clove garlic, finely chopped
- 2 lb 3 oz (1 kg) spinach, coarsely chopped
- ⅔ cup (60 g) grated Parmesan cheese
- Salt and black pepper

Preparation Time: 30 minutes
plus resting time
Cooking Time: 55 minutes
Serves: 4 to 6

In a large bowl, stir together the flour, ¼ cup (60 ml) of the olive oil, a pinch of salt, and ⅔ cup (150 ml) water, then knead the dough until it is smooth and soft. Wrap the dough in plastic wrap (cling film) and refrigerate for at least 30 minutes.

Preheat the oven to 350°F (180°C). Line an 11-inch (28 cm) round baking pan with parchment paper.

Meanwhile, in a nonstick frying pan, heat 4 to 5 tablespoons oil over medium-low heat. Add the onions and garlic and cook gently for 5 minutes. Add the spinach, a pinch of salt, and some pepper. Raise the heat to medium-high and cook for about 10 minutes, until all the liquid has evaporated. Add the Parmesan and stir.

Divide the dough in half. On a lightly floured surface, roll out half the dough into a thin sheet and transfer it to the prepared pan, pressing the dough into the corners. Pour in the spinach mixture and level the top with a spatula.

Roll the remaining dough into a thin sheet and place it over the filling, then roll the edges decoratively to seal. Prick the dough all over with a fork and bake the tart for about 35 minutes, then brush the top with a little oil and bake for another 5 minutes. Serve.

For a vegan version, replace the Parmesan cheese with ¼ cup (40 g) chia seeds. Chia seeds, from the *Salvia hispanica* plant, can be traced back to the Aztecs, and are rich in omega-3 and omega-6 fatty acids, which are powerful antioxidants, as well as iron, calcium, magnesium, potassium, vitamin C, and fiber.

Buckwheat Pizza with Green Beans and Tomatoes

Pizza di grano saraceno con fagiolini e pomodori

- ⅔ cup (100 g) rice flour
- 1¼ cups (150 g) buckwheat flour
- ⅓ oz (10 g) vegan powdered instant yeast for savory pies, sifted
- 2 tablespoons extra virgin olive oil, plus more as needed
- 5¼ oz (150 g) crescenza (stracchino) cheese, broken into small pieces
- 3½ oz (100 g) green beans, cut into small pieces and cooked
- 3½ oz (100 g) peeled roasted bell peppers, cut into small pieces
- 2 heirloom tomatoes, cut into wedges
- Basil leaves, for garnish
- Salt

Preparation Time: 20 minutes
plus resting time
Cooking Time: 25 minutes
Serves: 4

Preheat the oven to 400°F (200°C). Line a pizza pan with parchment paper.

In a large bowl, combine the rice flour, buckwheat flour, and yeast, then drizzle in ½ cup (120 ml) warm water and the olive oil and stir to combine. Knead the dough for at least 10 minutes. Turn the dough out onto a lightly floured surface and stretch it with your hands into a round, then cover it with a sheet of parchment paper and, using a rolling pin, roll it to a thickness of approximately ⅜ inch (5 mm).

Transfer the dough to the prepared pan, stretching it to fit the pan as needed, and spread half the crescenza cheese, the green beans, and the peppers evenly over the surface of the dough.

Sprinkle the pizza with a pinch of salt and drizzle with a little olive oil, then let it rest for 10 minutes.

Bake for about 15 minutes, then distribute the remaining crescenza cheese evenly over the pizza and bake for another 5 to 6 minutes.

Garnish with the tomatoes, a few basil leaves, a pinch of salt, and a drizzle of olive oil and serve.

If you prefer to use fresh yeast, let the dough rise for 2 hours after kneading, then transfer it to the prepared pan (no need to roll it out first) and stretch it to the edges of the pan. For a vegan version, use 2¾ oz (80 g) newly refreshed vegan sourdough starter (see page 56) and let the dough rise for 4 hours.

Basic Bread Dough

Pasta da pane

- ⅓ oz (10 g) fresh yeast, crumbled, or 1⅛ teaspoon active dry yeast
- 4¼ cups (500 g) "0" or bread flour (strong white flour)
- 1 teaspoon sugar
- 2 tablespoons extra virgin olive oil
- Salt

Preparation Time: 20 minutes plus 2 hours 30 minutes resting
Cooking Time: 30 minutes
Serves: 6
Makes 1 lb 2 oz (500 g) dough

Put the yeast in a bowl and add ⅓ cup (40 g) flour, the sugar, and ¼ cup (60 ml) water. Stir to mix the ingredients, cover the bowl with a clean cloth, and let the yeast bloom for 20 minutes, until foamy.

Sift the remaining flour onto your work surface, form it into a mound, and make a well in the center. Add the yeast mixture and the oil and sprinkle a teaspoon of salt around the sides. Add ¾ cup (175 ml) warm water and bring the ingredients together with your hands to make a dough. Knead for at least 10 minutes, keeping your fingers together as if they were a spatula and using your thumb to press down on the dough and stretch it. Slap the dough against the work surface occasionally to activate the gluten.

Shape the dough into a ball and put it in a large, lightly oiled bowl. Using a sharp knife, cut a cross in the top. Cover with a clean kitchen towel and let rise in a warm place for at least 2 hours.

Use the dough according to the recipe instructions or, to make bread, preheat the oven to 400°F (200°C). Lightly grease two 1-quart (1 l) loaf pans.

Punch down the dough without kneading it and divide it in half. Transfer one piece to each prepared pan. Cover and let rise for another 45 minutes.

Score the top of each loaf with a sharp knife and bake for about 30 minutes. Let the loaves rest in the pans for 10 minutes, then turn out of the pans and let cool completely before slicing and serving.

Tomato Pizza

Pizza rossa

- 2¼ lb (1 kg) very ripe plum tomatoes, chopped
- 4 to 5 tablespoons (60 to 75 ml) olive oil, plus more for greasing
- 2 to 3 tablespoons fresh basil leaves, torn into small pieces
- 2 cloves garlic, finely chopped
- 2 tablespoons fresh oregano leaves, or 1 generous pinch dried oregano
- 1 recipe Basic Bread Dough (recipe opposite)
- Salt

Preparation Time: 30 minutes
Cooking Time: 20 to 30 minutes
Serves: 4

Preheat the oven to 450°F (230°C) with a rack in the lowest position. Grease a 10 x 18-inch (25 x 45 cm) baking pan with oil.

In a large bowl, combine the tomatoes, olive oil, basil, garlic, and oregano and season with salt. Let stand for at least 30 minutes.

Drain off the juice released by the tomatoes and dampen the palms of your hands with a little of it. Using the palms of your hands, spread out the dough in the prepared baking pan. Sprinkle the tomato pieces over the surface of the dough and drizzle with oil. Bake on the lowest rack for 30 minutes, or until golden brown.

Oat Flour Pizza with Mushroom-Stuffed Crusts

Pizza d'avena col cornicione ai funghi shiitake

- 1¾ oz (50 g) vegan sourdough starter (see page 56), newly refreshed
- 1½ cups plus 1 tablespoon (200 g) all-purpose (plain) flour
- 1 cup plus 2 tablespoons (100 g) oat flour
- 1 teaspoon rice malt
- 5 tablespoons (75 ml) extra virgin olive oil, plus more as needed
- 1 teaspoon salt, plus more as needed
- 10½ oz (300 g) shiitake mushrooms, stemmed and finely chopped
- 1 small leek, washed well and finely chopped
- 7 oz (200 g) soy ricotta or other vegan ricotta cheese
- 4 or 5 basil leaves, thinly sliced, plus a few whole leaves for garnish
- ⅓ cup (80 ml) tomato purée (passata)
- 7 oz (200 g) vegan mozzarella, chopped

Preparation Time: 35 minutes plus resting time
Cooking Time: 25 minutes
Serves: 4

In a large bowl, combine the sourdough starter and ½ cup (120 ml) warm water and stir to dissolve the starter. Add the all-purpose (plain) flour, oat flour, rice malt, and 2 tablespoons of the olive oil and stir for 1 minute to combine. Add the salt, then knead the dough for 10 minutes. Cover the dough and let it rise in a warm place for 2 hours.

Preheat the oven to 450°F (230°C). Line a sheet pan with parchment paper.

In a nonstick frying pan, heat the remaining 3 tablespoons oil over low heat. Add the mushrooms, leek, and a pinch of salt and cook for 10 minutes.

Raise the heat to medium and cook until any remaining liquid has evaporated. Remove from the heat and let cool.

Add the ricotta and sliced basil to the cooled mushroom mixture and stir to combine. Transfer the mixture to a disposable piping bag.

Lightly punch down the dough and divide it into four equal pieces. Stretch each one into a thin round, putting them on the prepared pan as you go. On each round, pipe a ring of the ricotta mixture about 1 inch (2.5 cm) in from the edge of the dough and fold the edge over to enclose the filling, pressing with your fingertips to seal.

Spread the tomato purée (passata) over the bottom of each round and season with salt. Top with the mozzarella, dividing it evenly, then bake for about 15 minutes. Drizzle with oil, garnish with a few basil leaves, and serve.

The soy ricotta can be replaced with sheep's-milk ricotta, and the vegan mozzarella with fior di latte or another cow's-milk mozzarella.

White Pizza

Pizza bianca

- ¾ recipe Basic Bread Dough (page 74)
- 5 oz (150 g) mozzarella cheese, thinly sliced
- 5 oz (150 g) Taleggio cheese, thinly sliced
- A few fresh oregano leaves, chopped, or a generous pinch of dried oregano
- Olive oil, for drizzling
- Salt and pepper

Preparation Time: 15 minutes
Cooking Time: 20 minutes
Serves: 4

Preheat the oven to 425°F (220°C). Line a baking sheet with parchment (baking) paper.

On a lightly floured surface, roll out the dough thinly to fit the prepared baking sheet. Transfer the dough to the baking sheet and top with the mozzarella and Taleggio. Sprinkle with the oregano and season with salt and pepper. Drizzle with olive oil. Bake for about 20 minutes, then remove from the oven and serve.

If you like a thin crust for your pizza, follow the method above. If you prefer a thicker, softer crust, cover the dough and let it rise for an additional 45 minutes after placing it on the baking sheet.

Potato Pizza

Pizza di patate

- Olive oil, for brushing and drizzling
- 3 large waxy potatoes
- ¾ recipe Basic Bread Dough (page 74)
- Scant 1 cup (100 g) diced Taleggio cheese
- 2 oz (50 g) Parmesan cheese, shaved
- 1 tablespoon rosemary
- Salt and pepper

Preparation Time: 15 minutes
Cooking Time: 45 minutes
Serves: 4

Preheat the oven to 425°F (220°C). Brush a baking pan with olive oil.

Bring a large pot of salted water to a boil. Add the potatoes and cook for 12 minutes, or until tender. Drain and let cool, then peel the potatoes and thinly slice them.

Spread the dough out in the prepared baking pan so that it comes a little way up the sides. Top the dough with the potatoes and drizzle with a little oil.

Bake for about 15 minutes, then top evenly with the cheese, sprinkle with the rosemary, and season with salt and pepper. Return to the oven and bake for 7 to 8 minutes more, then serve hot.

Puglian Focaccia

Focaccia pugliese

- 1 potato
- 2 teaspoons active dry yeast
- 1 teaspoon sugar
- 2 cups (250 g) "00" flour
- 4 to 5 tablespoons (60 to 75 ml) extra virgin olive oil, plus more for greasing
- 12 cherry tomatoes
- Pinch of dried oregano
- Salt

Preparation Time: 20 minutes plus 1 hour 30 minutes rising
Cooking Time: 25 minutes
Serves: 6

Fill a medium saucepan with an inch or two of water, set a steamer basket inside, and bring the water to a simmer. Cut the potato into chunks, put them in the steamer, and steam for 15 minutes, until tender. Transfer the potato to a bowl and mash until smooth. Let cool.

In a small bowl, combine the yeast, sugar, and a scant ⅔ cup (150 ml) warm water. Sift the flour into a mound in a large bowl or directly onto a clean work surface and make a well in the center. Add the potato to the well, pour in the yeast mixture, and mix together to form a soft, smooth dough. Transfer to a lightly oiled bowl, cover with plastic wrap (cling film), and let rise in a warm place until doubled in volume.

Lightly grease a 13½-inch (34 cm) baking sheet. Transfer the dough to the baking sheet, pour over 2 to 3 tablespoons of the olive oil, and press the dough out with your hands to the edges of the baking sheet. Push the cherry tomatoes deep into the dough, sprinkle the oregano on top, and season with salt. Cover the focaccia and let rise for 1 hour.

Preheat the oven to 400°F (200°C).

In a small bowl, whisk 1 tablespoon water with the remaining 2 tablespoons oil and brush it over the dough. Bake for 25 minutes.

Avoid adding the yeast at the same time as the salt, because the salt interferes with the fermentation of the enzymes in the yeast if in direct contact. Begin by combining the yeast and its liquid together with the flour, and only after this season with salt.

Kamut Calzone with Asparagus and Egg

Calzone di kamut con asparagi e uovo

- 4 cups (500 g) whole-grain Kamut flour
- ⅓ oz (10 g) fresh yeast, crumbled, or ½ (¼ oz/7 g) packet active dry yeast (1⅛ teaspoons)
- 1 teaspoon sugar
- 3 tablespoons extra virgin olive oil
- 4 teaspoons salt
- 1 bunch asparagus, tough ends trimmed
- 4 eggs
- 5¼ oz (150 g) mozzarella cheese
- 1½ oz (40 g) Parmesan cheese, grated

Preparation Time: 30 minutes plus resting time
Cooking Time: 25 minutes
Serves: 4

Put the flour in a large bowl. In a small bowl, combine the yeast, sugar, and 1¼ cups (300 ml) warm water and stir to dissolve the yeast, then pour the mixture over the flour. Add the olive oil and stir to combine. Add the salt and knead the dough for at least 10 minutes. Cover the dough and let it rise in a warm place for 2 hours.

Slice the mozzarella and spread it on paper towels to dry.

Preheat the oven to 400°F (200°C). Line a sheet pan with parchment paper.

Lightly punch down the dough, divide it into four equal portions, and roll out each portion into a thin disk.

Place ¼ of the asparagus and the sliced mozzarella, and a cracked, raw egg on one-half of each disk. Sprinkle with salt, top with ¼ of the Parmensan and fold the dough over the filling to form a half-moon and press the edges to seal. Transfer the calzones to the prepared pan. Bake for about 20 minutes, then serve.

For a vegan version of this recipe, make the dough with 3½ oz (100 g) newly refreshed vegan sourdough starter (see page 56) in place of the yeast; replace the cow's-milk mozzarella with rice mozzarella and the Parmesan with 2 tablespoons ground flaxseeds (linseeds) and a pinch of salt, and omit the eggs.

Salads & Vegetable Sides

Cooked or raw vegetables (especially when in season), grains or pasta, and protein-rich foods such as legumes, cheese, eggs, oily seeds, and tofu—served with appetizing dressings, these are the ingredients needed to prepare tasty salads and side dishes, which can be served year-round as a single-course meal or, in smaller portions, as a delightful starter.

Rich single-course meals for all seasons

At one time, salads were almost exclusively composed of raw leafy vegetables and served as a side dish. Today, salads contain a wide spectrum of ingredients and can undoubtedly be a menu's main player.

The value of dressings

The word *salad* comes from the Latin *salada*, meaning "dressed," and as the translation implies, dressing is an essential component of a salad. Extra virgin olive oil is a common ingredient in dressings and is full of nutritional goodness (and also rich in calories, so it's best not to use *too* much). Less traditional dressing and seasoning ideas include tasty soy sauce, which has antioxidant properties, and gomasio, an Asian seasoning made from salt and toasted sesame seeds, which are rich in calcium and beneficial against heartburn.

A complete meal

Combining vegetables, grains of any type, and protein-rich foods in a big salad creates a balanced dish that supplies the body with the main nutrients it needs: vitamins, minerals, carbohydrates, fiber, and protein. The combination of grains and legumes is also beneficial: when eaten together, they can supply the essential amino acids your body needs, making a complete protein as good as those of animal origin.

Raw or steamed

Salads are a good way to eat raw vegetables, which, in a balanced vegetarian diet, should always be consumed alongside cooked vegetables. Serving vegetables raw allows us to appreciate their natural crunchiness and prevents the loss of nutrients, including water-soluble vitamins like vitamin C. Lightly steaming vegetables, if the recipe requires it, is an absolutely acceptable alternative to eating them raw, as steaming preserves the vegetables' flavor and visual appeal as well as their nutritional qualities.

Irreplaceable grains

Grains are also among the most balanced natural ingredients and represent an essential component of any diet, not just a vegetarian diet. Grains, including rice, wheat, farro, corn, and barley (to name but a few), are the body's main source of carbohydrates. They supply fiber, protein, B vitamins, and minerals such as potassium, iron, phosphorus, and calcium. Whole grains are preferable to refined grains, as they have not been subjected to processes that strip away their nutritional benefits.

Lots of great ideas for the table

Salads—the name may be the same, but the ways to prepare salads are many and varied. And as always, the most important ingredient is your imagination.

A crunchy note

Seeds impart a touch of crunchiness to salads, but they also have many beneficial qualities. Sesame seeds, for example, reactivate blood circulation and aid diuresis; flaxseeds (linseeds) promote good digestion; sunflower seeds have anti-inflammatory qualities; and pumpkin seeds are rich in iron and promote a feeling of fullness.

A special "dress"

The most classic salads are a combination of raw and cooked vegetables. Classic, however, does not mean boring. What can make the difference is the dressing. The most common ones are vinaigrette, based on vinegar, and citronette, prepared with lemon, oil, and salt, but give the imagination free rein and try dressings made from yogurt, honey, spices, aromatic herbs, mustard, and even gourmet touches such as almond oil or blackberry vinegar. One more idea? Indian chutney, prepared with fruit, vegetables, and spices.

Grains for all tastes

When we talk about salads made with grains, we often think of rice and pasta salads, but there are many alternatives. Farro, for example, goes well with almost all vegetables, and so does barley. Less common but equally versatile is millet, which works very well with vegetables such as spinach, artichokes, and celery. Middle Eastern cuisine gives us bulgur, a cracked wheat, and the classic grain salad tabbouleh, and North African couscous, made with semolina, can be wonderful in salads as well.

Plenty of protein

To stand on its own as a meal, a salad needs the addition of a protein-rich ingredient Both fresh and dried legumes provide protein contents that are on a par with those of meat, eggs, and dairy products. Unlike these animal products, however, they do not contain cholesterol and saturated fats; therefore they have no negative effects on the heart. Their carbohydrate content also makes them good sources of energy. Legumes also contain B vitamins and minerals, including iron. Their fiber content, approximately 10 g per portion on average (a third of the recommended daily intake for adults), promotes good digestion.

Best with grains

In a balanced vegetarian meal, legumes are often used in combination with grains in the main course, which offers precise nutritional benefits: legumes are poor in sulphates, essential amino acids that are found in grains. Combining them, therefore, ensures a complete protein mix.

To complete a meal

The main course can be accompanied by a vegetable side dish and a piece of fruit. Those rich in vitamin C (like tomatoes, cauliflowers, kiwis, and citrus fruits), which helps the body absorb the iron in legumes, are best. Alternatively, create a single-course meal that includes vegetables in addition to legumes and grains: the ideal proportions would be for the grains to occupy half the plate, with the rest divided between legumes (one-third) and vegetables (two-thirds).

The ingredients to always have on hand

Some grains and legumes have long been used in the preparation of salads, while others have only more recently been introduced.

Wheat

Wheat varieties can classified by hardness, color, and season. One common variety is durum wheat (a hard spring wheat), which is used in various preparations depending on how fine or coarse it was milled. Durum wheat can be cracked, parboiled, and dried to create bulgur, and semolina (a coarsely ground durum flour) is used to make couscous and pasta. As well as being a source of carbohydrates, wheat contains B vitamins and minerals.

Rice, farro, and barley

Compared to other grains, rice contains more starch, is gluten-free, and offers biologically more valuable protein. It is particularly easy to digest, so it is beneficial to those with digestive problems, and it is also slightly diuretic. Farro, one of the most ancient cultivated grains, is also very easy to digest and is rich in protein. Barley, as well as having diuretic and detoxifying properties, also reduces fat absorption thanks to the fiber it contains.

Corn, millet, and oats

The corn used in cooking is a sweet variety and contains good amounts of carbohydrates, phosphorus, and potassium. Millet is very rich in protein, carbohydrates, vitamins, fiber, and minerals, and is a natural tonic for stress and fatigue. Oats are a precious source of nutrients such as protein, fiber, calcium, phosphorus, and potassium but can be less easy to digest than most grains.

Amaranth

Used for centuries in Central and South America, amaranth is a small spherical and light-colored grain. It has significant nutritional benefits and is rich in lysine, an amino acid that improves tolerance to stress and promotes the production of antibodies.

Chickpeas and beans	Beans, including chickpeas, cannellini beans, and butter beans, are among the most commonly used legumes. Varieties originally from other parts of the world have started to find favor elsewhere, like adzuki beans from Japan, which are considered the "king of legumes" for their nutritional value and purifying properties, and mung beans from India, which are excellent in soups. Chickpeas, which can help lower cholesterol, have always been appreciated in salads and soups, but are also wonderful when puréed and served as hummus or formed into patties to make veggie burgers.
Lentils and peas	Lentils come in different shapes and colors, depending on the variety. Brown lentils are probably the most common, but split red lentils and smaller dark green varieties are also popular. They are the only legumes that do not require soaking prior to cooking. They are used in soups, but can also be used in many other preparations. There are 250 varieties of peas, which come in different sizes: extra small ones are sweet and tender, while larger ones require longer cooking times. They are the legumes with the lowest calorie count, at 70 calories per 3 ½ oz (100 g).
Fava (broad) beans and soybeans	A typical ingredient of Mediterranean cuisine, fava (broad) beans have a pleasant taste, slightly bitter and salty, and significant nutritional values in terms of protein (3½ oz/100 g of dried fava [broad] beans contain 27 g of protein) and carbohydrates. Soybeans, originally from China and Japan, have the highest percentage of protein and polyunsaturated fats. They can be processed into soybean oil, soybean flour, and soy milk, or used to make tofu and tempeh.

Fennel and Artichoke Salad

Insalata di Finocchi e Carciofi

- ½ cup (120 ml) olive oil
- Juice of 1 orange, strained
- 3 fennel bulbs, cored, tough outer layers removed
- Juice of 1 lemon, strained
- 2 globe artichokes
- 1 tablespoon very small capers, drained and rinsed
- Salt and pepper

Preparation Time: 30 minutes
Serves: 4

In a small bowl, whisk together the olive oil and orange juice and season with salt and pepper.

Very thinly slice the fennel, preferably using a mandoline.

Fill a large bowl with cool water and add the lemon juice. Trim the artichokes, remove the fuzzy chokes, and cut the artichokes into small pieces, dropping them into the bowl of lemon water as you go (this prevents browning).

Drain the artichokes thoroughly and put them in a salad bowl. Add the fennel and sprinkle with the capers.

Drizzle the orange dressing over the salad and serve.

Green Salad with Three Dressings

Insalatina con tris di dressing

- ¼ cup (60 ml) soy sauce
- 1 tablespoon balsamic vinegar
- 1 teaspoon honey mustard
- ¾ cup (175 ml) extra virgin olive oil
- 1 tablespoon finely chopped fresh chives
- Salt
- 1 (1¼-inch/3 cm) piece fresh ginger, peeled and finely grated
- Zest and juice of ½ orange
- Juice of 1 lemon
- 1 small hot chile, minced
- 1 tablespoon chopped cilantro (fresh coriander) leaves
- 1 small avocado, pitted and peeled
- Scant ½ cup (100 g) yogurt
- Juice of ½ lime
- Handful of basil leaves
- 2 cucumbers
- 2 slices rustic bread, cut into small cubes
- 1 small bunch radishes, thinly sliced
- 3 carrots, sliced into thin ribbons
- 1 yellow bell pepper, thinly sliced
- 3½ oz (100 g) mixed salad greens
- 2 tablespoons mixed seeds

Preparation Time: 25 minutes
Cooking Time: 4 minutes
Serves: 4

To make the balsamic dressing, in a jar, combine the soy sauce, balsamic vinegar, mustard, 3 tablespoons of the olive oil, chives, and a pinch of salt. Seal the jar and shake to combine.

To make the ginger dressing, in a small bowl, whisk together the ginger, orange zest, orange juice, lemon juice, chile, cilantro (fresh coriander), and ¼ cup (60 ml) of the olive oil.

To make the avocado dressing, in a food processor, combine the avocado, yogurt, 3 tablespoons of the olive oil, lime juice, and basil and pulse until well combined and smooth. Transfer to a serving bowl.

To assemble the salad, peel the cucumbers in alternating strips, cut them in half lengthwise, and seed them. Cut them crosswise into small chunks.

Drizzle the bread cubes with the remaining olive oil. Toast the bread in a frying pan over medium-high heat for 3 to 4 minutes, until golden and crunchy, then place them on paper towels to absorb excess oil.

In a large bowl, combine the cucumbers, radishes, carrots, bell pepper, and mixed greens. Top the salad with the seeds and croutons and serve with the three dressings alongside.

To enhance the flavor of the seeds, toast them in a heavy-bottomed nonstick frying pan, stirring them continuously, for 3 to 4 minutes, then let cool before adding them to the salad.

Composed Vegetable Salad with Tarragon Vinaigrette

Insalata di verdure con salsa al dragoncello

- 2 bunches asparagus, ends trimmed
- 7 oz (200 g) green beans
- 1½ cups (200 g) cauliflower florets
- Scant ½ cup (100 ml) plus 2 tablespoons extra virgin olive oil
- 2 egg yolks
- Juice of ½ lemon, strained
- Scant ½ cup (100 ml) peanut (groundnut) oil
- Leaves from 1 sprig tarragon, chopped
- 1 small beet, roasted, peeled, and sliced
- 1 lettuce heart, thinly sliced
- 1¾ oz (50 g) watercress, trimmed, leaves separated
- Salt and black pepper

Preparation Time: 20 minutes
Cooking Time: 12 minutes
Serves: 4

Bring a large pot of salted water to a boil. Add the asparagus and cook for 3 to 4 minutes, then use tongs to transfer it to a colander to drain and cool. Add the green beans and cauliflower to the boiling water and cook for 7 to 8 minutes, then drain and let cool slightly.

Chop the asparagus, green beans, and cauliflower into small chunks and combine them in a large bowl. Sprinkle them with a pinch of salt, drizzle with 2 tablespoons of the olive oil, and toss to coat.

In a blender cup or medium bowl, combine the egg yolks and lemon juice and blend briefly with a hand blender to combine. In a spouted measuring cup, combine the remaining olive oil and the peanut (groundnut) oil. With the blender running, very slowly stream in the oils and blend until the mayonnaise is emulsified and thickened. Season with salt and pepper and stir in the tarragon.

Just before serving, arrange the asparagus mixture on a serving dish and arrange the slices of beet alongside. Drizzle the mayonnaise on top of everything, garnish with the lettuce and the watercress leaves, and serve immediately.

For a vegan version of the recipe, replace the classic mayonnaise with vegan mayonnaise. To make your own, in a food processor, combine a scant ½ cup (100 ml) unflavored soy milk, a scant ½ cup (100 ml) peanut (groundnut) oil, the juice of ½ lemon, a pinch of salt, and 1 teaspoon honey mustard and process until emulsified and thickened.

Roasted Vegetable Salad

Insalata di verdure grigliate

- 2 round eggplants (aubergines), sliced ¼ inch (0.5 cm) thick
- 2 yellow bell peppers
- 1 red bell pepper
- 4 tomatoes on the vine
- ¼ cup (60 ml) extra virgin olive oil, plus more as needed
- Leaves from 1 sprig oregano
- Salt

Preparation Time: 20 minutes plus resting time
Cooking Time: 30 minutes
Serves: 4

Preheat the broiler.

In a very hot grill pan, cook the eggplant (aubergine) slices for 30 seconds per side. Transfer them to a cutting board, cut them into small strips, and place them in a large bowl.

Brush the bell peppers with a little oil and place them on a sheet pan. Broil, turning them to ensure they cook evenly, until charred and softened, 4 to 5 minutes. Remove from the oven (keep the broiler on), transfer to a bowl, cover with plastic wrap (cling film), and let cool. Peel and seed the peppers, then thinly slice the flesh and add it to the bowl with the eggplant.

Lightly oil the tomatoes and place them on a sheet pan. Broil for 5 minutes, turning them over from time to time, until their skin cracks and begins to peel off. Remove from the oven and let cool. Peel the tomatoes, transfer the flesh to a bowl, and mash with a fork until puréed. Sprinkle with a pinch of salt and drizzle with the olive oil, then add the tomato to the bowl with the eggplant and peppers.

Serve the salad sprinkled with the oregano.

The same quantity of plum tomatoes can be used in place of the tomatoes on the vine: slice them thickly and cook them on a grill pan for 30 seconds per side, then remove the skin and chop the flesh into small cubes. Enrich the salad with a scant ½ cup (20 g) arugula sprouts and 1 heaping tablespoon wheat germ.

Baby Zucchini Salad

Insalata di zucchine novelle

- 6 baby zucchini (courgettes), thinly sliced
- 2 oz (50 g) Parmesan cheese, shaved
- Pinch of dried oregano
- 1 tablespoon olive oil
- 2 tomatoes, peeled and sliced
- Salt and pepper

Preparation Time: 15 minutes plus 30 minutes resting time
Serves: 4

Put the zucchini (courgettes) in a salad bowl, add the Parmesan, oregano, and olive oil, and season with salt and pepper. Mix well and set aside in a cool place for at least 30 minutes to allow the flavors to mingle. Add the tomatoes just before serving.

Fennel and pink grapefruit

Finocchi e pompelmi rosa

- 4 tender fennel bulbs, cored, tough outer layers removed
- 2 pink grapefruits
- 7 oz (200 g) celery, blanched and julienned
- 5 tablespoons (75 ml) olive oil
- Juice of ½ lemon, strained
- 1 sprig mint, finely chopped
- Salt and pepper

Preparation Time: 15 minutes
Serves: 4

Thinly slice the fennel.

Peel the grapefruits, removing all the bitter white pith. Cut out the segments between the membranes and put them in a large salad bowl. Add the celery and the fennel.

In a small bowl, whisk together the olive oil and the lemon juice. Add the mint and season with salt and pepper. Drizzle the dressing over the salad, toss well, and serve.

Avocado Salad

Insalata di avocado

- 2 avocados
- Juice of 1 lemon, strained
- 2 mandarins or tangerines
- 1 head romaine lettuce, leaves separated
- 2 tomatoes, sliced
- 1 spring onion, sliced
- 2 tablespoons chopped flat-leaf parsley
- 2 teaspoons Dijon mustard
- 6 tablespoons (90 ml) olive oil
- Salt and pepper

Preparation Time: 25 minutes
Serves: 4

Halve, pit, and peel the avocados, then slice them and sprinkle with the lemon juice to prevent discoloration. Peel the mandarins, removing all traces of the white pith, and cut them into round slices.

Arrange the lettuce leaves on four individual serving dishes. Make a layer of tomato and spring onion slices on the leaves, cover with avocado slices in a circle, and top with slices of mandarin. Sprinkle with the parsley.

In a small bowl, whisk together the mustard, olive oil, a pinch of salt, and a pinch of pepper. Pour the dressing evenly over the salads and serve.

Spinach and Mushroom Salad

Insalata di spinaci e funghi

- 5 oz (150 g) mushrooms, thinly sliced
- Juice of 1 lemon, strained
- 11 oz (300 g) spinach, any thick stems removed
- 3 tablespoons pine nuts
- ¼ cup (60 ml) olive oil
- Salt and pepper

Preparation Time: 15 minutes
Serves: 4

Sprinkle the mushrooms with a little of the lemon juice and place in a salad bowl. Add the spinach and pine nuts.

In a small bowl, whisk together the olive oil and remaining lemon juice and season with salt and pepper. Pour the dressing over the salad, toss, and serve.

Asparagus and Herb Salad

Tartara d'asparagi alle erbette

- 16 asparagus spears, trimmed
- 2 tomatoes, peeled, seeded, and diced
- 1 bunch basil, finely chopped
- 2 bunches chervil, finely chopped
- 2 avocados
- Juice of 1 lemon
- 1 shallot, finely chopped
- 1 teaspoon capers
- ¼ cup (60 ml) olive oil
- 2 tablespoons apple cider vinegar
- Salt and pepper

Preparation Time: 30 minutes
Cooking Time: 20 minutes
Serves: 4

Bring a tall pot of lightly salted water to a boil. Trim the asparagus spears to the same length and tie them into a bundle with kitchen twine. Add the asparagus, standing it upright with the tips protruding above the water level. Cover and simmer for 15 minutes, or until tender. Lift out the asparagus and drain on paper towels, then let cool.

Put the tomatoes, basil, and chervil in a salad bowl. Halve, pit, and peel the avocados, then dice them and place them in a medium bowl. Toss with the lemon juice to prevent discoloration. Cut the asparagus spears into ¾-inch (2 cm) lengths, mix with the shallot and capers, and add to the salad bowl. Add the avocado and stir gently. Season with salt and pepper, drizzle with the olive oil and vinegar, toss gently, and serve.

Winter Salad with Mustard Dressing

Insalata invernale alla senape

- 1 small cauliflower, cut into small florets, any large florets quartered
- 10½ oz (300 g) broccoli, crown cut into florets, stem peeled and thinly sliced
- 2 medium potatoes
- 1¾ cups (300 g) cooked red kidney beans, drained and rinsed
- 2 endives, chopped
- 1 head Tardivo or Treviso radicchio, chopped
- 1 teaspoon whole-grain mustard
- 1 tablespoon apple cider vinegar
- 1 teaspoon acacia honey
- ¼ cup (60 ml) extra virgin olive oil
- 1 tablespoon coarsely chopped fresh parsley leaves
- Salt and black pepper

Preparation Time: 10 minutes
Cooking time: 20 minutes
Serves: 4

Fill a large saucepan with an inch or two of water, set a steamer basket inside, and bring the water to a simmer. Add the cauliflower and broccoli, cover, and steam for 5 to 6 minutes, until they are just tender but still crunchy. Transfer the cauliflower and broccoli to a large bowl and set aside.

Fill a large bowl with cool water. Peel the potatoes and cut them into small pieces, dropping them into the bowl as you go. Drain the potatoes, transfer to the steamer basket, cover, and steam for 10 to 12 minutes. Turn off the heat and transfer the potatoes to the bowl with the cauliflower and broccoli.

Add the beans, endives, and radicchio to the bowl with the vegetables.

In a small bowl, whisk together the mustard, vinegar, honey, olive oil, parsley, a pinch of salt, and some pepper.

Drizzle the salad with the dressing and serve.

For a vegan version, replace the honey with the same quantity of date syrup or rice malt. The salad can be prepared with various raw or cooked vegetables, depending on the season. Dress the salad just before serving, so that the vegetables are not left to marinate in the salt and vinegar for too long.

Farmhouse Salad

Insalata del contadino

- 1 lb 2 oz (500 g) cooked potatoes, diced
- 7 oz (200 g) cooked haricots verts (French beans)
- 7 oz (200 g) cooked or canned borlotti beans, drained, if canned
- 1 small onion, thinly sliced into rings
- 2 tablespoons white wine vinegar
- 6 tablespoons (90 ml) olive oil
- 4 to 6 basil leaves, torn
- Salt

Preparation time: 10 minutes
Serves: 4

In a serving dish, toss together the potatoes, haricots verts (French beans), and borlotti beans and sprinkle with the onion. Pour the vinegar into a small bowl and whisk in a generous pinch of salt. Add the olive oil and whisk well to combine. Pour the dressing over the salad, sprinkle with the basil, and serve.

Warm Couscous Salad with Tomatoes and Peppers

Insalata tiepida di cuscus, pomodori, e peperoni

- 1 yellow bell pepper
- 1 red bell pepper
- 1⅓ cups (200 g) cherry tomatoes, halved
- 1 clove garlic, thinly sliced
- 5 to 6 tablespoons (75 to 90 ml) extra virgin olive oil, plus more as needed
- 2 carrots, cut on an angle into small chunks
- 1 spring onion
- 1⅔ cups (400 ml) vegetable stock
- 1½ cups (300 g) farro couscous
- Scant 2 cups (300 g) canned chickpeas, drained and rinsed
- Juice of ½ lemon
- Pinch of fennel seeds
- Crushed pink peppercorns
- Salt

Preparation Time: 25 minutes
plus resting time
Cooking Time: 30 minutes
Serves: 4

Preheat the broiler. Bring a large pot of salted water to a boil.

Brush the bell peppers with a little oil and place them on a sheet pan. Broil, turning them to ensure they cook evenly, until lightly charred and softened, 4 to 5 minutes. Remove from the oven (keep the broiler on), transfer to a bowl, cover with plastic wrap (cling film), and let cool.

In a medium bowl, combine the tomatoes, garlic, 1 tablespoon of the olive oil, and a pinch of salt. Spread them over a sheet pan and broil for 10 minutes.

Add the carrots and the spring onion to the boiling water and cook for 5 minutes, then drain and let cool.

In a medium saucepan, bring the stock to a boil. Put the couscous in a medium bowl and pour into the hot stock. Cover and let stand for about 10 minutes, until the couscous has absorbed the stock.

Place the chickpeas in a clean kitchen towel and rub gently to remove their skins; discard the skins. Peel and seed the roasted bell peppers, then finely dice the flesh.

In a food processor, combine the blanched spring onion, remaining 4 to 5 tablespoons (75 to 90 ml) oil, the lemon juice, fennel seeds, and a pinch of salt. Process until well combined and smooth.

In a large bowl, combine the carrots, roasted peppers, tomatoes, and chickpeas. Drizzle with the spring onion dressing.

Fluff the couscous with a fork and add it to the bowl with the vegetables. Toss the couscous and vegetables to combine, sprinkle with the pink pepper, and serve.

If you prefer to cook the chickpeas yourself, combine ¾ cup (150 g) dried chickpeas and a ¾-inch (2 cm) square of kombu seaweed in a large bowl, add cold water to cover, and set aside to soak overnight. Drain them and transfer the chickpeas and kombu to a saucepan. Add cold water to cover, 1 garlic clove, and a bay leaf, then cook for about 2 hours, until the chickpeas are tender. Let cool before using.

Farro Salad with Poached Eggs

Insalata di farro con uovo in camicia

- 1½ cups (300 g) pearled farro, rinsed
- 1 head puntarelle
- Leaves from 1 small bunch basil
- Leaves from 3 sprigs marjoram
- Leaves from 3 sprigs thyme
- 5 tablespoons (40 g) raw almonds
- 4 to 5 tablespoons (60 to 75 ml) extra virgin olive oil
- 3½ oz (100 g) wild radicchio, leaves separated
- 7 oz (200 g) baby zucchini (courgettes), sliced into thin ribbons
- 1 tablespoon distilled white vinegar
- 1 teaspoon salt, plus more as needed
- 4 eggs
- Black pepper

Preparation Time: 20 minutes
Cooking Time: 45 minutes
Serves: 4

Bring a medium saucepan of salted water to a boil. Add the farro and cook for about 25 minutes.

Fill a large bowl with ice and water. Core the puntarelle, separate the leaves, and cut them into thin strips. Put them in the ice water and set aside to curl.

In a food processor, combine the basil, marjoram, thyme, almonds, olive oil, a pinch of salt, and a generous sprinkle of pepper. Pulse until well combined.

Drain the farro in a colander, run it under cold running water to cool it, then transfer it to a large bowl. Add the pesto and stir to coat the farro.

Drain the puntarelle. Divide the radicchio and puntarelle among individual plates and divide the farro and zucchini (courgettes) on top.

Fill a large shallow saucepan with 2 inches (5 cm) of water and bring to a boil. Add the vinegar and the salt and stir the water in a circular motion to create a gentle whirlpool. Crack an egg into a small bowl and gently slide the egg into the center of the whirlpool (this helps the egg white wrap around the yolk). Cook for 4 minutes, then use a slotted spoon to gently transfer the egg to paper towels to drain excess water. Repeat to poach the remaining eggs.

Arrange a poached egg over the farro on each plate and serve.

Pearled farro has had its bran layer removed, which allows it to cook faster than semi-pearled and whole-grain farro. For a vegan version, replace the egg with 7 oz (200 g) tempeh, cubed and marinated in a bowl with the juice of 1 lime and ¼ cup (60 ml) soy sauce, then drained and sautéed in a frying pan with 3 tablespoons olive oil.

Rice Salad with Artichokes and Fennel

Insalata di riso, carciofi e finocchi

- 1¼ cups (250 g) brown rice, rinsed
- Juice of 1 lemon, strained
- 2 artichokes
- 3 tablespoons roasted peanuts, coarsely chopped
- 3½ oz (100 g) smoked scamorza cheese, cut into small cubes
- 2 fennel bulbs, bulbs cut into small cubes, fronds finely chopped
- Juice of 1 orange, strained
- 4 to 5 tablespoons (60 to 75 ml) extra virgin olive oil
- Heaping 1½ teaspoons sweet paprika
- Salt

Preparation Time: 20 minutes
Cooking Time: 45 minutes
Serves: 4

Bring a medium pot of salted water to a boil. Add the rice and cook for about 25 minutes, until it is just tender but still firm. Drain it in a sieve, rinse under cold running water to cool, then drain and transfer it to a large bowl.

Fill a large bowl with cool water and add half the lemon juice. Trim the artichokes, halve them, and cut the fuzzy choke from the center, then thinly slice them, dropping the slices into the bowl of lemon water as you go (this prevents them from browning).

Add the peanuts, scamorza, and fennel and fennel fronds to the rice. Drain the artichokes, add them to the rice mixture, and stir thoroughly to combine.

In a small bowl, whisk together the remaining lemon juice with the orange juice, olive oil, paprika, and a pinch of salt.

Drizzle the dressing over the salad, stir, and serve.

The smoked scamorza can be replaced with the same quantity of smoked tofu, chopped into small cubes. It can be added directly to the salad, or it can first be sautéed in a frying pan with 2 tablespoons olive oil and a pinch of salt, then added to the salad while still warm.

Pasta Salad with Peas and Mint Pesto

Insalata di pasta con piselli al pesto di menta

- 1 lb 2 oz (500 g) fresh fava (broad) beans, shelled
- 1 lb 2 oz (500 g) fresh peas, shelled
- 7 oz (200 g) green beans, cut into small pieces
- 1 small red onion, such as Tropea or torpedo, very thinly sliced
- 8¾ oz (250 g) Kamut fusilli
- 5 or 6 mint leaves
- 3 tablespoons chopped wild fennel or fennel fronds
- Juice of ½ lemon
- 4 to 5 tablespoons (60 to 75 ml) extra virgin olive oil
- Salt and black pepper

Preparation Time: 20 minutes
Cooking Time: 35 minutes
Serves: 4

Bring a large pot of salted water to a boil. Add the fava (broad) beans and cook for 15 minutes. Use a spider (skimmer) to transfer them to a colander to drain and cool. Add the peas to the boiling water and cook for 7 to 8 minutes. Use the spider (skimmer) to transfer them to a colander to drain and cool. Add the green beans to the boiling water and cook for 5 minutes, then drain and let cool. Remove the fava (broad) beans from their skins and set aside.

Put the onion in a medium bowl, add cold water to cover, and set aside to soak for 10 minutes. Drain the onion and pat dry.

Bring a large pot of water to a boil. Salt the water, add the pasta, and cook according to the package instructions until al dente. Drain the pasta, rinse it under cold running water to cool, then drain it again and transfer it to a large bowl.

In a food processor, combine the mint, fennel, lemon juice, olive oil, and a generous sprinkle of pepper and process until smooth and well combined.

Dress the pasta with the mint pesto, add the fava (broad) beans, peas, and green beans, and toss to combine.

Arrange the pasta on individual serving plates, garnish with the red onion, and serve.

If small and very tender, fava (broad) beans can be used raw in salads. Out of season, frozen fava (broad) beans and peas can be used instead.

Harvest Salad Sandwiches

Insalata del mietitore

- 4 crusty rolls
- ¼ cup (60 ml) plus 2 tablespoons extra virgin olive oil
- 2 cucumbers
- 4 tomatoes on the vine, cut into wedges
- 1 white onion, finely diced
- 1 small hot chile, seeded and minced
- Pinch of dried oregano
- Salt

Preparation time: 15 minutes plus resting time
Serves: 4

Cut off the tops of the rolls and set the tops aside; pull out the soft bread inside the rolls, creating a cup. Finely chop the bread you removed, put it in a small bowl, and drizzle it with 2 tablespoons of the olive oil.

Peel the cucumbers in alternating strips and cut them into small chunks.

Put the tomatoes in a large bowl. Add the cucumbers, onion, and chile and drizzle with the remaining ¼ cup (60 ml) oil. Season with the oregano and a pinch of salt and toss to combine.

Divide the salad among the four rolls and sprinkle with the chopped bread. Place the tops back on the rolls, press gently, and let them rest for 30 minutes before serving.

To moderate the heat of the chile, remove and discard the ribs and seeds, which contain the highest concentration of capsaicin, the chemical compound that makes peppers hot. To enrich the salad, add a sliced hard-boiled egg or 3½ oz (100 g) herbed tofu, cut into small cubes.

Farro Salad with Olives and Tomatoes

Insalata di farro, pomodori e olive

- 1½ cups (300 g) pearled farro
- 1 clove garlic
- Pinch of dried oregano
- Pinch of cayenne pepper
- ¼ cup (60 ml) extra virgin olive oil
- 2 cups (300 g) large ripe cherry tomatoes, halved
- 20 Tuscan or other black olives, pitted
- 2 spring onions, thinly sliced
- 1¾ oz (50 g) semiaged Pecorino Toscano cheese, cut into small cubes
- Handful of basil leaves, torn, plus whole leaves for garnish if desired
- Salt

Preparation Time: 20 minutes
plus soaking time
Cooking Time: 45 minutes
Serves: 4

Soak the farro in cold water to cover for 12 hours. Drain, rinse under cold running water, then drain again.

Fill a large pot with water, salt the water, and add the garlic. Bring the water to a boil. Add the farro and cook for about 45 minutes, until tender. Drain the farro and transfer it to a large bowl. Sprinkle it with the oregano, cayenne, and a pinch of salt, then drizzle with the olive oil. Mix well and let cool.

Add the tomatoes, olives, spring onions, pecorino, and basil to the cooled farro and stir to combine. Let stand for 30 minutes to allow the flavors to combine.

Serve garnished with a few whole basil leaves, if desired.

For a vegan version of this dish, omit the pecorino cheese and add 7 oz (200 g) cooked lupini beans: drain and rinse them, remove and discard their skins, coarsely chop them, then add them to the cooled farro with the vegetables.

Rice Salad with Black Olives

Insalata di riso alle olive nere

- 4 plum tomatoes
- ¼ cup (60 ml) plus 2 tablespoons extra virgin olive oil
- 1 yellow onion, finely chopped
- 1 tablespoon white vinegar
- Scant ½ cup (100 ml) white wine
- Juice of 3 lemons, strained
- 1½ cups (300 g) Arborio rice
- ½ cup (80 g) black olives, pitted and chopped
- Leaves from 2 sprigs marjoram, chopped
- Salt

Preparation Time: 20 minutes
Cooking Time: 25 minutes
Serves: 4

 (DF) (GF) (VG)

Bring a large pot of water to a boil. Add the tomatoes and blanch for a few seconds, then drain them and let cool. Peel and seed the tomatoes, then chop the flesh into small cubes.

In a small saucepan, heat 2 tablespoons of the olive oil over medium-low heat. Add the onion and cook for 1 to 2 minutes, then add the vinegar and cook until it has evaporated. Add the wine and the lemon juice and cook for 5 minutes, then turn off the heat. Strain the mixture through a fine-mesh sieve set over a bowl and let the liquid cool (discard the solids).

Bring a large pot of salted water to a boil. Add the rice and cook until al dente, about 20 minutes, then drain it in a sieve and rinse it under cold running water to cool. Transfer the rice to a large bowl and sprinkle with a pinch of salt. Drizzle with the lemon-onion sauce and remaining ¼ cup (60 ml) oil. Add the olives and the marjoram and stir to combine.

Sprinkle the tomato over the rice and serve.

This salad goes very well with thin slices of pecorino pepato cheese or, if you are on a vegan diet, with 5¼ oz (150 g) tempeh, cut into very small cubes and fried in ¼ cup (60 ml) extra virgin olive oil and seasoned with a pinch of salt.

Bread Salad with Cucumbers and Tomatoes

Pane molle di Prato

- Scant 1 cup (200 ml) white wine
- 1 bay leaf, broken into pieces
- 1 sprig rosemary
- 1 whole clove
- 4 tomatoes on the vine, cut into small wedges
- 1 cucumber, peeled and thinly sliced
- 8 radishes, cut into small wedges
- 1 celery heart, thinly sliced
- 1 red onion, sliced into thin rings
- 4 to 5 tablespoons (60 to 75 ml) extra virgin olive oil
- 1 tablespoon white wine vinegar
- 10½ oz (300 g) slightly stale Tuscan bread, cut into 4 slices
- Salt

Preparation time: 20 minutes plus resting time
Serves: 4

In a medium bowl, combine the wine, bay leaf, rosemary, clove, and 2 cups (500 ml) water. Set aside to infuse for 1 hour.

In a large bowl, combine the tomatoes, cucumber, radishes, celery, and onion. Sprinkle the vegetables with a pinch of salt, then drizzle them with the olive oil and vinegar and toss well to combine.

Strain the wine mixture and discard the solids. Dip the bread quickly in the wine mixture, and arrange one slice on each of four individual serving plates. Top the bread evenly with the vegetable salad and serve.

You can replace the Tuscan bread with multigrain whole wheat (wholemeal) bread and add 3½ oz (100 g) tofu, grated on the large holes of a box grater, or 1 cup (100 g) grated Pecorino Toscano Fresco cheese.

Sprouted Lentil Salad with Three Dressings

Germogli con tris di salse

- ¼ cup (50 g) dried chickpeas
- ¼ cup (50 g) dried lentils,
- 1 cucumber
- 1 small daikon, peeled and cut into small cubes
- 4 baby zucchini (courgettes), cut into small cubes
- 4 squash blossoms (courgette flowers), pistils removed, coarsely chopped
- ¼ cup (10 g) watercress sprouts
- ½ canteloupe, peeled, seeded, and cut into cubes
- ½ teaspoon miso paste
- Juice of ½ lemon, strained
- 1 tablespoon tahini
- 3 tablespoons olive oil
- Salt
- 2 tablespoons tamari
- 1 ripe red plum, pitted
- 1 tablespoon apple cider vinegar
- 1 teaspoon raw sugar
- 5 or 6 coriander seeds, crushed
- Pinch of cayenne pepper
- ¼ cup (60 ml) pomegranate juice
- ¼ cup (60 ml) peanut (groundnut) oil
- 1 heaping tablespoon gomasio

To prepare tahini at home, toast ⅔ cup (100 g) white sesame seeds in a heavy-bottomed nonstick frying pan over low heat until they start to release their aroma. Let cool, then transfer them to a food processor and add a pinch of salt. With the motor running, drizzle in 4 to 5 tablespoons (60 to 75 ml) sesame oil and process until the seeds break down into a smooth paste.

Preparation time: 20 minutes plus soaking time
Serves: 4

Combine the chickpeas and lentils in a medium bowl and add cold water to cover. Cover and set aside to soak for 8 hours. Drain and rinse them, then return them to the bowl, still damp. Cover them and set aside to sprout for 1 to 2 days more.

Peel the cucumber in alternating stripes, halve it lengthwise and remove the seeds, then cut it into small cubes and put them in a large bowl. Add the daikon, zucchini (courgette), squash blossoms (courgette flowers), chickpeas, lentils, sprouts, and melon and mix together.

To make the miso sauce, in a small bowl, whisk together the miso, lemon juice, tahini, olive oil, a pinch of salt, and 2 tablespoons water.

To make the tamari sauce, in a blender, combine the tamari, plum, vinegar, sugar, coriander seeds, cayenne, and a pinch of salt and blend briefly, then transfer to a small bowl.

To makee the pomegranate sauce, in a small bowl, whisk together the pomegranate juice, peanut (groundnut) oil, gomasio, and a pinch of salt until emulsified.

Serve the salad with the dressings alongside.

Millet Salad with Beets and Romanesco

Insalata di miglio con barbabietola e cavolo cimone

- 1½ cups (300 g) millet, rinsed
- 1 bunch parsley
- 1 clove garlic
- 1 bay leaf
- 10½ oz (300 g) frozen edamame (in the pod)
- 1 small head romanesco, cut into florets
- ¼ cup (40 g) hazelnuts, toasted and coarsely chopped
- 4 to 5 tablespoons (60 to 75 ml) extra virgin olive oil
- 3½ oz (100 g) raw beet, peeled and very thinly sliced
- Salt and black pepper

Preparation Time: 20 minutes
Cooking Time: 35 minutes
Serves: 4

Put the millet in a large saucepan and add 4 or 5 parsley sprigs, the garlic, bay leaf, a pinch of salt, and 3¾ cups (940 ml) water. Bring the water to a boil, then reduce the heat to low, cover, and cook the millet for 20 minutes. Turn off the heat and let cool, covered, then fluff it and discard the parsley, garlic, and bay leaf.

Bring a medium pot of salted water to a boil. Add the edamame and let the water return to a boil, then cook for 5 minutes. Drain and let cool.

Fill a large saucepan with an inch or two of water, set a steamer basket inside, and bring the water to a simmer. Put the romanesco in the steamer basket, cover, and steam for 7 to 8 minutes.

Put the millet in a large bowl. Coarsely chop a handful of the parsley leaves and add them to the millet. Add the edamame, hazelnuts, and romanesco, then sprinkle the salad with a pinch of salt and some pepper and drizzle with the olive oil.

Divide the beet slices among individual serving plates, arrange the millet salad on top, and serve.

Edamame, or green soybeans, are a good source of vegetable protein. They are sold shelled or in the pod in the freezer section of most grocery stores and Asian specialty shops.

Pasta Salad with Tomato and Avocado

Insalata di pasta con pomodori e avocado

- 3 eggs
- 3½ oz (100 g) baby spinach
- 6 tablespoons (50 g) pumpkin seeds
- 4 to 5 tablespoons (60 to 75 ml) extra virgin olive oil
- 1 avocado
- Juice of 1 lemon
- 10½ oz (300 g) corn fusilli pasta
- 2 cups (300 g) small black cherry tomatoes, cut into small wedges
- 1 purple spring onion, sliced
- Salt

Preparation Time: 15 minutes
Cooking Time: 20 minutes
Serves: 4

Put the eggs in a medium saucepan and add cold water to cover. Bring the water to a boil, then cook for 7 minutes from the time the water starts boiling. Drain the eggs and run them under cold running water to cool, then crack the shells lightly and place the eggs in a bowl of cold water to soak for 5 minutes.

In a food processor, combine 1 oz (30 g) of the spinach, the pumpkin seeds, olive oil, and a pinch of salt and process until smooth and well combined.

Halve and pit the avocado, then peel it, cut it into small cubes, and place them in a small bowl. Drizzle the avocado with the lemon juice to prevent it from browning.

Bring a large pot of water to a boil. Salt the water, add the pasta, and cook according to the package instructions until al dente. Drain the pasta, rinse it under cold running water to cool, then drain it again and transfer it to a large bowl.

Add the spinach pesto, the tomatoes, spring onion, and the remaining spinach and toss to combine. Peel and halve the hard-boiled eggs, arrange them next to the salad, and serve.

For a vegan version, omit the eggs and, for the pesto, process the spinach and pumpkin seeds with 3½ oz (100 g) silken tofu, then season with a pinch of salt and some pepper.

Warm Black Rice Salad with Tofu

Insalata tiepida di riso nero, tofu e verdure

- 1¼ cups (250 g) black rice, rinsed
- 1 lb 2 oz (500 g) turnip greens
- ¼ cup (60 ml) extra virgin olive oil
- 1 clove garlic, smashed and peeled
- 1⅓ cups (200 g) cherry tomatoes
- 1 teaspoon raw sugar
- 7 oz (200 g) tofu, cut into cubes
- ¼ cup (30 g) coarsely chopped pistachios
- Salt

Preparation Time: 15 minutes
Cooking Time: 40 minutes
Serves: 4

Bring a large saucepan of salted water to a boil. Add the rice and cook for 40 minutes.

In the meantime, bring a separate large pot of salted water to a boil. Add the turnip greens and cook for 5 minutes. Drain them and let cool slightly, then coarsely chop them.

In a large frying pan, heat the olive oil over medium heat. Add the garlic and cook until golden, then discard the garlic. Add the tomatoes and the sugar to the pan and cook for 10 minutes. Add the turnip greens and the tofu, then turn off the heat and let stand for 5 minutes. Taste and season with salt.

Drain the rice in a sieve, run it under cold running water to cool slightly, then drain again and transfer to a large bowl. Add the tofu and vegetables and stir to combine.

Sprinkle the rice salad with the pistachios and serve.

Whole-grain black rice, which retains the bran (the grain's outermost layer), has a low glycemic index. It contains more minerals than white rice and guarantees a high intake of anthocyanins, useful for strengthening immune defenses.

Black Chickpea Salad with Apple and Sunchoke

Insalata di ceci neri con mele e topinambur

- Scant 1 cup (150 g) dried black chickpeas
- 1 (1¼-inch/3 cm) square kombu seaweed
- ¼ cup (60 ml) plus 2 tablespoons extra virgin olive oil
- 1½ lemons
- 3½ oz (100 g) sunchokes (Jerusalem artichoke)
- 1 Gala apple
- 1 (14 oz/400 g) can corn kernels, drained and rinsed
- 2 heads red Verona or Treviso radicchio, cored and leaves separated
- Handful of parsley leaves, finely chopped
- Salt and black pepper

Preparation Time: 20 minutes plus soaking time
Cooking Time: 2 hours
Serves: 4

Put the chickpeas and kombu in a large bowl, add cold water to cover, and set aside to soak for 48 hours, then drain them and transfer the chickpeas and kombu to a large saucepan. Add cold water to cover by approximately 2 inches (5 cm) and cook over low heat, without letting the water come to a boil, for about 2 hours. Add a pinch of salt, then drain the chickpeas, discard the kombu, and transfer to a large bowl. Drizzle with 2 tablespoons of the olive oil and sprinkle with a pinch of salt.

Peel the zest from the lemon half with a vegetable peeler, slice the zest into long, very thin strips, and set aside. Squeeze the juice from the lemon half into a large bowl and fill the bowl with cold water. Peel the sunchokes (Jerusalem artichokes) and thinly slice them, dropping them into the bowl of lemon water as you go to prevent browning.

Core the apple, then cut it into small cubes, place them in a small bowl, and drizzle them with the juice of one lemon half.

Drain the sunchokes (Jerusalem artichokes) and add them to the bowl with the chickpeas. Add the corn, apple, radicchio, and parsley and toss to combine.

In a small bowl, whisk together the juice of the remaining lemon half, remaining ¼ cup (60 ml) oil, a pinch of salt, and some pepper.

Drizzle the salad with the dressing, sprinkle with the lemon zest, and serve.

When you cook chickpeas or other beans and legumes, use very low heat, without letting the water ever reach its boiling point, and only add salt to the pot toward the end of the cooking time to prevent the skin of the beans or legumes from getting tough.

Sautéed Chicories with Fava Purée

Crema di fave e catalogna

- 1⅔ cups (250 g) dried split fava (broad) beans
- 1 small white onion, thinly sliced
- 1 bunch puntarelle or other chicory, coarsely chopped
- 4 to 5 tablespoons (60 to 75 ml) extra virgin olive oil
- 1 clove garlic, smashed and peeled
- Pinch of cayenne pepper
- Salt

Preparation Time: 10 minutes plus soaking time
Cooking Time: 1 hour 25 minutes
Serves: 4

Soak the fava (broad) beans in warm water to cover for 12 hours, then drain and rinse them. Transfer them to a large saucepan and add 3 cups (750 ml) cold water and the onion. Bring the water to a boil over high heat, then reduce the heat to medium, cover, and cook for about 1 hour 15 minutes, until the beans are tender.

In the meantime, bring a large pot of salted water to a boil. Add the puntarelle and cook for 5 to 6 minutes, then drain and set aside.

When the beans are almost cooked, in a small frying pan, heat the olive oil over medium heat. Add the garlic, a pinch of salt, and the cayenne and cook, stirring, until fragrant. Turn off the heat and let the flavor develop for 10 minutes, then discard the garlic.

Add a pinch of salt to the beans, then purée them directly in the pot with a hand blender until smooth.

Divide the fava (broad) bean purée among individual serving plates, drizzle with the garlic oil, top with the puntarelle, and serve.

If dried whole fava (broad) beans are used with their skin still on, increase the soaking time to 48 hours, changing the water two or three times. Cook them in boiling water, then remove their skins to make them easier to digest.

Sauteed Spring Vegetables

Padellata di verdure primaverilli

- 1⅓ cups (200 g) shelled fresh fava (broad) beans
- Juice of 1 lemon
- 4 artichokes
- 1 cup (250 ml) vegetable stock
- ¼ cup (60 ml) extra virgin olive oil
- 1 small red onion, such as Tropea or torpedo, cut into small wedges
- 4 young carrots (not baby carrots), halved lengthwise, then cut into wedges
- 1⅓ cups (200 g) shelled fresh peas
- Leaves from 2 sprigs marjoram
- Salt and black pepper

Preparation Time: 25 minutes
Cooking Time: 25 minutes
Serves: 4

Bring a large pot of water to a boil. Add the fava (broad) beans and blanch for 1 minute, then drain them and let cool. Remove the beans from their skins and set aside in a bowl.

Fill a large bowl with cool water and add the lemon juice. Trim the artichokes, cut them into wedges, and cut the fuzzy choke from the center, dropping the wedges into the bowl of lemon water as you go (this prevents them from browning).

In a small saucepan, bring the stock to a boil.

In a large nonstick frying pan, heat the olive oil over medium heat. Add the onion and carrots and cook, stirring, for 2 to 3 minutes.

Drain the artichokes and add them to the pot. Add the peas and the fava (broad) beans, then add the hot stock. Cover and cook for 15 minutes. Remove the lid, raise the heat to medium-high, and cook until the remaining liquid has evaporated. Turn off the heat.

Add the marjoram and season with salt and pepper, then serve.

You can enrich this recipe and turn it into a single course meal by adding 7 oz (200 g) tofu, cut into cubes, coated in flour, and pan-fried in 3 tablespoons olive oil for 3 to 4 minutes.

White Beans and Tomato with Toast

Fagioli alla maruzzara

- 1⅔ cups (250 g) cherry tomatoes
- ¼ cup (60 ml) extra virgin olive oil
- 2 stalks celery, finely diced
- 1 clove garlic, smashed and peeled
- 3¼ cups (500 g) cooked cannellini beans, drained and rinsed
- Dried oregano
- ⅓ cup (30 g) grated Parmesan cheese
- 4 slices rustic bread, toasted, for serving
- Salt and black pepper

Preparation Time: 10 minutes
Cooking Time: 1 hour
Serves: 6

Preheat the broiler.

Lightly crush the tomatoes or prick them with the tip of a small knife.

In a clay cooking pot or heavy-bottomed saucepan, heat the olive oil over medium heat. Add the tomatoes, celery, and garlic and cook for 3 to 4 minutes to let the flavor develop, then add 4 cups (1 l) hot water and cook for about 20 minutes. Season with salt, then add the beans. Cook for 30 minutes, then season with oregano and pepper.

Set six individual oven-safe ramekins on a sheet pan. Ladle the tomato-bean mixture into the ramekins and top evenly with the Parmesan. Broil for 10 minutes, until the cheese has melted.

Serve hot, with the toast alongside.

If using dried cannellini beans, soak them for 12 hours in cold water to cover, then drain and rinse them, transfer them to a large saucepan, and add cold water to cover. Bring the water to a boil, then reduce the heat to maintain a simmer and cook for about 1 hour. Season with salt at the end of the cooking time.

Sautéed Vegetables with Sprouts and Seeds

Verdure saltate in padella con semi e germogli

- 8¾ oz (250 g) baby zucchini (courgettes)
- ¼ cup (60 ml) extra virgin olive oil
- 2½ tablespoons pumpkin seeds
- 2½ tablespoons sunflower seeds
- 3 tablespoons black sesame seeds
- 2 tablespoons brown flaxseeds (linseeds)
- 1 (1¼-inch/3 cm) piece fresh ginger, peeled and grated
- 2 spring onions, finely chopped
- 7 oz (200 g) green beans, thinly sliced on an angle
- 8 young carrots (not baby carrots), thinly sliced on an angle
- 1 teaspoon sweet paprika
- 7 oz (200 g) baby spinach
- 2 tablespoons soybean sprouts
- ¼ cup (10 g) radish sprouts
- Salt

Preparation Time: 20 minutes
Cooking Time: 15 minutes
Serves: 4

Quarter each zucchini (courgette) lengthwise and then halve them crosswise.

In a large frying pan or a wok, heat the olive oil over medium-high heat. Add the seeds and toast, stirring continuously, for a few seconds. Add the ginger, spring onions, green beans, and carrots and cook for 3 to 4 minutes. Add the zucchini (courgettes), season with salt, and cook for another 3 to 4 minutes.

Add the paprika and stir, then add the spinach and cook for 1 minute more. Turn off the heat, sprinkle with the sprouts, and serve.

Flaxseeds (linseeds) need to be ground or crushed before use for them to be digested. For a single course dish, at the end of the cooking time add 10½ ounces (300 g) of cooked black beans and 5 ounces (150 g) whole wheat (wholemeal) farro cooked in boiling water for 45 minutes.

Vegetable Stir-Fry

Casseruola di bok choy, daikon e lattuga

- 1 orange
- 2 tablespoons toasted sesame oil
- 2 tablespoons peanut (groundnut) oil
- 1 clove garlic, smashed and peeled
- 1 daikon, peeled and sliced into ¼-inch-thick (0.5 cm) matchsticks
- 4 heads bok choy, cut into 1½- to 2-inch (4 to 5 cm) pieces
- 1 head romaine lettuce, cut into ½-inch-wide (1 cm) strips
- 10½ oz (300 g) smoked tofu, cut into cubes
- ¼ cup (60 ml) soy sauce

Preparation Time: 20 minutes
Cooking Time: 15 minutes
Serves: 4

Remove a strip of zest from the orange with a vegetable peeler and set aside. Juice the orange and strain the juice into a small bowl.

In a large frying pan or a wok, heat the sesame oil and the peanut (groundnut) oil over medium-high heat. Add the garlic and the strip of orange zest, then add the daikon and cook for 2 to 3 minutes. Add the bok choy, raise the heat to high, and cook for 3 to 4 minutes.

Add the lettuce, tofu, soy sauce, and orange juice. Cook until the liquid has reduced by half. Discard the garlic and the orange zest and serve.

Daikon is a root vegetable that can be used raw, grated and mixed with other vegetables, or cooked, cubed or cut into sticks. It has diuretic and draining qualities. Bok choy, also known as Chinese cabbage, is now available in almost all supermarkets, including in Italy, and it is a good source of vitamins A and C.

Spring Ratatouille

Ratatouille di primavera

- 1 bunch asparagus, ends trimmed
- Juice of 1 lemon
- 4 artichokes
- 7 oz (200 g) baby zucchini (courgettes)
- 1⅓ cups (200 g) cherry tomatoes
- ¼ cup (60 ml) extra virgin olive oil
- 1 small red onion, such as Tropea or torpedo, cut into thin wedges
- 10½ oz (300 g) new potatoes, scrubbed and halved
- Salt
- ¼ cup (40 g) coarsely chopped salted peanuts
- Handful of basil leaves

Preparation Time: 20 minutes
Cooking Time: 30 minutes
Serves: 4

Peel the asparagus stalks with a vegetable peeler and slice them on an angle.

Fill a large bowl with cool water and add the lemon juice. Trim the artichokes, cut them into wedges, and cut the fuzzy choke from the center, dropping the wedges into the bowl of lemon water as you go (this prevents them from browning).

Wash the zucchini (courgettes) and slice them thickly on an angle. Prick the tomatoes with the tip of a small knife.

In a large saucepan, heat the olive oil over medium heat. Add the onion and potatoes and cook for 2 to 3 minutes to let the flavor develop, then add a scant 1 cup (200 ml) boiling water. Season with salt and cook for 10 minutes. Drain the artichokes and add them to the pot. Add the tomatoes and cook for 6 to 7 minutes.

Add the zucchini (courgettes) and asparagus and season with salt. Cover and cook for another 5 minutes, then turn off the heat.

Sprinkle with the peanuts and basil, then serve.

To make this a main dish, serve it over a bed of bulgur wheat. Rinse 1½ cups (200 g) bulgur wheat with cold water and put it in a medium saucepan. Add 3 cups (750 ml) water, salt the water, and bring to a boil, then reduce the heat to maintain a simmer and cook for 10 minutes. Turn off the heat and let rest for another 10 minutes before serving.

Roasted Balsamic Tomatoes

Pomodori al forno all'aceto balsamico

- ¼ cup (60 ml) olive oil, plus more for brushing
- 1 teaspoon balsamic vinegar
- 8 tomatoes, halved
- 1 sprig thyme
- Salt and pepper

Preparation Time: 15 minutes
Cooking Time: 1 hour 15 minutes
Serves: 4

Preheat the oven to 350°F (180°C). Brush a baking dish with oil.

In a small bowl, whisk together the olive oil and vinegar and season with salt and pepper. Put the tomatoes in the prepared baking dish, arranging them in a single layer, and brush them with the oil-vinegar mixture. Sprinkle evenly with the thyme.

Bake for 15 minutes, then reduce the oven temperature to 225°F (110°C) and bake for at least 1 hour more.

Remove from the oven, transfer the tomatoes to a serving dish, and serve hot or at room temperature.

Green Beans with Tomato

Fagiolini al pomodoro

- 1 lb 5 oz (600 g) haricots verts (French beans), trimmed
- 2 tablespoons olive oil
- 1 onion, chopped
- 1 clove garlic, peeled
- 5 tomatoes, peeled, seeded, and chopped
- 6 green olives, pitted and quartered
- 6 basil leaves, chopped
- Salt and pepper

Preparation Time: 15 minutes
Cooking Time: 25 minutes
Serves: 4

Bring a large pot of water to a boil. Add the beans and cook for 5 to 10 minutes, or until just tender.

Meanwhile, in a large frying pan, heat the olive oil over low heat. Add the onion and garlic and cook, stirring occasionally, for 5 minutes.

Drain the beans, add them to the pan with the onion, and mix well. Stir in the tomatoes, season with salt and pepper, then remove and discard the garlic. Simmer over low heat for about 10 minutes, then stir in the olives and basil and cook for another 5 minutes. Serve warm.

Warm Asparagus Salad

Insalata al forno di asparagi e zucchine

- 5 tablespoons (75 ml) olive oil
- 1 red onion, very thinly sliced
- 1 chile, seeded and cut into strips
- 2 zucchini (courgettes), diced
- 1 lb 2 oz (500 g) asparagus tips
- 2 tablespoons soy sauce
- 2 tablespoons honey
- Salt and pepper

Preparation Time: 30 minutes
Cooking Time: 30 minutes
Serves: 6

Preheat the oven to 350°F (180°C).

Pour 2 tablespoons of the olive oil into a large baking dish. Add the onion and chile, toss to coat, and roast for 20 minutes. Remove the dish from the oven and add the zucchini (courgettes) and asparagus tips, then toss gently. Return to the oven and roast for another 8 to 10 minutes.

In a small bowl, whisk together the soy sauce, honey, and remaining 3 tablespoons oil and season with pepper. Remove the vegetables from the oven, pour the soy sauce dressing over, toss lightly, and serve.

Soups & Stews

Some people view soup as an exclusively winter dish, to be served steaming hot when it is freezing outside. But many soups can be served warm or cold, even during the summer, when soup can be a valuable source of hydration and minerals lost in the summer heat. Enriched with grains, legumes, and other protein-rich foods such as cheese and eggs, irresistible vegetable soups are nutritious, comforting, and refreshing.

A concentration of minerals, vitamins, and fiber

Soups are among the most traditional and versatile dishes, and offer significant nutritional benefits.

Many nutrients

Vegetable soups, even better if prepared with seasonal produce, are rich in minerals and vitamins, and usually contain negligible fat and no cholesterol. They also provide an abundance of fiber and liquids, which ensure that the digestive system functions well and make the dish more filling.

A tasty one-course meal

If, in addition to vegetables, a recipe for soup calls for grains (bread, pasta, or rice, but not exclusively these), legumes, or other protein-rich ingredients such as eggs, dairy products, tofu, tempeh, or seitan, the soup's nutritional content will be affected. Similar preparations can become main courses or single-course meals, preferably to be served in the evening. To complete the meal in a balanced way, just add a side portion of vegetables and a piece of fruit. Soups made with just vegetables can be accompanied by a protein-rich dish and a fruit salad or fruit-based dessert.

Flavor boost

To fully take advantage of the benefits of a vegetarian soup, add a little more flavor. Drizzling extra virgin olive oil over the soup just before serving boosts flavor and also provides antioxidants and monosaturated fatty acids that help prevent heart problems. Salt can also be used to enhance flavor, but it's best to limit your intake of sodium, as it promotes water retention, among other things. Aromatic herbs; edible seaweeds such as kombu, wakame, and agar-agar; and soy sauce or tamari make excellent alternatives to salt.

Great ideas for the table

Minestra or *zuppa*? *Crema* or *vellutata*? What does *minestrone* mean? These Italian terms for different styles of soup can be confusing because the differences between them are often very subtle.

Minestra
The name derives from the Latin *ministrare*, "to serve at the table." It started as a humble dish based on stock, which, in addition to vegetables, also includes pasta, rice, or other grains. There are many varieties, in which the use of vegetables is linked to regional culinary traditions and locally available produce. Brothier preparations are called *minestre chiare* ("clear soups").

Minestrone
Minestrone is said to have been introduced after the discovery of America and the subsequent arrival of New World ingredients such as potatoes and beans, which, when used in the preparation of *minestre*, gave rise to a richer and more substantial dish. The classic Italian minestrone is characterized by the use of green, red, and yellow vegetables and the inclusion of a grain, which varies in type depending on where the recipe originated: rice in the minestrone from Milan, broken linguine pasta in the one from Genoa, maltagliati pasta in Tuscany, and short pasta shapes in Apulia.

Zuppa
Compared to the *minestra*, the main difference is that it does not include pasta or rice, but is served with bread or toast. It is usually thicker than a *minestra*.

Vellutata, crema, and passato
A *vellutata* is a puréed soup that contains a thickener such as béchamel sauce, cream, or yogurt. A *crema*, very similar to a *vellutata*, is a puréed soup thickened slightly with rice flour, starch, or milk. A *passato* is simply a puréed vegetable soup, without any thickening agents.

The ingredients to always have on hand

Soups represent a simple way to prepare and serve the precious ingredients nature has provided. Many soup recipes start with a *soffritto*, a mixture of finely chopped onion, garlic, celery, carrot, and parsley, which is cooked in a frying pan in a little oil over low heat for 10 to 15 minutes.

Vegetable stock   A tasty soup starts with flavorful stock—and for the recipes in this book, that's obviously vegetable stock. It is not difficult to make it at home: sweat fresh vegetables in butter or olive oil, then add copious amounts of water, black pepper, garlic, and a bouquet garni, or skip the sweating and put the vegetables right in the pot. Bring the water to a simmer, then reduce the heat to maintain a simmer and cook for about 1 hour. Strain the stock, discarding the solids, and use it immediately, or let it cool and then store it in airtight containers in the freezer. You can also pour some into an ice cube tray and freeze it so you'll have small quantities of stock on hand, ready to add to sauces and other dishes to enhance their flavor.

Vegetables   It is best to use fresh vegetables in season, which retain most of their nutrients. In autumn and winter, cook soups based on cabbage, pumpkin, carrots, beets (beetroot), or onions; in spring and summer, ingredients such as asparagus, tomatoes, and eggplants (aubergines) will play a leading role. More tender vegetables will be added toward the end of the cooking time to prevent them from overcooking. Generally speaking, however, vegetable soups should never be cooked for too long, to avoid compromising the nutritional properties of the vegetables.

Grains

Pasta and rice are essential ingredients in many soups, but farro and barley are common as well—and let's not forget bread, which can be added to soups to act as a thickener and make the final dish heartier. Grains and grain-based products enrich recipes not only with their flavor and texture, but also with the excellent carbohydrate content, B vitamins, minerals, and fiber. Try to use unrefined whole grains in soups for the most nutritional benefits.

Legumes

Beans, peas, lentils, and chickpeas contain little fat and lots of fiber. They are also a good source of vitamins, minerals, and, above all, protein that is as valuable as animal-derived protein. If you want to serve a nutritious soup, particularly one that can be served for dinner as a single-course meal, you cannot leave out legumes. If your soup also contains grains, even better: legumes and grains complement each other, creating a high-quality nutritional combination. Protein-rich tofu, seitan, or tempeh can also be added to soups.

Summer Vegetable Soup

Minestrone estivo

- 4 plum tomatoes
- 1¾ cups (300 g) shelled fresh borlotti beans
- 3 spring onions, thinly sliced into rounds
- ¾ cup (150 g) brown rice
- 10½ oz (300 g) potatoes, peeled and cut into small cubes
- 10½ oz (300 g) green beans, sliced
- 1 bunch Swiss chard, coarsely chopped
- Leaves from 2 sprigs marjoram
- Leaves from 2 sprigs thyme
- Leaves from 1 bunch parsley
- Leaves from 2 sprigs mint
- 3 tablespoons wild fennel or fennel fronds
- 4 to 5 tablespoons (60 to 75 ml) extra virgin olive oil
- Salt

Preparation Time: 30 minutes
Cooking Time: 1 hour 30 minutes
Serves: 4

Bring a large pot of water to a boil. Add the tomatoes and blanch for 1 to 2 minutes, then drain them and let cool slightly. Peel and seed the tomatoes, then chop the flesh.

In a large saucepan, combine the borlotti beans and 8 cups (2 l) water. Bring to a simmer over medium-high heat, then reduce the heat to low and cook for about 40 minutes. Add a pinch of salt, the spring onions, and the rice and cook for 30 minutes. Add the potatoes, tomatoes, green beans, and chard and cook for about 20 minutes more, until the vegetables are tender.

In the meantime, in a food processor, combine the marjoram, thyme, parsley, mint, fennel, olive oil, and a pinch of salt. Process until well combined.

Let the soup cool slightly and serve warm, or let cool completely and serve at room temperature. Top each serving with a spoonful of the herb pesto.

Once it has cooled, you can enrich the soup with 1 tablespoon nutritional yeast (yeast flakes) or wheat germ. Add 1 tablespoon gomasio to the pesto instead of the salt. For a vegetarian (no longer vegan) version, add a Parmesan rind to the soup; remove and discard it before serving. If you like, you can replace the brown rice with 7 oz (200 g) small pasta shapes; add them to the soup 10 minutes before the end of the cooking time.

Cream of Asparagus Soup

Crema di asparagi alla milanese

- 4¼ cups (1 l) vegetable stock
- 2 bunches asparagus, woody ends trimmed
- 3 tablespoons (40 g) butter
- Scant ½ cup (50 g) all-purpose (plain) flour
- 2 cups plus 2 tablespoons (500 ml) milk
- 3 slices bread, cut into small cubes
- 2 eggs
- 6 tablespoons (40 g) grated Parmesan cheese
- Scant ½ cup (100 ml) heavy (whipping) cream
- Pinch of freshly grated nutmeg
- Salt

Preparation Time: 20 minutes
Cooking Time: 35 minutes
Serves: 4

In a medium saucepan, bring the stock to a boil over high heat, then reduce the heat to maintain a simmer.

Bring a small pot of salted water to a boil. Peel the asparagus stalks with a vegetable peeler, then separate the tips and slice the stalks into small rounds. Add 12 of the asparagus tips to the boiling water and cook for 3 to 4 minutes, then drain and set aside for garnish.

In a large saucepan, melt the butter over medium heat. Add the flour and toast it in the butter, stirring continuously, for 2 to 3 minutes. While whisking continuously, slowly pour in the hot stock, then the milk, and whisk until combined. Bring the mixture just to a boil, then reduce the heat to maintain a simmer. Add the uncooked asparagus and cook for about 20 minutes.

Preheat the broiler.

Put the bread cubes on a baking sheet and toast them under the broiler for 1 to 2 minutes, until golden brown (do not let them burn).

In a medium bowl, whisk together the eggs, Parmesan, cream, and nutmeg. While whisking, slowly pour in a ladleful of the asparagus soup to temper the eggs. Pour the egg mixture into the pot with the soup and blend with a hand blender until creamy and smooth.

Ladle the soup into bowls. Arrange the cooked asparagus tips on top and sprinkle with the croutons, then serve.

This soup is very nutritious and can almost serve as a single-course meal; to complete it, add a portion of cooked or raw vegetables to taste. To prepare a vegan version, replace the cow's milk with nondairy milk, the Parmesan with 1¾ oz (50 g) grated vegan cheese, and the heavy (whipping) cream with a scant ½ cup (100 ml) nondairy cream.

Tomato and Sweet Pepper Soup

Crema di pomodori e peperoni

- 1¾ lb (800 g) plum tomatoes
- ¼ cup (60 ml) extra virgin olive oil, plus more as needed
- 1 yellow bell pepper, finely chopped
- 1 shallot, thinly sliced
- 1 large potato, peeled and cut into small cubes
- Handful of basil leaves
- 2 tablespoons tahini
- 3 tablespoons yogurt
- 2 tablespoons mixed seeds
- Pinch of cayenne pepper
- Salt

Preparation Time: 20 minutes
Cooking Time: 35 minutes
Serves: 4

Bring a large pot of water to a boil. Add the tomatoes and blanch for a few seconds, then transfer them to a colander to drain and let them cool slightly (keep the water at a boil). Peel and seed the tomatoes, then coarsely chop them.

In a large saucepan, heat the olive oil over medium-low heat. Add the tomatoes, bell pepper, shallot, and potato and cook for 4 to 5 minutes.

Add 4¼ cups (1 l) of the boiling water and a pinch of salt, then cook for 30 minutes.

Let the soup cool slightly, or let cool to room temperature, if you prefer, then taste and season with salt. Add the basil, tahini, and yogurt and blend directly in the pot with a hand blender until smooth.

Ladle the soup into bowls and sprinkle with the seeds and cayenne, then drizzle with a little olive oil and serve.

You can replace the cow's-milk yogurt with the same quantity of soy yogurt. After sprinkling the soup with the seeds, add a scant ½ cup (20 g) mixed red beet sprouts and alfalfa sprouts sprinkled with a few drops of shoyu. If you like, you can serve the soup accompanied by whole wheat (wholemeal) toast.

Beet and Fennel Gazpacho

Gazpacho di barbabietola al finocchietto

- 1 lb 2 oz (500 g) beets (beetroot), peeled and thinly sliced
- 2 cucumbers, peeled and diced
- 2 scallions, sliced, 1 tablespoon reserved for garnish
- 1 small hot chile, seeded and finely chopped
- ¼ cup (60 ml) extra virgin olive oil
- Juice of 1 lemon
- 3½ oz (100 g) stale bread
- 3 tablespoons chopped wild fennel or fennel fronds
- Salt

Preparation time: 15 minutes
Serves: 4

In a food processor, combine the beets (beetroot), cucumbers, scallions, chile, olive oil, lemon juice, a pinch of salt, and 1¼ cups (300 ml) cold water, then process until smooth and homogeneous. Break the stale bread into small pieces and add them to the food processor. Process for 2 to 3 minutes, until well combined.

Pour the gazpacho into four bowls, add a few ice cubes to each, and serve garnished with the reserved scallions and the fennel.

If you can't find raw beets, you can use pre-cooked, steamed beets instead. To soften the strong taste of the scallions, soak in cold water for 10 minutes before use. Remember that gazpacho is always served cold.

Green Creamed Soup

Crema verde

- 2 tablespoons (30 g) butter
- 2 leeks, white parts only, thinly sliced
- 3 potatoes, diced
- 4½ cups (1 l) vegetable stock
- 9 oz (250 g) watercress, chopped
- Pinch of freshly grated nutmeg
- Scant ⅔ cup (150 ml) heavy (whipping) cream
- Salt and pepper
- Buttered toasted croutons, for serving

Preparation Time: 15 minutes
Cooking Time: 30 minutes
Serves: 4

In a large saucepan, melt the butter over low heat. Add the leeks and cook, stirring occasionally, for 5 minutes, or until softened. Add the potatoes, pour in the stock, and cook for 10 minutes. Add the watercress and nutmeg, season with salt and pepper, and cook for another 10 minutes.

Carefully transfer the soup to a food processor and puree until smooth. Return the soup to the pot, stir in the cream, and reheat briefly.

Serve with buttered toasted croutons.

Pea and Lettuce Soup

Zuppa di piselli con lattuga

- 2 small heads lettuce, shredded
- 3 potatoes, peeled and diced
- 3 large spring onions, thinly sliced
- 2 cups (300 g) shelled peas
- 1 small bunch mixed herbs, such as parsley, fennel, and sage
- 3 tablespoons (40 g) butter
- 1 sprig parsley, finely chopped
- Salt and pepper

Preparation Time: 40 minutes
Cooking Time: 30 minutes
Serves: 4

Put the lettuce, potatoes, spring onions, peas, the mixed herbs, and half the butter in a large saucepan, pour in 3 cups (720 ml) water, and season with salt and pepper. Cover and cook over medium heat, stirring occasionally, for 30 minutes.

Remove and discard the bunch of herbs and pour the soup into a serving bowl or tureen. Stir in the remaining butter and the parsley and season with salt and pepper. Serve immediately.

Carrot and Paprika Soup

Carote alla paprika in brodo

- 4½ cups (1 l) vegetable stock
- 1 lb 5 oz (600 g) carrots, grated
- 7 oz (200 g) potatoes, diced
- Pinch of sweet paprika
- Salt
- 2 tablespoons (30 g) butter
- Juice of 1 lemon, strained
- 4 slices rye bread, for serving
- Grated Parmesan cheese, for serving
- Basil, for serving

Preparation Time: 25 minutes
Cooking Time: 30 minutes
Serves: 4

In a large saucepan, bring the stock to a boil. Add the carrots and potatoes, stir in the paprika, and season with salt. Reduce the heat to maintain a simmer and cook for 30 minutes. Remove from the heat. Carefully transfer the soup to a food processor or blender and process until smooth. Pour the soup into a bowl and stir in the butter and lemon juice.

Put one slice of the bread into each of four individual soup bowls and sprinkle with some Parmesan. Ladle the carrot soup over the bread and top with more Parmesan and the basil. Serve immediately.

Carrot Soup with Zucchini Salsa

Vellutata di carote con tartare di zucchine

- 2½ cups (600 ml) vegetable stock
- ¼ cup (60 ml) plus 1 tablespoon extra virgin olive oil
- 1¾ lb (800 g) carrots, sliced
- 1 shallot, chopped
- 3 tablespoons all-purpose (plain) flour
- 1 bay leaf
- 2 sprigs thyme
- 4 zucchini (courgettes), cut into very small cubes
- 1 small red bell pepper, cut into small cubes
- Grated zest of ½ lemon
- Juice of 1 lemon, strained
- 4 squash blossoms (courgette flowers), pistils removed, thickly sliced
- Salt and black pepper

Preparation Time: 25 minutes
Cooking Time: 25 minutes
Serves: 4

In a small saucepan, bring the stock to a boil over high heat.

In a medium saucepan, heat ¼ cup (60 ml) of the olive oil over medium-high heat. Add the carrots and the shallot and cook, stirring, for 2 to 3 minutes, then sprinkle with the flour and let it toast for 2 to 3 minutes. While stirring with a wooden spoon, slowly pour in the hot stock.

Tie the bay leaf and the thyme together with kitchen twine to make a bouquet garni and add it to the pot. Reduce the heat to low, cover the pot with the lid ajar, and cook for about 20 minutes, until the carrots are tender. Discard the bouquet garni.

In the meantime, in a medium bowl, combine the zucchini (courgettes) and the bell pepper. Drizzle with the remaining 1 tablespoon oil, then sprinkle with the lemon zest and a pinch of salt.

Working in batches, carefully transfer the carrot soup to a blender and purée until smooth. Return it to the pot, stir in the lemon juice, and season with salt and black pepper.

Ladle the soup into bowls, then top with the zucchini and pepper salsa and the squash blossoms (courgette flowers) and serve.

You can serve the soup hot or warm. You could also enrich the zucchini and pepper salsa with 1¾ oz (50 g) smoked tofu, cubed, or with 2¾ oz (80 g) semisoft sheep's-milk cheese.

Chickpea Soup with Tagliatelle

Zuppa di ceci con tagliatelle

- Scant 1 cup (150 g) dried chickpeas
- 1 (¾-inch/2 cm) square kombu seaweed
- ¼ cup (60 ml) extra virgin olive oil
- 1 leek, washed well and finely chopped
- 1 stalk celery, finely chopped
- 1 carrot, finely chopped
- Leaves from 1 sprig rosemary, finely chopped
- 2 tablespoons tomato sauce
- 8¾ oz (250 g) tagliatelle pasta
- Salt and black pepper

Preparation Time: 10 minutes plus soaking time
Cooking Time: 2 hours 30 minutes
Serves: 4

Put the chickpeas and kombu in a large bowl, add warm water to cover, and set aside to soak for 48 hours. Drain and transfer the chickpeas and kombu to a large saucepan. Add cold water to cover them by approximately 2 inches (5 cm), cover, and cook over low heat, without letting the water come to a boil, for about 2 hours, until tender, adding hot water to the pot if necessary to keep the chickpeas submerged. Discard the kombu, then use a slotted spoon to transfer half the chickpeas to a food processor. Process until broken down, then return the chickpeas to the pot and stir to combine.

In a large saucepan, heat the olive oil over medium heat. Add the leek, celery, and carrot and cook for 5 to 6 minutes. Add the rosemary, tomato sauce, and the chickpeas with their cooking liquid, and season with salt. Reduce the heat to low, cover, and cook for 15 minutes. Break the tagliatelle noodles in half and add them to the pot. Bring the soup to a boil and cook according to the package instructions until the tagliatelle is al dente.

Ladle the soup into bowls, drizzle with oil, sprinkle generously with pepper, and serve.

Soaking chickpeas and other legumes in warm water before cooking them starts the sprouting process, which makes them easier to digest. Adding kombu to the pot also makes legumes easier to digest, as well as reducing their cooking time.

Winter Vegetable Soup

Zuppe di verdure d'inverno

- 4 sun-dried tomatoes
- ¼ cup (60 ml) extra virgin olive oil, plus more as needed
- 1 yellow onion, finely chopped
- 7 oz (200 g) peeled pumpkin, cut into ½-inch (1 cm) cubes
- 1 small celeriac, peeled and cut into ½-inch (1 cm) cubes
- 10½ oz (300 g) cauliflower, cut into small florets
- 10½ oz (300 g) broccoli, cut into small florets
- 7 oz (200 g) whole-wheat tubetti pasta
- 6 tablespoons (40 g) grated Parmesan cheese
- Salt and black pepper

Preparation Time: 20 minutes
Cooking Time: 45 minutes
Serves: 4

In a medium saucepan, bring 6 cups (1.5 l) water to a boil over high heat.

Put the sun-dried tomatoes in a medium bowl, add warm water to cover, and set aside to soak for 10 minutes, then drain. Finely dice the tomatoes and set aside.

In a large saucepan, heat the olive oil over medium-low heat. Add the onion, reduce the heat to low, and cook for 3 to 4 minutes. Add the pumpkin and celeriac and cook for 2 to 3 minutes.

Add the cauliflower, broccoli, sun-dried tomatoes, a pinch of salt, and the boiling water. Cook for 30 minutes. Add the pasta and cook according to the package instructions until al dente.

Serve the soup topped with a drizzle of oil, some pepper, and the Parmesan cheese.

For a vegan version of this recipe, omit the Parmesan cheese; in a food processor, combine 2 tablespoons toasted pumpkin seeds, 1 tablespoon nutritional yeast (yeast flakes), and, if desired, the grated zest of ½ orange and process into a coarse pesto. Use this in place of the Parmesan.

Millet and Buckwheat Soup

Minestra di miglio e grano saraceno

- ¼ cup (60 ml) extra virgin olive oil
- ½ cup (100 g) millet, rinsed and drained
- ⅓ cup (100 g) buckwheat, rinsed and drained
- 1 leek, washed well and sliced into thin rounds
- 2 fennel bulbs, cut into small cubes, fronds reserved
- 1 lemon
- Salt and black pepper

Preparation Time: 10 minutes
Cooking Time: 35 minutes
Serves: 4

In a large saucepan, heat the olive oil over medium-high heat. Add the millet and the buckwheat and toast them, stirring continuously, for 2 to 3 minutes. Add about 3½ cups (800 ml) hot water and a pinch of salt and bring to a boil. Reduce the heat to low, cover, and cook for 5 minutes. Add the leek and fennel and cook for another 20 minutes.

Remove the zest of the lemon with a vegetable peeler and finely chop it. Finely chop the fennel fronds and mix them with the lemon zest.

Ladle the soup into bowls and sprinkle with the lemon zest and fennel fronds. Add a generous sprinkle of pepper and serve.

In addition to carbohydrates, millet has the highest protein content of all grains. It is also a good source of salicylic acid and vitamins A, B, and B3. Buckwheat is not part of the Graminae family, so, like millet, it does not contain gluten and can be eaten by those with celiac disease (just check the label to make sure it wasn't processed in a facility where they also process grains that contain gluten).

Kale-and-Potato Bread Soup

Zuppa gratinata di cavolo e patate

- 1 bunch Swiss chard
- ¼ cup (60 ml) extra virgin olive oil
- 1¾ lb (800 g) Tuscan kale (cavolo nero), stemmed, leaves thinly sliced
- 2 medium potatoes, peeled and cut into small cubes
- 1 leek, washed well and sliced into thin rounds
- Pinch of cayenne pepper
- 6 cups (1.5 l) vegetable stock
- 4 slices Tuscan bread
- 3½ oz (100 g) Pecorino Toscano Fresco cheese, sliced
- 1 oz (30 g) semiaged Pecorino Toscano cheese
- Salt

Preparation Time: 20 minutes
Cooking Time: 45 minutes
Serves: 4

Separate the chard stems and leaves. Chop the stems and cut the leaves into strips.

In a large saucepan, heat the olive oil over medium-low heat. Add the chard, kale, potatoes, leek, and cayenne and cook gently for 4 to 5 minutes. Add the stock and season with salt. Cover and cook for 25 minutes.

Preheat the oven to 425°F (220°C).

Set four individual ovenproof bowls on a baking sheet. Toast the bread and place one piece in the bottom of each bowl.

Divide the pecorino fresco evenly among the bowls, placing it over the bread. Ladle the vegetable soup into the bowls, then sprinkle with the grated pecorino. Bake for about 15 minutes, then serve.

For a vegan version of this recipe, replace the pecorino fresco with a vegan cheese for melting and use a hard vegan cheese for grating on top of the soup in place of the Pecorino Toscano. You can replace the Tuscan bread with sliced rye bread.

Bread and Potato Stew with Arugula

Pancotto con rucola e patate

- 1 lb 2 oz (500 g) potatoes, peeled and sliced ¼ inch (0.5 cm) thick
- 10½ oz (300 g) arugula (rocket), chopped
- 4 to 5 tablespoons (60 to 75 ml) extra virgin olive oil
- 1 clove garlic, smashed and peeled
- 1 hot red chile, sliced into thin rounds
- 10½ oz (300 g) stale bread
- Salt

Preparation Time: 20 minutes
Cooking Time: 30 minutes
Serves: 4

Put the potatoes in a large saucepan, add abundant cold water, and bring to a boil over high heat. When the water comes to a boil, add salt and cook for 5 minutes, then add the arugula (rocket) and cook for 5 minutes more.

Meanwhile, in a small frying pan, heat the olive oil over medium heat. Add the garlic and cook until golden. Discard the garlic, then add the chile to the pan with the oil and turn the heat off.

Break the stale bread into small pieces and add them to the pot with the potatoes. Let it soften for a few minutes, then remove from the heat and pour the entire contents of the pot through a colander.

Divide the potato-bread mixture among individual serving bowls, drizzle with the garlic-chile oil, stir, and serve.

You can enrich the stew with 5¼ oz (150 g) tofu, cut into small cubes: first sauté it in oil flavored with garlic, chile pepper, and salt until golden, then add it to the pot just before draining and stir to combine.

Barley and Porcini Soup

Zuppa d'orzo e porcini

- 1½ oz (40 g) dried porcini mushrooms
- ¾ cup (150 g) pearled barley
- 2 tablespoons olive oil
- 1 onion, chopped
- 7 oz (200 g) zucchini (courgettes), thinly sliced
- 6½ cups (1.5 l) vegetable stock
- Salt

Preparation Time: 30 minutes
Cooking Time: 35 minutes
Serves: 4 to 6

Put the mushrooms in a small bowl, add warm water to cover, and let soak for 20 minutes.

Meanwhile, bring a large pot of salted water to a boil. Add the barley and cook for 10 minutes, then drain.

In a large saucepan, heat the olive oil over low heat. Add the onion and cook, stirring occasionally, for 5 minutes.

Drain the mushrooms and squeeze out the excess moisture. Tear them into small pieces and add them to the pan. Cook for a few minutes, then add the zucchini (courgettes) and cook for a few more minutes. Stir in the barley and the stock, season with salt, and cook, stirring occasionally, for 20 minutes, or until the barley, mushrooms, and vegetables are tender. Ladle into warmed soup bowls and serve immediately.

Cornmeal and Vegetable Soup

Bordatino livornese

- 1¾ lb (800 g) fresh borlotti beans, shelled
- 1 sage leaf
- 1 clove garlic
- 1 carrot
- 1 yellow onion
- 1 stalk celery
- ¼ cup (60 ml) extra virgin olive oil
- Scant ½ cup (100 ml) tomato purée (passata)
- 10½ oz (300 g) Tuscan kale (cavolo nero), stemmed, leaves thinly sliced
- 1½ cups (200 g) cornmeal
- Handful of parsley leaves, finely chopped
- Salt

Preparation Time: 20 minutes
Cooking Time: 2 hours 10 minutes
Serves: 4

In a large saucepan, combine the beans, sage leaf, and garlic. Add water to cover, bring to a simmer over medium-high heat, then reduce the heat to low and cook for about 1 hour, until the beans are tender. Remove and discard the sage and the garlic, then purée the beans directly in the pot with a hand blender. Measure the purée and add enough water to make about 8 cups (2 l). Taste and season with salt.

In a food processor, combine the carrot, onion, and celery and pulse until very finely chopped.

In a large saucepan, heat the olive oil over low heat. Add the chopped vegetable mixture and a pinch of salt and cook for 15 minutes. Add the tomato purée (passata) and cook for 10 minutes.

Add the bean purée and mix well. Raise the heat to medium-high to bring the mixture to a boil. Add the kale and stir to combine. While stirring, pour in the cornmeal and stir until incorporated, then reduce the heat to maintain a simmer and cook, stirring frequently, for 45 minutes.

Remove from the heat and stir in the parsley. Taste and season with salt, then serve.

To speed up the cooking times, you can use precooked cornmeal for polenta. For a richer vegetarian (but not vegan) version of the recipe, pour the soup into a casserole dish, adding layers of thinly sliced fresh pecorino or Asiago cheese, and bake in a preheated 350°F (180°C) oven for 10 minutes.

Genovese Minestrone

Minestra alla genovese

- 5 cups (1.2 l) vegetable stock
- ¼ cup (60 ml) plus 2 to 3 tablespoons extra virgin olive oil
- 1 stalk celery, finely diced
- 2 carrots, finely diced
- 1 onion, finely diced
- 7 oz (200 g) savoy cabbage, tough ribs removed, sliced into strips
- 1 bunch Swiss chard, coarsely chopped
- 5 or 6 lettuce leaves, coarsely chopped
- Scant ½ cup (100 ml) tomato purée (passata)
- ⅔ cup (100 g) cooked fresh borlotti beans
- Handful of basil leaves
- Handful of parsley leaves
- Leaves from 1 sprig rosemary
- 1 clove garlic
- Pinch of red pepper flakes
- 1 oz (30 g) Parmesan cheese, grated
- 5¼ oz (150 g) fresh tagliatelle pasta
- Salt

Preparation Time: 20 minutes
Cooking Time: 40 minutes
Serves: 4

In a medium saucepan, bring the stock to a boil over high heat.

In a large saucepan, heat ¼ cup (60 ml) of the olive oil over medium heat. Add the celery, carrots, and onion and cook, stirring, for 3 to 4 minutes. Add the cabbage, chard, lettuce, and tomato purée (passata), then pour in the hot stock. Cover the pot with the lid ajar and cook for about 30 minutes, then add the beans and season with salt.

Meanwhile, in a food processor, combine the basil, parsley, rosemary leaves, garlic, red pepper flakes, remaining 2 to 3 tablespoons oil, the Parmesan, and a pinch of salt, and process until smooth.

Add the tagliatelle and the pesto to the soup, and cook until the pasta is al dente, 1 to 3 minutes. Ladle into bowls and serve.

The tagliatelle can be replaced with ½ cup (50 g) rolled oats, to be added to the soup 5 minutes before the end of the cooking time. For a vegan version, replace the Parmesan in the pesto with 1 heaping tablespoon wheat germ and add the pesto just before serving.

Chard and Chickpea Soup with Tofu

Zuppa di cicerchie, erbette borragine e tofu

- 5¼ oz (150 g) dried cicerchie (Umbrian chickpeas) or chickpeas
- 7 oz (200 g) tofu, cut into small cubes
- Juice of 1 lemon
- ¼ cup (60 ml) plus 3 tablespoons extra virgin olive oil
- 4 spring onions, sliced
- 1 bunch Swiss chard, stemmed, leaves thinly sliced
- 10½ oz (300 g) borage, thinly sliced
- 4¼ cups (1 l) vegetable stock
- Pinch of red pepper flakes
- Salt

Preparation Time: 15 minutes plus soaking time
Cooking Time: 2 hours 30 minutes
Serves: 4

Soak the cicerchie in cold water to cover for 24 hours, changing the water twice. Drain and rinse them, then place them in a large saucepan with abundant cold water. Bring to a boil over high heat, then reduce the heat to medium-low and simmer for 2 hours, or until they are tender and cooked through but not mushy.

Meanwhile, combine the tofu and lemon juice in a small bowl and set aside.

In a medium saucepan, bring the stock to a boil over high heat.

In a large frying pan, heat ¼ cup (60 ml) of the olive oil over medium-low heat. Add the onions and cook for 1 to 2 minutes. Add the chard and borage and let them wilt, then add the hot stock. Raise the heat to medium-high and bring the stock to a boil.

Drain the cicerchie, add them to the soup, and season with salt. Reduce the heat to maintain a simmer and cook for 20 minutes.

Meanwhile, in a medium frying pan, heat the remaining 3 tablespoons oil. Drain the tofu and add it to the pan. Cook, stirring, until the tofu is golden, then season with salt and the red pepper flakes.

Stir the tofu into the soup, ladle into bowls, and serve.

To make cicerchie easier to digest, after soaking, put them in a saucepan, cover them in cold water, bring to a boil, and cook for 20 minutes. Drain them, then add them to a saucepan of boiling water and cook for 1 hour 40 minutes.

Tofu and Vegetable Soup

Zuppa di tofu e verdure

- 1 (1½-inch/4 cm) piece fresh ginger, peeled and thinly sliced
- 3 tablespoons peanut (groundnut) oil
- 5¼ oz (150 g) tofu, cut into cubes
- 4 baby zucchini (courgettes), thinly sliced on an angle
- 2 spring onions, thinly sliced on an angle
- 1 carrot, thinly sliced on an angle
- ½ cup (50 g) soybean sprouts
- 1¾ oz (50 g) baby spinach
- 3 tablespoons soy sauce
- ¼ cup (40 g) coarsely chopped unsalted roasted peanuts

Preparation Time: 10 minutes
Cooking Time: 10 minutes
Serves: 4

In a small saucepan, combine the ginger and 2 cups (500 ml) water and bring it to a boil. Cook for 1 minute, then turn off the heat and strain the water, discarding the ginger.

In a large saucepan, heat the oil over medium heat. Add the tofu, zucchini (courgettes), spring onions, and carrot and cook for 2 to 3 minutes to allow the flavor to develop.

Add the ginger-infused water, the bean sprouts, and the spinach and cook for 5 minutes. Turn off the heat and stir in the soy sauce.

Ladle into individual serving bowls, garnish with the peanuts, and serve.

To vary the flavor of the soup, hemp tofu or chile-seasoned tofu can be used instead. The peanuts can be replaced with 1 tablespoon salted peanut butter and the spinach with arame seaweed.

Fresh Pasta and Beans in Tomato Broth

Malmaritati

- 10½ oz (300 g) plum tomatoes
- ¼ cup (60 ml) extra virgin olive oil, plus more as needed
- 1 clove garlic, smashed and peeled
- 3 cups (500 g) shelled fresh borlotti beans
- 8¾ oz (250 g) fresh egg lasagna noodles
- Handful of parsley leaves, chopped
- Salt and black pepper

Preparation Time: 15 minutes
Cooking Time: 1 hour 40 minutes
Serves: 4

Bring a large pot of water to a boil. Add the tomatoes and blanch for 30 seconds, then drain them and let cool slightly. Peel and seed the tomatoes, then cut the flesh into cubes.

In a large clay cooking pot, heat the olive oil over low heat. Add the garlic and cook until golden, then discard the garlic. Add the tomatoes and the beans, then add about 8 cups (2 l) cold water, cover, and cook over low heat for about 1 hour 30 minutes.

Use a spider (skimmer) to transfer one-third of the beans to a food processor. Process until broken down, then return them to the pot. Season with salt and bring the soup to a simmer over medium heat.

Cut the pasta sheets into diamond shapes and add them to the soup, then cook for 3 to 4 minutes, or until the pasta is al dente.

Ladle the soup into individual serving bowls and garnish with the parsley and some pepper, then drizzle with a little oil and serve.

If using dried borlotti beans, soak them in warm water for 24 hours before cooking them. This pasta-and-bean dish can be served with grated Parmesan cheese. A bay leaf can be added to the bean cooking water for extra flavor.

Cabbage Soup with Pasta and All the Beans

Millecosedde

- 10½ oz (300 g) mixed dried legumes including peeled fava (broad) beans, chickpeas, cannellini beans, and lentils
- ¾ ounce (20 g) dried porcini mushrooms
- ¼ cup (60 ml) extra virgin olive oil
- 1 large carrot, peeled and diced
- 1 yellow onion, cut into small dice
- 1 stalk celery, thinly sliced
- 10½ oz (300 g) savoy cabbage, tough ribs removed, leaves sliced
- 10½ oz (300 g) rigatoni pasta
- ⅓ cup (30 g) grated Pecorino Romano cheese
- Salt and black pepper

Preparation Time: 20 minutes plus soaking time
Cooking Time: 2 hours 15 minutes
Serves: 4

Soak the legumes in cold water for 36 hours, changing the water two or three times. Drain and set aside.

Put the mushrooms in a bowl, add 1½ cups (350 ml) warm water to cover, and set aside to soak for 10 minutes. Drain them and coarsely chop the mushrooms, reserving the soaking liquid.

In an earthenware pot or heavy-bottomed saucepan, heat the olive oil over medium heat. Add the carrot, onion, celery, and a pinch of salt and cook until the onion is translucent, 5-10 minutes. Add the reserved mushrooms and the cabbage and cook for 1–2 minutes, or until the cabbage just starts to soften. Add 4 cups (1 l) water and the reserved mushroom liquid to the pot and season with salt and pepper. Bring the soup to a boil, then cover and reduce the heat to low. Cook for 2 hours, or until the legumes are tender, adding water as needed to ensure the legumes stay submerged.

About 30 minutes before the legumes have finished cooking, bring a large pot of water to a boil. Salt the water, add the pasta, and cook according to the package instructions, then drain it and add it to the pot with the legumes. Add the pecorino and a generous sprinkle of pepper and serve.

For a vegan version of this recipe, replace the pecorino cheese with a heaping tablespoon of nutritional yeast (yeast flakes) or miso paste. To facilitate the cooking of the legumes and make them easier to digest, add 1 (1¼-inch/3 cm) piece of kombu to the soaking and cooking water; discard it before serving.

Pumpkin Stew with Adzuki Beans

Stufato di azuki e zucca

- 1 cup (200 g) dried red adzuki beans, rinsed
- 1 (¾-inch/2 cm) square kombu
- ¼ cup (60 ml) extra virgin olive oil
- 1 leek, washed well and sliced into thin rounds
- 10½ oz (300 g) peeled pumpkin, cut into small cubes
- 1 sprig rosemary
- 2 sprigs thyme
- 1 (14 oz/400 g) can whole peeled tomatoes, chopped
- Salt

Preparation Time: 10 minutes plus soaking time
Cooking Time: 1 hour 10 minutes
Serves: 4

Put the beans and kombu in a large bowl, add cold water to cover, and set aside to soak for 8 hours, then drain them and transfer the beans and kombu to a large saucepan. Add cold water to cover by approximately 2 inches (5 cm), bring to a boil, then reduce the heat to maintain a simmer and cook for 40 minutes. At the end of the cooking time, season with salt and discard the kombu.

In the meantime, in a large saucepan, heat the olive oil over medium heat. Add the leek and cook for 2 to 3 minutes. Add the pumpkin to the pot and stir. Tie the rosemary and 1 sprig of the thyme together with kitchen twine to make a bouquet garni and add it to the pot. Season with salt, then add the tomatoes and stir. Reduce the heat to low and cook for 20 minutes.

Drain the beans, return them to the pot, and add the pumpkin-tomato mixture. Cook over medium-low heat for 5 to 6 minutes to let the flavor develop, then turn off the heat and discard the bouquet garni.

Garnish with the leaves from the remaining sprig of thyme, drizzle with a little oil, and serve.

According to macrobiotic principles, the adzuki beans' soaking water can be drunk, as it is rich in mineral salts and vitamins. Because of their sweet flavor, vaguely similar to that of chestnuts, these beans are used for the preparation of some desserts in Japanese cuisine.

Vegetable Stew with Peppers and Tomatoes

Ciammotta di peperoni, pomodori e melanzane

- Extra virgin olive oil, for frying
- 2 purple eggplants (aubergines), sliced into ¼-inch-thick (0.5 cm) rounds
- 10½ oz (300 g) potatoes
- 1 red bell pepper, thinly sliced
- 1 yellow bell pepper, thinly sliced
- 1 lb 2 oz (500 g) ripe plum tomatoes
- 1 clove garlic
- Salt

Preparation Time: 20 minutes
Cooking Time: 55 minutes
Serves: 4

Fill a high-sided frying pan with about 1 inch (2.5 cm) of olive oil and heat the oil over medium-high heat to 350°F (180°C). Working in batches, add the eggplant (aubergine) slices to the hot oil and fry for 3 to 4 minutes, until they start to turn golden. Using tongs, transfer the eggplant to paper towels to absorb excess oil.

Bring the oil back up to temperature. Peel the potatoes, cut them into cubes, and add them to the hot oil. Fry until tender and golden, about 10 minutes, then use a slotted spoon to transfer them to paper towels to drain. Bring the oil back up to temperature, add the bell peppers, and fry for 5 minutes, then drain on paper towels as well.

Meanwhile, bring a large pot of water to a boil. Add the tomatoes and blanch for 1 minute, then drain them and let cool slightly. Peel, seed, and coarsely chop the tomatoes, then place them in a large saucepan. Add the fried eggplant, potatoes, and peppers, the garlic, and a pinch of salt. Cook over very low heat for 30 minutes, discard the garlic, and serve.

Much like caponata and ratatouille, this recipe can be turned into a full meal by adding a source of protein such as fresh cheese or eggs (for a vegetarian diet) or sautéed tofu or seitan (for a vegan diet).

Tomato and Mushroom Stew

Pancotto di pomodori e funghi

- ¾ oz (20 g) dried porcini mushrooms
- ½ cup (120 ml) extra virgin olive oil
- 7 oz (200 g) seitan, cut into small chunks
- 1 leek, washed well and sliced into thin rounds
- 2 carrots, chopped
- 1 stalk celery, tough strings removed, chopped
- 1 (14 oz/400 g) can whole peeled tomatoes, coarsely chopped
- 1 tablespoon tomato paste (purée)
- Leaves from 2 sprigs marjoram
- 3½ oz (100 g) stale bread
- Salt and black pepper

Preparation Time: 15 minutes plus soaking time
Cooking Time: 30 minutes
Serves: 4

Preheat the oven to 350°F (180°C).

Put the dried mushrooms in a bowl, add warm water to cover, and set aside to soak for 10 minutes, then drain, clean, and coarsely chop them.

In a large saucepan, heat ¼ cup (60 ml) of the olive oil over medium heat. Add the seitan and cook for 1 to 2 minutes, then add the mushrooms, leek, carrots, and celery and cook for 4 to 5 minutes. Add the chopped tomatoes, tomato paste (purée), and marjoram and stir. Season with salt and add about 3½ cups (800 ml) hot water. Bring to a simmer, then reduce the heat to low and cook for 20 minutes.

Meanwhile, cut the bread into small cubes, spread them over a sheet pan, and drizzle with the remaining ¼ cup (60 ml) oil. Toast in the oven for about 10 minutes, until golden brown.

Ladle the soup into bowls. Top each bowl with croutons and let them soften slightly, then sprinkle with some pepper and serve.

The water used to soak the mushrooms can be strained to remove any grit and added to the soup to enhance its flavor. The seitan can be replaced with 2½ cups (400 g) cooked cannellini beans or chickpeas.

Pasta, Dumplings, &

Crêpes

A bowl of pasta topped with a tasty sauce can be a perfect dish. Already an integral part of the Italian meal, supplemented with vegetables, legumes, or cheese, a simple pasta dish or irresistible filled pastas can be transformed into a balanced and complete meal.

The perfect mix

Pastas can be dried, fresh, or filled, and the flavor of the dish will also depend on the sauce used and the way the pasta is prepared.

Dried or fresh, with a sauce

Industrially produced dried pastas are typically made from a durum wheat semolina-and-water dough. Some shapes are formed by extruding the dough through a die; many producers use nonstick-coated dies, which result in smoother noodles. The dies used for bronze-cut pasta varieties are uncoated, so the surface of the noodles is rougher and therefore holds sauce better; seek out bronze-cut pastas when you can. Homemade or store-bought fresh pasta is prepared with soft wheat flour, to which eggs may or may not be added. Available in many shapes, lengths, and widths, pasta can be served with elaborate sauces but also simply with butter and Parmesan cheese. For every 3½ oz (100 g) pasta, use 4 cups (1 L) water and 1½ teaspoons salt; bring the water to a boil, add the salt, then add the pasta and cook as directed in the recipe. Fresh pasta will cook much faster than dried.

Homemade pasta

All-purpose (plain) flour and Italian "00" flour are the most commonly used types for the preparation of fresh pasta, but also have the least nutritional value. Pasta can be made at home using different flours, alone or in combination, to boost nutrition (especially fiber, minerals, and vitamins). Some good varieties to try for homemade pasta include whole wheat (wholemeal), chickpea, chestnut, farro, barley, and quinoa flours. Some of these are also gluten-free.

A treasure chest of flavors

Filled pastas include lasagna, cannelloni (pasta rectangles rolled up around a filling), ravioli, tortelli, and tortellini. One rule applies to them all: the sauce used must take into account the filling and enhance its flavors, not overwhelm them.

Whole wheat is best

Pasta made with wheat semolina (in particular durum wheat) is rich in carbohydrates and does not contain any harmful fats or cholesterol. It is even better if it is made with whole wheat (wholemeal) flour, which contains more minerals, vitamins, and fiber than more refined flours. Its higher fiber content means whole wheat pasta aids digestion, increases the feeling of fullness, and slows down the absorption of sugars, preventing insulin spikes that encourage the accumulation of body fat. Furthermore, whole wheat (wholemeal) flour has a higher protein content—more than 12 percent—than white flour.

Not just wheat

Durum wheat pasta is the best-known and most commonly used type, but for more varied nutrition and a greater variety of flavors, try other types of pasta, made from different grains or even legumes such as chickpeas. Each type has specific nutritional values, so experiment with pastas made from farro, corn, or buckwheat flour, and also those made with special wheat varieties such as Senatore Cappelli or Kamut.

Au gratin for a crunchy note

Cooking a pasta dish au gratin enhances its flavor. Typically, dishes prepared au gratin are baked at high temperatures (over 350°F/180°C) or broiled, to form a wonderful golden brown crust on top. The browning occurs because of the Maillard reaction (named for the French chemist who discovered it), a chemical reaction between amino acids and sugars when they are exposed to heat. This is why, to obtain the classic gratin crust, it is necessary to add Parmesan cheese, butter, or other protein-rich fats to the pasta before baking or broiling. Some recipes also include an egg yolk.

The ingredients to always have on hand

In addition to pastas made from durum wheat, other types are available, each with its own properties and nutritional values.

Senatore Cappelli wheat and buckwheat
Much of the flour used to make pasta is ground from wheat species that have been industrialized or genetically modified. Senatore Cappelli, however, which is cultivated organically in the Marche, Apulia, and Basilicata regions of Italy, has not been subjected to any engineering and therefore retains its distinct taste and nutritional properties. Look for pastas made from this variety in specialty stores. Buckwheat, in spite of its name, is neither wheat nor technically a grain (it belongs to the Polygonaceae family, the same family as rhubarb). Buckwheat flour can be used to produce gluten-free pasta rich in protein, antioxidants, and minerals.

Corn and farro
Gluten-free corn pasta is a favorite choice for those suffering from celiac disease. It has a pleasant taste that lends itself to many combinations. From a nutritional point of view, it is an excellent source of folates, B vitamins, and fiber. Farro pasta has a fiber content ten times higher than that of wheat, and pastas made from farro flour typically contain the fewest calories. Furthermore, farro is a naturally hardy grain, and is therefore often cultivated without pesticides.

Kamut
Kamut is the commerical name for red Khorasan wheat, originally from Iran, which is grown organically and has never been cross-cultivated to create a hybrid variety. Kamut pasta contains amino acids, selenium, and B vitamins. It is easy to digest and helps protect the lining of the gut. Its flavor is distinct, reminiscent of hazelnuts, but more delicate than whole wheat (wholemeal) pasta, so Kamut pasta should be served with full-flavored and complex sauces.

Doughs, shapes, and sauces

Gnocchi and crêpes are delicious and very versatile dishes that, depending on how they are served, can take on different roles in a balanced vegetarian meal.

As a side dish

In spite of the fact that gnocchi is more often served as a first course or main dish, it can also be served as a side dish to accompany recipes featuring vegetables, legumes, or dairy products, or as a contrast to vegetable salads. Among the varieties most often served as a side dish is spaetzle, gnocchi from the Tyrol area made with flour and eggs.

A treasure chest of flavors

Crêpes, originally from France (and known as *crespelle* in Italy), are very thin pancakes prepared with basic ingredients such as flour, milk, eggs, and oil or butter. They can be filled in various ways, and the filling you choose will affect their nutritional value. In a vegetarian menu, fresh vegetable fillings play a leading role, as does cheese or protein-rich alternatives such as tofu or seitan. Depending on the richness of the filling, crêpes can be served as a starter, a second course, or even a snack.

To each its own shape

Gnocchi can be categorized by shape. There are three different types: "rolled" gnocchi, like potato gnocchi, made with a soft dough shaped into a ball or a little log; flattened gnocchi, like Roman gnocchi, which are shaped when hot, flattened, and allowed to cool before being cut; and spoonable gnocchi, made with a batter, not a dough, that is dropped by spoonfuls into boiling water and takes shape as it cooks.

Beyond potatoes

Pumpkin and spinach can also be used as the base for vegetable gnocchi. Bread-based gnocchi, historically a dish of *la cucina povera* (or peasant cooking), uses stale bread mixed with eggs and milk. Ricotta gnocchi are softer and creamier than potato gnocchi and can be served with any type of sauce, but are at their best with simple sauces such as tomato and basil or butter and sage. Gnocchi can also be made with flour—not just wheat flour, but also buckwheat, chestnut, and chickpea flours and cornmeal, among others.

Crêpes without eggs

Crêpes can be made using different types of flour, and can be modified to fit a vegan diet. The cow's milk called for in many crêpe recipes, for example, can be replaced with soy milk. There are also many crêpe recipes that do not use eggs.

How to fold a crêpe

The word *crêpe* derives from the Latin *crispus* ("curly") or the Greek *krìspos* ("rolled"), and crêpes can be folded in different ways. For example, they can be folded into a cone, making a pocket into which the filling is placed; or they can be filled and folded into triangles or rolled up around the filling like a cigar; they can also be gathered into a pouch around the filling and the top cinched with a fresh chive or two.

More ingredients to keep on hand

Some basic ingredients recur in the preparation of gnocchi and crêpes.

Eggs

In vegetarian diets, eggs are important because they provide complete protein; in fact, they contain all nine essential amino acids, which our bodies do not produce and must therefore be obtained from foods.

Bread

It is an excellent source of carbohydrates, which, according to nutritionists, should account for more than 50 percent of our daily calories. Breads also contain protein, B vitamins, potassium, and magnesium.

Potatoes

Floury white-fleshed potatoes (as opposed to waxy potatoes) are the most suitable for the preparation of gnocchi. Excellent results can be achieved using russet, Kennebec, and Majestic varieties. It is also important to use mature potatoes: small new potatoes contain too little starch and have a higher water content, so they require too much flour to make a workable dough.

Ricotta

Though it's referred to as "cheese," ricotta is obtained by heating the whey left over from cheese production, and derives its name, meaning "re-cooked" in Italian, from this process. Cow's-milk ricotta has a protein content markedly superior to that of cheese and a lower fat content; it is also a good source of protein and minerals. It is an easily digestible food and relatively low in calories.

Whole Wheat Tagliatelle with Avocado Pesto

Tagliatelle integrali con pesto di avocado

- 10½ oz (300 g) farro tagliatelle or other long pasta
- Handful of cilantro (fresh coriander)
- Scant ½ cup (50 g) walnuts
- Grated zest of ½ lime
- 1 avocado, pitted, peeled, and chopped
- 1 shallot, thinly sliced
- Juice of 1 lime
- 3 tablespoons extra virgin olive oil
- 1 fresh hot chile, seeded, membrane removed, and very finely diced
- Salt

Preparation Time: 15 minutes
Cooking Time: 5 minutes
Serves: 4

Bring a large pot of water to a boil. Salt the water, add the pasta, and cook according to the package instructions until al dente. Reserve but do not drain the pasta.

On a cutting board, combine the cilantro (fresh coriander), walnuts, and lime zest and coarsely chop. Transfer to a small bowl, stir to combine well, and set aside.

In a blender cup or tall jar, combine the avocado, shallot, lime juice, and a pinch of salt and purée with a hand blender.

Add a small ladleful of the pasta cooking water and the olive oil to the avocado purée and blend briefly to combine, then stir in the chile.

Drain the pasta and transfer it to a serving bowl. Add the avocado sauce and toss to coat, then sprinkle with the cilantro-walnut mixture and serve.

Avocados are very rich in vitamins A, D, and E. They have antioxidant properties and high levels of linoleic acid and omega-3 fatty acids. Buy avocados when they're soft to the touch, which means they're perfectly ripe.

Farro Spaghetti with Vegetables and Fresh Herbs

Spaghetti di farro con ragù di verdure e erbe

- 11¼ oz (320 g) farro spaghetti
- ¼ cup (60 ml) extra virgin olive oil
- 2 spring onions, sliced
- 4 bell peppers, thinly sliced
- 3½ oz (100 g) grape tomatoes, halved
- 6 zucchini (courgettes), cut into very small cubes
- Grated zest and juice of 1 lemon
- 6 squash blossoms (courgette flowers), cleaned and sliced
- Leaves from 1 sprig mint, finely chopped
- 3 tablespoons finely chopped wild fennel or fennel fronds
- Salt

Preparation Time: 20 minutes
Cooking Time: 20 minutes
Serves: 4

Bring a large pot of water to a boil. Salt the water, add the spaghetti, and cook according to the package instructions until al dente.

In the meantime, in a large nonstick frying pan, heat the olive oil over low heat. Add the onions and cook for 2 to 3 minutes.

Add the bell peppers and raise the heat to medium. Cook for 3 to 4 minutes, then add the tomatoes and cook for a few minutes. Add the zucchini (courgettes), season with salt, and cook for another 5 minutes.

Drain the pasta and add it to the pan with the vegetables to absorb flavor. Add the lemon zest, lemon juice, squash blossoms (courgette flowers), mint, and fennel. Stir to combine, then serve.

For a gluten-free and very low-carb first course, replace the farro spaghetti with shirataki spaghetti (cook as directed on the package). Shirataki noodles are made from konjac yam flour, or glucomannan, a soluble fiber, and are very low in calories.

Pici with Walnut Pesto

Pici alla fornaia

- 11¼ oz (320 g) pici pasta or thick spaghetti
- Leaves from 1 small bunch basil
- 3½ oz (100 g) aged Pecorino Toscano cheese, grated
- 1 cup (100 g) walnuts
- 5 to 6 tablespoons (75 to 90 ml) extra virgin olive oil
- Salt

Preparation Time: 10 minutes
Cooking Time: 20 minutes
Serves: 4

Bring a large pot of water to a boil. Salt the water, add the pasta, and cook for about 18 minutes (or as directed on the package), stirring gently only when the pasta has softened to avoid breaking it.

Meanwhile, in a food processor, combine the basil (reserve a few leaves for serving, if desired), pecorino, walnuts, olive oil, and a pinch of salt and process until well combined, then transfer the pesto to a serving bowl.

Stir a small ladleful of the pasta cooking water into the pesto. Drain the pasta, add it to the bowl with the pesto, and stir quickly to coat. Serve garnished with a few basil leaves, if desired.

To soften the intense flavor of the walnuts, blanch them in boiling water for 2 to 3 minutes, then drain them and remove their skins before incorporating them into the pesto.

Pasta with Cauliflower and Pine Nuts

Pasta con cavolfiore rimestata

- ⅓ cup (50 g) Passolina raisins (Zante currants)
- 12¼ oz (350 g) cauliflower, cut into florets
- 4 to 5 tablespoons (60 to 75 ml) extra virgin olive oil
- 1 yellow onion, finely chopped
- Pinch of saffron (one 0.4 g sachet)
- ¼ cup (40 g) pine nuts
- 11¼ oz (320 g) maccheroni pasta
- ⅓ cup (40 g) grated pecorino pepato cheese
- Handful of basil leaves, sliced
- Salt

Preparation Time: 10 minutes
Cooking Time: 20 minutes
Serves: 4

Put the raisins in a small bowl, add warm water to cover, and set aside to soak for 10 minutes, then drain.

Bring a large pot of salted water to a boil. Add the cauliflower and cook for 5 to 6 minutes. Using a slotted spoon, transfer the cauliflower to a colander to drain; reserve the cooking water.

In a large frying pan, heat the olive oil over medium-low heat. Add the onion and cook for a few minutes, until softened. In a small bowl, dissolve the saffron in a small ladleful of water, then pour it into the pan with the onion. Cover and cook over low heat for 10 minutes, then add the cauliflower, raisins, and pine nuts and season with salt.

Meanwhile, return the cauliflower cooking water to a boil, add the pasta, and cook according to the package instructions until al dente. Drain the pasta and add it to the frying pan. Add the pecorino and basil, stir to combine, and serve.

Passolina raisins (Zante currants) are a type of dark raisin produced from a very small grape typical of Sicily and Lipari. They have a slightly sour taste. If you can't find them, use regular black raisins and soak as directed.

Pappardelle with Walnuts

Pappardelle alle noci

- 3 tablespoons (40 g) butter
- ⅔ cup (80 g) walnuts, coarsely chopped
- 1 tablespoon freshly ground pink peppercorns
- 1 tablespoon chopped fresh flat-leaf parsley
- 8 ounces (250 g) fresh pappardelle
- Salt

Preparation Time: 10 minutes
Cooking Time: 15 minutes
Serves: 2

In a large saucepan, melt the butter over low heat. Add the walnuts and peppercorns and cook, stirring continuously, for 4 minutes. Remove from the heat and add the parsley.

Bring a large pot of salted water to a boil. Add the pasta and cook for 2 to 3 minutes, until al dente. Drain the pasta and add it to the walnut sauce, stirring until the pasta is well coated. Transfer to a hot serving dish and serve immediately.

If you have the time and patience, blanch the walnuts in boiling water for a few seconds, drain and let cool, then transfer them to a clean kitchen towel and rub them to remove their brown skins, which can be bitter.

Spaghetti with Fava-Tomato Sauce

Macco di fave

- 7 oz (200 g) dried split fava (broad) beans
- 1 white onion, sliced
- 2 canned whole peeled tomatoes, chopped
- 7 oz (200 g) spaghetti
- Extra virgin olive oil
- ⅓ cup (30 g) grated Pecorino Romano cheese
- Salt and black pepper

Preparation Time: 10 minutes plus soaking time
Cooking Time: 1 hour 25 minutes
Serves: 4

Soak the fava (broad) beans in warm water to cover for 12 hours, then drain and rinse them. Transfer them to a large saucepan and add 6 cups (1.5 l) cold water, the onion, and the tomatoes. Bring to a boil, then reduce the heat to maintain a simmer, cover, and cook for about 1 hour. Season with salt, then raise the heat to medium-high to bring the liquid to a simmer. Break the spaghetti noodles in half, add them to the pot, and cook according to the package instructions until the pasta is al dente.

Season generously with pepper, then divide the spaghetti among individual serving bowls. Drizzle with a little oil, sprinkle with the pecorino, and serve.

For a vegan version of this recipe, replace the pecorino cheese with 1 heaping tablespoon wheat germ. Wheat germ must always be added at the end of the cooking time, as heat from cooking will affect its nutritional value.

Pasta with Favas and Peas

Pasta con ragù di fave e piselli alla santoreggia

- 1⅓ cups (200 g) shelled fresh fava (broad) beans
- 2 tomatoes on the vine
- ¼ cup (60 ml) extra virgin olive oil
- 1 stalk celery, very finely diced
- 1 carrot, very finely diced
- 2 red spring onions, sliced into thin rounds
- 1 sprig savory, plus a few whole leaves for garnish
- 1⅓ cups (200 g) shelled fresh peas
- Scant 1 cup (200 ml) vegetable stock
- 11¼ oz (320 g) Kamut fusilli
- Salt and black pepper

Preparation Time: 20 minutes
Cooking Time: 40 minutes
Serves: 4

Bring a large pot of water to a boil. Add the fava (broad) beans and the tomatoes and blanch for 1 minute, then drain them and let cool. Remove the beans from their skins and set aside in a bowl. Peel and seed the tomatoes, then cut the flesh into cubes.

In the meantime, in a large saucepan, heat the olive oil over medium-low heat. Add the celery, carrot, and spring onions and cook for 4 to 5 minutes. Add a sprig of savory, the fava (broad) beans, peas, and stock. Reduce the heat to low, cover, and cook for 15 minutes. Season with salt, then add the tomatoes and cook for 2 to 3 minutes.

Bring a large pot of water to a boil. Salt the water, add the pasta, and cook according to the package instructions until al dente. Drain the pasta, return it to the pot, and add the fava (broad) bean ragù.

Garnish with a few savory leaves and some pepper, and serve.

Cooking beans with savory makes them easier to digest. The pasta can be served with grated Parmesan cheese or, for a vegan version, sprinkled with 1 teaspoon nutritional yeast (yeast flakes) or gomasio just before serving.

Pasta with Parsley and Breadcrumbs

Vermicelli alla carrettiera

- 11¼ oz (320 g) vermicelli pasta
- ¼ cup (60 ml) plus 1 tablespoon extra virgin olive oil
- 1 white onion, very thinly sliced
- 1 clove garlic, finely chopped
- Handful of parsley, finely chopped
- Pinch of dried oregano
- ¾ cup (80 g) breadcrumbs
- Salt and black pepper

Preparation Time: 10 minutes
Cooking Time: 20 minutes
Serves: 4

Bring a large pot of water to a boil. Salt the water, add the pasta, and cook according to the package instructions until al dente.

Meanwhile, in a large frying pan, heat ¼ cup (60 ml) of the olive oil over low heat. Add the onion, garlic, and parsley and cook for 10 minutes. Add the oregano and season with salt and pepper.

In a separate frying pan, heat the remaining 1 tablespoon oil over medium heat. Add the breadcrumbs and toast until golden.

Drain the pasta, then add it to the pan with the onion mixture and toss to combine. Transfer to a serving bowl, sprinkle with the toasted breadcrumbs, and serve.

In this recipe, the toasted breadcrumbs replace Parmesan cheese. Instead of the bread-crumbs, you can use 3½ oz (100 g) pane guttiau, a paper-thin Sardinian flatbread; coarsely chop it and sprinkle it on the pasta before serving. (Look for pane guttiau at specialty food shops.)

Saffron Gnocchi

Ciciones al pomodoro di farina e zafferano

- 2 pinches of saffron (two 4 g sachets)
- Scant 2¼ cups (400 g) semolina flour
- Salt
- 1¾ lb (800 g) plum tomatoes
- ¼ cup (60 ml) extra virgin olive oil
- 1 clove garlic, finely chopped
- 1½ oz (40 g) mature Pecorino Sardo cheese, shaved

Preparation Time: 30 minutes
Cooking Time: 30 minutes
Serves: 4

In a spouted measuring cup, dissolve the saffron in a scant 1 cup (200 ml) warm water.

Put the semolina directly on your work surface, form it into a mound, and make a well in the center. Add the saffron mixture to the well with a pinch of salt and use a fork to gradually incorporate it into the flour until the dough comes together. Knead for 5 minutes, until the dough is firm and smooth.

Roll the dough into long, ½-inch-diameter (1 cm) cylinders, then cut these into ½-inch-long (1 cm) gnocchi. Roll each piece on a gnocchi board or the tines of a fork.

Bring a large pot of water to a boil. Add the tomatoes and blanch for 30 seconds, then drain them and let cool slightly. Peel and seed the tomatoes and cut the flesh into cubes.

In a medium frying pan, heat the olive oil over medium heat. Add the garlic and cook until fragrant, then add the tomatoes and a pinch of salt and cook for 10 minutes.

Bring a large pot of salted water to a boil. Add the gnocchi and cook until they start to float, then cook for 15 minutes more. Drain them and return them to the pot. Add the tomato sauce and toss to coat.

Divide the gnocchi and sauce among individual serving plates, then sprinkle with the pecorino and serve.

Semolina is a pale yellow flour obtained from durum wheat using a milling process more complex than that used to make other durum wheat flours. It is commonly used in bread and pasta doughs prepared without eggs. If it is milled to a finer texture, it is called *semolina rimacinata* (remilled semolina) and is used mainly for making bread.

Pumpkin Gnocchi with Almond-Sage Pesto

Gnocchi di zucca con pesto di mandorle e salvia

- 1 (1¾ lb/800 g) Mantuan pumpkin or butternut squash, halved, seeded, and cut into wedges
- Scant ¾ cup (100 g) all-purpose (plain) flour
- Pinch of freshly grated nutmeg
- 12 sage leaves
- ⅓ cup (50 g) raw almonds
- 1 clove garlic
- 1 teaspoon nutritional yeast (yeast flakes)
- 4 to 5 tablespoons (60 to 75 ml) extra virgin olive oil
- 1¾ oz (50 g) oil-packed semi-dried or sun-dried tomatoes, drained, patted dry, and finely chopped
- Salt and black pepper

Preparation Time: 30 minutes
Cooking Time: 45 minutes
Serves: 4

Preheat the oven to 400°F (200°C). Line a sheet pan with parchment paper.

Spread the pumpkin over the prepared pan. Cover with foil and bake for 20 minutes, then remove the foil and bake for about 20 minutes more, until the pumpkin is tender. Remove from the oven and let cool, then scoop the flesh of the pumpkin into a bowl and mash it with a potato ricer.

Bring a large pot of salted water to a boil.

Add the flour, nutmeg, and a pinch of salt to the bowl with the pumpkin and stir briefly to combine. On a lightly floured surface, roll the mixture into long cylinders around ¾ inch (2 cm) in diameter, then cut the cylinders into 1¼-inch-long (3 cm) gnocchi.

In a food processor, combine the sage, almonds, garlic, nutritional yeast, olive oil, a pinch of salt, and some pepper and process until the mixture is well combined and smooth.

Add the gnocchi to the boiling water and cook until they start to float, then cook for 1 minute more. Drain the gnocchi and return them to the pot.

Toss the gnocchi with the sage pesto, add the tomatoes, and serve.

There are many varieties of sage, but the most common is *Salvia officinalis*. It has digestive and anti-inflammatory qualities, and it can be used to flavor ingredients during cooking, or dipped in batter and fried.

Gnocchi with Cocoa and Raisins

Gnocchi di patate con cacao e uvette

- 1¾ lb (800 g) white-fleshed potatoes
- 5 tablespoons (40 g) raisins
- 1½ oz (40 g) candied citron, finely chopped
- Scant 2½ cups (300 g) all-purpose (plain) flour, sifted, plus more for dusting
- 2 eggs, lightly beaten
- 3 tablespoons (40 g) butter
- 1¾ oz (50 g) smoked ricotta cheese, grated
- 1½ tablespoons unsweetened cocoa powder
- ½ teaspoon ground cinnamon
- 1 teaspoon sugar
- Salt

Preparation Time: 30 minutes
Cooking Time: 35 minutes
Serves: 4

Put the potatoes in a large saucepan and add cold water to cover. Bring the water to a boil over high heat and cook for 30 minutes, until the potatoes are tender and easily pierced with a fork. Drain them and let cool.

Meanwhile, put the raisins in a small bowl, add warm water to cover, and set aside to soak for 10 minutes, then drain and return them to the bowl. Add the candied citron and set aside.

Peel the potatoes and mash the flesh with a potato ricer, letting it fall directly onto a lightly floured surface. Form it into a mound and make a well in the center.

Add the flour and the eggs to the well and knead until the mixture is well combined. Roll the dough into long, ¾-inch-diameter (1.5 cm) cylinders, then cut these into ¾-inch (1.5 cm) gnocchi. Roll each piece over the tines of a fork.

Bring a large pot of salted water to a boil. Add the gnocchi and cook until they start to float, then cook for 1 minute more. Use a spider (skimmer) to transfer them directly to individual serving plates.

In a small saucepan, melt the butter over medium heat until foaming, then remove from the heat.

Drizzle the gnocchi with the melted butter and sprinkle it with the ricotta, the raisin-citron mixture, and the cocoa powder, cinnamon, and sugar. Serve right away.

White-fleshed potatoes have the highest quantity of starch and dry flesh, ideal for the preparation of gnocchi, croquettes, and pies.

Sweet Spiced Tortelli

Tortelli alla cremasca

- Scant 2½ cups (300 g) all-purpose (plain) flour
- 4 eggs
- ⅓ cup (50 g) raisins
- 3 tablespoons (40 g) butter
- ½ cup (50 g) breadcrumbs
- 3½ oz (100 g) amaretti cookies (biscuits)
- 1 spice cookie (biscuit), such as a speculoos
- ⅔ cup (60 g) grated Parmesan cheese, plus 1½ oz (40 g), shaved, for garnish
- 1¾ oz (50 g) candied citron, cut into small cubes
- Pinch of freshly grated nutmeg
- Vegetable stock
- Salt

Preparation Time: 15 minutes plus resting time
Cooking Time: 25 minutes
Serves: 4

In a large bowl, stir together the flour, 3 eggs, and a pinch of salt. Shape the dough into a loaf, then wrap it in plastic wrap (cling film) and let it rest for 30 minutes.

Put the raisins in a small bowl, add warm water to cover, and set aside to soak for 10 minutes, then drain.

In a nonstick frying pan, melt half the butter over medium heat. Add the breadcrumbs and toast until golden, then transfer them to a medium bowl and let cool.

In a food processor, pulse the amaretti and spice cookies (biscuits) until broken down into crumbs, then add them to the bowl with the breadcrumbs. Add the ⅔ cup (60 g) grated Parmesan, the remaining egg, and the raisins, candied citron, and nutmeg, and stir to combine. If the filling is too dry, add a little vegetable stock until it is soft.

Bring a large pot of water to a boil.

On a lightly floured surface, roll out the dough into a thin sheet and cut it into 2½-inch (6 cm) squares. Place 1 teaspoon of the filling at the center of each square, fold the dough over to form a triangle, and press the edges to seal. Salt the boiling water, add the tortelli, and cook for 5 to 7 minutes, depending on the thickness of the dough.

Meanwhile, in a small saucepan, melt the remaining butter until foamy.

Drain the tortelli and transfer to a serving dish. Top with the melted butter and the shaved Parmesan, then serve.

The spice cookie (biscuit) often used in this preparation is a *mostaccino*, typical of the Cremona region. Another spice cookie (biscuit), such as a ginger snap or speculoos, can be used instead.

Kamut Gnocchi with Fava Purée

Gnocchetti di farina di Kamut con crema di fave

- ¼ cup (60 ml) plus 2 tablespoons extra virgin olive oil
- Scant 3 cups (350 g) Kamut flour
- 2⅓ cups (350 g) shelled fresh fava (broad) beans
- 2 plum tomatoes
- 1 shallot, finely chopped
- 1 cup (250 ml) vegetable stock
- 2 young carrots (not baby carrots), sliced into 2 mm-thick rounds, then finely diced
- Salt and black pepper

Preparation Time: 20 minutes
Cooking Time: 15 minutes
Serves: 4

In a medium saucepan, combine 2 cups (500 ml) water, 2 tablespoons of the olive oil, and a pinch of salt. Bring the water to a boil over high heat, then add the flour all in one go and stir with a wooden spoon until the dough comes away from the side of the pan. Turn the dough out onto a lightly floured surface and let it cool. Roll the dough into long, ¾-inch-diameter (1.5 cm) cylinders, then cut these into ¾-inch (1.5 cm) lengths. Roll each piece over the tines of a fork or down a gnocchi board.

Bring a large pot of water to a boil. Add the fava (broad) beans and the tomatoes and blanch for 1 minute, then use a slotted spoon to transfer them to a colander to drain (keep the water at a boil). Let cool slightly. Remove the beans from their skins and set aside in a bowl. Peel and seed the tomatoes and chop the flesh into small cubes.

In a small frying pan, heat the remaining ¼ cup (60 ml) oil. Add the shallot and cook for 1 to 2 minutes. Set aside 2 tablespoons of the fava (broad) beans and add the rest to the pan with the shallot. Season with salt. Add the stock and cook, covered, for 5 minutes.

Using a hand blender, purée the cooked fava (broad) beans directly in the pot until smooth.

Add the gnocchi to the boiling water and cook until they start to float, then cook for 1 minute more. Drain them and return them to the pot, then add the reserved 2 tablespoons whole fava (broad) beans, the carrots, and the tomatoes, and season with pepper.

Spread some of the fava (broad) bean purée over each serving plate, top with the gnocchi and vegetables, and serve.

Kamut is the name for Khorasan wheat, named for a historical region in Iran. It is grown organically and has nutritional qualities superior to those of common wheat.

Baked Farro Gnocchi with Cauliflower

Gratin di gnocchi di cuscus al cavolfiore

- 3¼ cup (30 g) raisins
- 14 oz (400 g) cauliflower, cut into small florets
- ¼ cup (60 ml) peanut (groundnut) oil
- 1 small yellow onion, very thinly sliced
- 1 (1¼-inch/4 cm) piece fresh ginger, peeled and grated
- 1 heaping tablespoon curry powder
- Scant 1 cup (200 ml) vegetable stock
- ¼ cup (10 g) fresh cilantro (fresh coriander)
- 1½ cups (300 g) farro couscous
- 1 cup (120 g) farro flour
- 6 tablespoons (40 g) breadcrumbs
- Salt

Preparation Time: 30 minutes plus soaking time
Cooking Time: 35 minutes
Serves: 4

Preheat the oven to 400°F (200°C).

Put the raisins in a small bowl, add warm water to cover, and set aside to soak for 10 minutes, then drain.

Bring a large pot of salted water to a boil. Add the cauliflower and cook for 5 minutes, then drain and let cool.

In a large nonstick frying pan, heat the oil over medium-low heat. Add the onion, ginger, and curry powder and cook for 2 to 3 minutes. Add the cauliflower, raisins, and stock, reduce the heat to low, and cook for 7 to 8 minutes. Add the cilantro (fresh coriander) and stir to combine. Turn the heat off.

In a small saucepan, combine a scant 2 cups (450 ml) water and a pinch of salt and bring it to a boil, then turn the heat off. Add the couscous to the water and let stand for 15 minutes to absorb the liquid. Transfer the couscous to a medium bowl and let it cool.

Add the flour to the bowl with the couscous and knead until the dough comes together. Roll the dough into ¾-inch-diameter (1.5 cm) cylinders, then cut the cylinders into ¾-inch-long (1.5 cm) gnocchi.

Bring a large pot of salted water to a boil. Add the gnocchi and cook until they start to float, about 2–3 minutes. Use a spider (skimmer) to transfer them to the pan with the cauliflower curry and stir to coat. Transfer the mixture to a baking dish and sprinkle the top with the breadcrumbs. Bake for about 15 minutes, until golden brown.

Cauliflower can be eaten raw, sliced thinly, grated, or broken into florets to be served with a dip; or cooked: boiled, steamed, or roasted. It is rich in potassium, folic acid, calcium, iron, phosphorus, and vitamin C, and it has purifying and mineralizing properties.

Buckwheat Cannelloni with Eggplant

Cannelloni di grano saraceno con melanzane

- 4 plum tomatoes
- Scant 1¾ cups (200 g) buckwheat flour
- 2 eggs
- ¼ cup (60 ml) plus 2 tablespoons extra virgin olive oil, plus more as needed
- 1 clove garlic
- 1¾ lb (800 g) round purple eggplants (aubergines), cut into ½-inch (1 cm) cubes
- Leaves from 2 sprigs thyme, chopped
- ¼ cup (10 g) chopped chives
- 8¾ oz (250 g) crescenza (stracchino) cheese
- Scant ½ cup (100 ml) milk
- Salt

Preparation Time: 20 minutes plus resting time
Cooking Time: 50 minutes
Serves: 4

Bring a large pot of water to a boil. Add the tomatoes and blanch for 1 to 2 minutes, then drain them and let cool slightly. Peel and seed the tomatoes, then cut the flesh into small cubes.

In a large bowl, stir together the flour, eggs, 2 tablespoons of the olive oil, and a pinch of salt. Knead the dough for a few minutes, then shape it into a loaf, wrap it in plastic wrap (cling film), and refrigerate for at least 30 minutes.

Preheat the oven to 350°F (180°C).

In a large frying pan, heat the remaining ¼ cup (60 ml) oil over medium heat. Add the garlic and cook until golden. Add the eggplant (aubergine) and a pinch of salt, cover, and cook, stirring occasionally, for 10 minutes. Remove the lid, raise the heat to medium-high, and cook for another 5 minutes. Stir in the thyme and chives, remove from the heat, and let cool.

Bring a large pot of water to a boil.

On a lightly floured surface, roll out the dough into a thin sheet, then cut it into 4-inch (10 cm) squares. Salt the boiling water, add the squares of dough, and cook for 2 to 3 minutes. Drain the noodles and lay them flat on a sheet of parchment paper to dry.

Divide the eggplant among the noodles, spooning it in a line along one side, and roll up the noodles to enclose the eggplant. Place the cannelloni in a baking dish and drizzle with oil.

In a blender, combine the crescenza and the milk and purée. Pour the cheese mixture over the cannelloni and bake for about 25 minutes.

Sprinkle the tomato cubes with a pinch of salt, then arrange them on the cannelloni and serve.

Instead of sautéing the eggplants (aubergines), try roasting them: prick them in a few places with a fork, place them on a sheet pan, and roast in a preheated oven at 400°F (200°C) for about 30 minutes, until they are tender. Remove from the oven and let cool slightly. Peel the eggplants (aubergines), squeeze out any excess liquid, and cut the flesh into cubes. Place them in a bowl; drizzle with 1 tablespoon olive oil, sprinkle with salt, and stir in the thyme and chives, then proceed as directed.

Oat, Spinach, and Ricotta Dumplings

Polpettine di fiocchi d'avena con spinacini

- Scant ½ cup (100 ml) milk
- 1 bay leaf
- 1 shallot, thinly sliced
- 3 cups (250 g) quick-cooking oats
- 7 oz (200 g) sheep's-milk ricotta cheese
- 6 tablespoons (40 g) grated Parmesan cheese
- 1 egg yolk
- 7 oz (200 g) baby spinach
- 2 eggs
- 1 cup (100 g) breadcrumbs
- 1 head wild radicchio
- Extra virgin olive oil
- 1 tablespoon balsamic vinegar
- Salt and black pepper

Preparation Time: 20 minutes
plus resting time
Cooking Time: 40 minutes
Serves: 4

Preheat the oven to 350°F (180°C). Line a sheet pan with parchment paper.

In a small saucepan, combine the milk, bay leaf, shallot, and a pinch of salt and heat over very low heat for 5 to 6 minutes, until the milk is just steaming. Discard the bay leaf.

Put the oats in a medium bowl and pour the milk mixture over them, then let stand for 5 minutes.

Transfer the oats to a food processor and add the ricotta, Parmesan, egg yolk, spinach, and some pepper. Process until the mixture is well combined and smooth. Let stand for 10 minutes.

In a small bowl, beat the eggs with a pinch of salt. Put the breadcrumbs in a shallow dish. Shape the oat-ricotta mixture into walnut-size balls and flatten them lightly with your palm. Dip the balls into the beaten egg, letting any excess drip off, then roll them in the breadcrumbs to coat completely and set them on the prepared pan. Drizzle the balls with a little olive oil and bake for about 30 minutes.

Meanwhile, put the radicchio in a medium bowl and dress it with the vinegar, some oil, and a pinch of salt.

Serve the dumplings hot, with the radicchio alongside.

The oats can be replaced with whole-grain barley flakes or farro flakes. For a vegan version, replace the milk with nondairy milk or vegetable stock. Replace the eggs and the egg yolk with 1 teaspoon ground flaxseed (linseed) mixed with 3 tablespoons water. The breadcrumbs can be replaced with ⅓ cup (50 g) toasted sesame seeds, if desired.

Bread Dumplings in Broth

Canederli di magro in brodo

- 2 cups plus 2 tablespoons (500 ml) milk
- 10½ oz (300 g) stale bread
- Handful of parsley leaves, chopped, plus more for garnish
- 3 eggs
- Pinch of freshly grated nutmeg
- 1½ tablespoons (20 g) butter
- 1 yellow onion, finely chopped
- 4¼ cups (1 l) vegetable stock
- Scant ½ cup (50 g) all-purpose (plain) flour
- Salt and black pepper

Preparation Time: 20 minutes
Cooking Time: 25 minutes
Serves: 4

In a small saucepan, warm the milk over medium-low heat until just steaming, then remove from the heat.

Break the bread into small chunks and place them in a large bowl. Pour the milk over the bread and set aside to soak for 10 minutes. Squeeze any excess milk out of the bread, then transfer to a clean large bowl and add the parsley, eggs, nutmeg, a pinch of salt, and some pepper.

In a small frying pan, melt the butter over medium heat. Add the onion and ¼ cup (60 ml) of the stock and cook until the stock has completely evaporated and the onion is tender. Let cool.

In a large saucepan, bring the stock to a boil over high heat.

Meanwhile, add the onion and the flour to the bowl with the bread, then knead the ingredients together until the mixture is homogeneous. Shape the bread mixture into apricot-size dumplings.

Reduce the heat under the stock to medium, then add the dumplings and cook for 10 to 12 minutes. Using a spider, transfer the dumplings to serving bowls. Strain the stock, then ladle it into the bowls over the dumplings. Garnish with parsley and serve.

You can enrich the dumplings by adding 1¾ oz (50 g) cooked chopped spinach or Swiss chard, and 3½ oz (100 g) cheese, such as semi-matured Montasio, cut into small cubes.

Ricotta and Greens Dumplings

Rabatòn

- 1 lb 2 oz (500 g) Swiss chard
- 7 oz (200 g) Piedmontese ricotta cheese (seirass)
- 1 cup (100 g) breadcrumbs
- 6 tablespoons (40 g) grated Parmesan cheese
- 2 eggs, beaten
- 1 clove garlic, passed through a garlic press
- All-purpose (plain) flour, for dusting
- 6 cups (1.5 l) vegetable stock
- 3 tablespoons (40 g) butter
- 8 sage leaves
- Salt

Preparation Time: 30 minutes
Cooking Time: 15 minutes
Serves: 4

Preheat the oven to 425°F (220°C).

Bring a large pot of salted water to a boil. Add the chard and cook for 2 to 3 minutes, then drain it and let cool. Squeeze out any excess water, then finely chop the chard.

In a large bowl, combine the chard, ricotta, breadcrumbs, Parmesan, eggs, garlic, and a pinch of salt and stir well until the dough comes together.

On a lightly floured surface, roll the dough into 1½- to 2-inch-long (4 to 5 cm) pieces, about ½ inch (1 cm) in diameter, then roll them in flour to lightly coat.

In a large pot, bring the stock to a boil. Add the gnocchi and cook until they start to float, then use a spider (skimmer) to transfer them to a baking dish.

In a small saucepan, melt the butter over medium heat until foaming. Add the sage and cook for 30 to 60 seconds, until fragrant.

Drizzle the gnocchi with the sage butter. Bake for about 10 minutes.

Unlike other types of ricotta, Piedmontese ricotta, also known as *seirass*, is a cow's-milk whey cheese. It is soft and smooth and has a sweet flavor.

Bread Gnocchi with Zucchini Salsa

Gnocco di pane e zucchine

- 2 cups (500 ml) milk
- 1 heaping tablespoon sweet paprika
- 8¾ oz (250 g) stale bread
- ¼ cup (60 ml) plus 3 tablespoons extra virgin olive oil, plus more as needed
- 2 spring onions, sliced
- 2 eggs, beaten
- 1 tablespoon chopped fresh parsley
- Leaves from 3 sprigs thyme, chopped
- 1 lb 2 oz (500 g) zucchini (courgettes), cut into very small cubes
- 2 cups (300 g) cherry tomatoes, halved
- 8 squash blossoms (courgette flowers), pistils and stems removed, coarsely chopped
- Salt and black pepper

Preparation Time: 30 minutes plus resting time
Cooking Time: 1 hour 10 minutes
Serves: 4

In a small saucepan, combine the milk and paprika and heat over low heat until the milk is just steaming.

Break the bread into small chunks and place it in a medium bowl. Pour in the hot milk, cover the bowl, and set aside to soak for 1 hour.

In a medium frying pan, heat 3 tablespoons of the olive oil over medium-low heat. Add half the spring onions and a pinch of salt and cook for 5 to 6 minutes. Turn off the heat and let cool.

Knead the softened bread until the mixture is smooth. Add the eggs, onion, parsley, thyme, a pinch of salt, and some pepper. Mix until well combined. Turn the bread mixture out onto a sheet of dampened parchment paper. Mold it into a loaf, then wrap it in the parchment and tie it with kitchen twine.

Transfer the loaf to an oval pan with abundant, gently boiling water and cook over medium-low heat for about 1 hour.

In a large nonstick frying pan, heat the remaining ¼ cup (60 ml) oil over medium-high heat. Add the remaining spring onion, the zucchini (courgettes), and the tomatoes, season with salt, and cook the vegetables for 5 minutes. Add the chopped squash blossoms (courgette flowers), then turn the heat off.

Drain the loaf and remove the parchment paper, then slice the loaf.

Serve the vegetables arranged on top of the slices and drizzled with olive oil.

Paprika is made from ground dried peppers. It is available sweet (if the seeds have been removed before grinding), hot (if the seeds have been left in), or smoked.

Chickpea Ravioli with Tomato Sauce

Mezzelune di ceci con salsa di pomodoro

- 1½ cups plus 1 tablespoon (200 g) all-purpose (plain) flour
- 2 eggs
- 1 leek, white and light green parts only, washed well
- 1 lb 2 oz (500 g) tomatoes, peeled
- ½ cup (120 ml) extra virgin olive oil, plus more as needed
- 2½ cups (400 g) cooked chickpeas, rinsed
- 1½ oz (40 g) Fiore Sardo (smoked pecorino) cheese, grated
- Leaves from 2 sprigs marjoram
- Salt and black pepper

Preparation Time: 55 minutes plus resting time
Cooking Time: 30 minutes
Serves: 4

Sift the flour and a pinch of salt onto your work surface, form it into a mound, and make a well in the center. Add the eggs to the well, then use a fork to gradually incorporate them into the flour until the dough comes together. Knead the dough for 5 minutes, then wrap it in plastic wrap (cling film) and set aside in a cool place to rest for 30 minutes.

Slice the light green portion of the leek lengthwise into very thin strips and set aside; coarsely chop the white portion and place it in a medium saucepan. Add the tomatoes, ¼ cup (60 ml) of the olive oil, and a pinch of salt to the saucepan and cook over medium-high heat for 20 minutes. Using a hand blender, purée the sauce directly in the pan.

In a medium frying pan, heat a tablespoon or two of oil over high heat. Add the green portion of the leek and fry for a few seconds, then use a slotted spoon to transfer the leek to paper towels to drain; cover to keep warm until ready to serve.

Place the chickpeas in a clean kitchen towel and rub gently to remove their skins; discard the skins and transfer the chickpeas to a food processor. Add the cheese, marjoram, remaining ¼ cup (60 ml) oil, a pinch of salt, and some pepper and process until smooth.

Bring a large pot of water to a boil.

On a lightly floured surface, roll out the dough into a thin sheet and cut out 1½-inch (4 cm) disks with a scallop-edge cutter. Place 1 teaspoon of the chickpea filling at the center of each disk. Fold the dough over the filling to form a half-moon and press the edges to seal.

Salt the boiling water, add the ravioli, and cook for 5 to 7 minutes, then drain. Serve topped with the tomato sauce and garnished with the fried leek.

The ravioli can be prepared ahead of time and frozen for later use: Place them in a single layer on a lightly floured sheet pan and freeze until solid, then transfer them to a zip-top bag and store in the freezer. Cook them as directed, straight from the freezer.

Buckwheat Crêpe Cake with Chard and Artichokes

Timballo di crespelle di grano saraceno con carciofi ed erbette

- 1 cup (130 g) buckwheat flour
- 1 cup (250 ml) milk
- 1 teaspoon white wine vinegar
- 2 eggs
- ½ cup (120 ml) plus 1 tablespoon extra virgin olive oil
- 1 lb 2 oz (500 g) Swiss chard, stemmed
- Juice of 1 lemon
- 4 artichokes
- 1 leek, washed well and sliced into thin rounds
- Leaves from 3 sprigs thyme
- ⅓ cup (40 g) all-purpose (plain) flour
- 2 cups (500 ml) unsweetened almond milk
- 1 oz (30 g) Grana Padano cheese, grated
- Salt

Preparation Time: 30 minutes plus resting time
Cooking Time: 55 minutes
Serves: 4

Preheat the oven to 350°F (180°C). Line an 8-inch (20 cm) springform pan with parchment paper.

In a food processor, combine the buckwheat flour, milk, vinegar, eggs, 1 tablespoon of the olive oil, and a pinch of salt. Pulse until well combined, then let the batter rest for 30 minutes.

Meanwhile, bring a large pot of salted water to a boil. Add the chard and blanch for 2 minutes, then drain and let cool. Coarsely chop the chard.

Fill a large bowl with cool water and add the lemon juice. Trim the artichokes, cut them into thin wedges, and cut the fuzzy choke from the center, dropping the wedges into the bowl of lemon water as you go (this prevents them from browning).

In a large frying pan, heat ¼ cup (60 ml) of the oil over medium heat. Add the leek, thyme, and a pinch of salt. Drain the artichokes and add them to the pan, then cook for 5 minutes. Add the chard and cook for another 5 minutes.

In a small saucepan, heat the remaining ¼ cup (60 ml) oil over medium heat. Add the all-purpose (plain) flour and cook, stirring, for 1 minute. While whisking, drizzle in the almond milk, then cook the béchamel sauce, stirring continuously, for 7 to 8 minutes.

Heat an 8-inch (20 cm) nonstick frying pan over medium heat. Pour in a small ladleful of batter, then lift and tilt the pan to allow the batter to spread uniformly over the surface. Cook the crêpe for 1 minute on each side, then transfer it to a plate and let cool. Repeat with the remaining batter.

In the prepared springform pan, layer the crêpes, béchamel sauce, and cooked vegetables, ending with a layer of the béchamel. Sprinkle the top with the Grana Padano. Bake for about 25 minutes, until golden brown. Remove from the oven and let cool in the pan for 5 minutes, then remove the springform ring, transfer to a serving plate, and serve.

Buckwheat is highly nutritious and energizing. It is part of the same family as rhubarb and sorrel, so it is not a grain like true wheat. It is rich in potassium, magnesium, and flavonoids and has antioxidant properties.

Ravioli with Ricotta, Spinach, and Marjoram

Mezzelune di ricotta di soia e spinaci alla maggiorana

- ½ cup plus 1 tablespoon (100 g) durum wheat semolina
- 1 cup (100 g) soy flour
- 1 teaspoon ground turmeric
- 5 tablespoons (75 ml) extra virgin olive oil
- 1 small red onion, such as Tropea or torpedo, finely chopped
- 1 lb 2 oz (500 g) spinach
- 3½ oz (100 g) soy ricotta cheese
- Grated zest of ½ orange
- 2 tablespoons (30 g) vegan butter
- Juice of 1 orange
- 1 tablespoon gomasio
- 1 teaspoon nutritional yeast (yeast flakes)
- Leaves from 2 sprigs marjoram, chopped
- Salt

Preparation Time: 25 minutes
plus resting time
Cooking Time: 20 minutes
Serves: 4

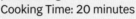

In a large bowl, stir together the semolina, soy flour, turmeric, a pinch of salt, 2 tablespoons of the olive oil, and a scant ½ cup (100 ml) water. Wrap the dough in plastic wrap (cling film) and let it rest for at least 30 minutes.

In a large frying pan, heat the remaining 3 tablespoons oil over medium-low heat. Add the onion and cook for a few minutes, until softened. Add the spinach and season with salt, then raise the heat to medium-high and cook until all the liquid has evaporated. Remove from the heat and let cool.

In a medium bowl, stir together the ricotta and the orange zest. Add the cooled spinach mixture and stir to combine.

Bring a large pot of water to a boil.

On a lightly floured surface, roll out the dough into a thin sheet and cut it into 2½-inch (6 cm) disks. Place a heaping teaspoon of the ricotta filling at the center of each disk, then fold the dough over to form half-moons and press the edges to seal.

Salt the boiling water, add the ravioli, and cook for 4 to 5 minutes.

Meanwhile, in a small saucepan, melt the butter over low heat. Add the orange juice, raise the heat to medium-high, and whisk until emulsified.

Use a slotted spoon or spider/skimmer to transfer the ravioli to a serving dish. Pour the melted butter mixture over them and toss gently to coat. Sprinkle with the gomasio, nutritional yeast (yeast flakes), and marjoram, then serve.

The ravioli filling must be dry so as not to dampen the pasta too much. If there is still quite a bit of liquid left after cooking the spinach mixture, stir in 2 tablespoons breadcrumbs, lightly toasted without any oil.

Crêpes with Green Peas

Crespelle con ragù di piselli

- 2 cups (250 g) all-purpose (plain) flour
- 1⅔ cups (400 ml) soy milk
- 9 to 10 tablespoons (135 to 150 ml) extra virgin olive oil
- 1¼ cups (100 g) textured soy protein
- Leaves from 3 sprigs marjoram
- 3 spring onions, sliced
- 2¾ cups (400 g) shelled fresh peas
- 2 tablespoons wheat germ
- Salt and black pepper

Preparation Time: 25 minutes plus resting time
Cooking Time: 25 minutes
Serves: 4

Sift the flour directly into a large bowl. In a spouted measuring cup, whisk together the soy milk, 3 tablespoons of the olive oil, and ⅔ cup (150 ml) water. While whisking, drizzle the milk mixture into the flour and whisk until combined. Add a pinch of salt and let the batter rest for 30 minutes.

In the meantime, soak the soy protein in boiling water for 30 minutes, then drain and squeeze out any excess water.

In a blender, combine 4 to 5 tablespoons (60 to 75 ml) of the oil, the marjoram, and a pinch of salt. Set the marjoram oil aside.

In a medium saucepan, heat the remaining 2 tablespoons oil over medium-low heat. Add the spring onions and cook for 1 to 2 minutes. Add a scant 1 cup (200 ml) cold water and the peas and cook for 5 minutes. Add the soy protein and season with salt. Cook for 5 to 6 minutes. Finish with a generous sprinkle of pepper.

Heat an 8-inch (20 cm) nonstick frying pan over medium heat. Pour in a small ladleful of batter, then lift and tilt the pan to allow the batter to spread uniformly over the surface. Cook the crêpe for 1 minute on each side, then transfer it to a plate and cover to keep warm. Repeat with the remaining batter.

Fill the crêpes with the pea mixture, then fold them in half and then into quarters to form triangles. Drizzle with the marjoram oil, sprinkle with the wheat germ, and serve.

Peas are in season from April to June. Look for them fresh at your local market and enjoy them for the brief period that they are available. During the rest of the year, frozen can be substituted.

Rye Crepe Noodles with Celeriac

Crespelle di farina di segale con sedano rapa

- 1½ cups (160 g) rye flour
- 2½ cups (600 ml) milk
- 1 egg
- Juice of 1 lemon
- 10½ oz (300 g) celeriac
- ¼ cup (60 ml) extra virgin olive oil, plus more as needed
- 1 leek, washed well and sliced into thin rounds
- Zest of ½ orange
- Juice of 1 orange, strained
- 3 tablespoons chopped wild fennel or fennel fronds
- Black pepper

Preparation Time: 30 minutes
Cooking Time: 25 minutes
Serves: 4

(CT)

In a food processor, combine the flour, milk, egg, and a pinch of salt and process until the mixture is smooth and well combined.

Fill a large bowl with water and add the lemon juice. Peel the celeriac and grate it on the large holes of a box grater. Put the grated celeriac in the lemon water to prevent it from browning.

In a large nonstick frying pan, heat the olive oil over low heat. Drain the celeriac and add it to the pan. Add the leek and a pinch of salt, cover, and cook for 10 minutes. Add the orange zest and juice and cook until the liquid has evaporated, then add the fennel and stir. Turn the heat off.

Lightly grease an 8-inch (20 cm) nonstick frying pan and heat it over medium heat. Pour in a small ladleful of batter, then lift and tilt the pan to allow the batter to spread uniformly over the surface. Cook the crêpe for 1 minute on each side, then transfer it to a plate. Repeat with the remaining batter.

Stack two or three crêpes and cut them into ½-inch-wide (1 cm) strips. Repeat with the remaining crêpes. Transfer them to the pan with the vegetables and cook over medium-high heat for 1 minute to warm through.

Sprinkle with pepper and fennel fronds and serve.

Leeks can be used much like onions. Each leek has a white portion, which was the part of the leek that remained underground while the leek was growing, and dark green tops, which are usually discarded. Leeks contain iron, magnesium, calcium, potassium, and a good amount of vitamin A. They are most often eaten cooked but can be eaten raw, with a dip, or added to salads. In this case it is best to use its tender heart.

Pasta Bundles with Ratatouille

Fagottini integrali con ratatuia di verdure

- ⅔ cup (80 g) whole-wheat (wholemeal) flour
- 2 eggs
- ½ cup plus 1 tablespoon (130 ml) milk
- 2 tablespoons (30 g) butter, melted and cooled
- 1¾ lb (800 g) plum tomatoes
- ½ cup (120 ml) extra virgin olive oil
- 1 yellow bell pepper, cut into small cubes
- 1 red bell pepper, cut into small cubes
- 1 purple eggplant (aubergine), cut into small cubes
- 2 zucchini (courgettes), cut into small cubes
- ⅔ cup (100 g) cherry tomatoes
- 1 spring onion, finely diced
- 4 mint leaves, very thinly sliced
- 1 small bunch chives
- Salt

Preparation Time: 30 minutes plus resting time
Cooking Time: 35 minutes
Serves: 4

Preheat the oven to 300°F (150°C). Line a sheet pan with parchment paper.

In a food processor, combine the flour, eggs, milk, melted butter, a pinch of salt, and 5 tablespoons (70 ml) water. Pulse until well combined, then let the batter rest for 30 minutes.

In the meantime, bring a large pot of water to a boil. Add the plum tomatoes and blanch for 30 seconds, then drain them and let cool slightly. Peel and seed the tomatoes, then transfer the flesh to a medium saucepan and use a hand blender to purée it. Add a pinch of salt and ¼ cup (60 ml) of the olive oil, then cook the sauce over low heat for 15 minutes.

In a large nonstick frying pan, heat the remaining ¼ cup (60 ml) oil over medium-high heat. Add the bell peppers, eggplants (aubergine), zucchini (courgettes), cherry tomatoes, spring onion, and a pinch of salt, then cook for 6 to 7 minutes. Stir in the mint, turn off the heat, and let the vegetables cool.

Bring a small pot of water to a boil. Add the chives and blanch for a few seconds, then drain them.

Heat an 8-inch (20 cm) nonstick frying pan over medium heat. Pour in a small ladleful of batter, then lift and tilt the pan to allow the batter to spread uniformly over the surface. Cook the crêpe for 1 minute on each side, then transfer it to a plate. Repeat with the remaining batter.

Divide the cooled vegetable mixture among the crêpes, placing it in the center of each. Gather the edges of the crêpes around the filling to form little bundles and tie the tops closed with the chives. Set the crêpes on the prepared sheet pan and bake for 10 minutes to warm through.

Spread the warm tomato sauce over individual serving plates, arrange the stuffed crêpes on top, and serve.

It is important to let the batter rest so that the liquid is fully absorbed and the gluten relaxes. This will give the batter a thicker consistency and the crêpes a more delicate texture.

Crêpes with Spinach and Ricotta

Crespelle alla Fiorentina

- 1⅓ cups (170 g) all-purpose (plain) flour
- 3 eggs
- 3½ cups (800 ml) milk
- 1 lb 2 oz (500 g) spinach
- 8¾ oz (250 g) sheep's-milk ricotta cheese
- Scant 1 cup (80 g) grated Parmesan cheese
- Pinch of freshly grated nutmeg
- 3 tablespoons (40 g) butter, plus more for greasing
- 3½ tablespoons tomato purée (passata)
- Salt and black pepper

Preparation Time: 30 minutes
plus resting time
Cooking Time: 40 minutes
Serves: 4

In a food processor, combine 1 cup (120 g) of the flour, 2 eggs, 1 cup (250 ml) of the milk, and a pinch of salt. Pulse until well combined, then let the batter rest for 30 minutes.

Preheat the oven to 400°F (200°C).

Bring a medium saucepan of salted water to a boil. Add the spinach and cook for 3 to 4 minutes, then drain it and let cool. Squeeze out any excess water, then finely chop the spinach and transfer it to a medium bowl.

Add the ricotta, 1 egg, half the Parmesan, the nutmeg, a pinch of salt, and some pepper and stir well to combine.

In a medium saucepan, melt the butter over medium heat. Add the remaining flour all at once and toast it, stirring with a wooden spoon, for about 1 minute. While whisking, drizzle in the remaining milk and whisk until well combined. Reduce the heat to low and cook the béchamel sauce, stirring frequently, for 7 to 8 minutes. Turn off the heat, season with salt, and stir in the remaining Parmesan.

In an 8-inch (20 cm) nonstick frying pan, melt a small pat of butter over medium heat. Pour in a small ladleful of batter, then lift and tilt the pan to allow the batter to spread uniformly over the surface. Cook the crêpe for 1 minute on each side, then transfer it to a plate. Repeat with the remaining batter.

Spread a layer of the béchamel sauce over the bottom of a baking dish. Fill the crêpes with the ricotta mixture and roll them up around the filling. Place them in the baking dish over the béchamel, then cover them with the remaining béchamel and the tomato purée (passata) and bake for about 20 minutes. Serve hot.

Ricotta can be made not only from cow's milk, but also from sheep's milk, which has a firm and grainy consistency and a strong flavor; buffalo milk, which is soft and creamy; and goat's milk, which is soft and has a distinctive flavor.

Baked Crêpes with Tomato and Eggplant

Crespelle alla napoletana

- 4 eggs
- Scant ¾ cup (100 g) all-purpose (plain) flour
- ⅔ cup (60 g) grated Parmesan cheese
- Scant 1 cup (200 ml) milk
- 1 tablespoon extra virgin olive oil
- 7 oz (200 g) buffalo ricotta cheese
- Handful of parsley leaves, chopped
- 1 clove garlic
- 2 purple eggplants (aubergines), cubed
- 20 Gaeta or other black olives, pitted
- Scant 1 cup (200 ml) tomato purée (passata)
- 7 oz (200 g) buffalo mozzarella cheese, cut into cubes
- Salt and black pepper

Preparation Time: 30 minutes
Cooking Time: 45 minutes
Serves: 4

Preheat the oven to 350°F (180°C). Lightly oil an oval baking dish.

In a large bowl, beat the eggs with a fork. Add the flour, half the Parmesan, a pinch of salt, and some pepper and whisk to combine. While whisking, drizzle in the milk and whisk until the batter is well combined.

In an 8-inch (20 cm) frying pan, heat the olive oil over medium-high heat. Pour in a small ladleful of batter, then lift and tilt the pan to allow the batter to spread uniformly over the surface. Cook the crêpe for 1 minute on each side, then transfer it to a plate and cover to keep warm. Repeat with the remaining batter.

In a medium bowl, stir together the ricotta, the remaining Parmesan, and the parsley and season with salt. Spread this mixture over the crêpes, roll them up around the filling, and place them in the prepared baking dish.

In a nonstick medium frying pan, cook the garlic over medium-low heat until golden (do not let it burn). Add the eggplant (aubergines) and a pinch of salt. Cover and cook for 5 minutes. Add the olives, tomato purée (passata), and a pinch of salt, then reduce the heat to low and cook for 10 minutes.

Pour the eggplant-tomato sauce over the rolled crêpes and bake them for 20 minutes. Sprinkle the top with the mozzarella, then bake for 5 minutes more, until the cheese has melted. Serve.

In November, when Gaeta olives are picked, they are green with dark dots. They are then pickled in brine, which turns them their characteristic purplish color.

Chestnut Crêpes with Sweet Peppers and Robiola Cheese

Crespelle di castagne ai peperoni e robiola

- 2 cups plus 2 tablespoons (250 g) chestnut flour
- 2 cups (500 ml) milk
- 2 eggs, beaten
- 2 yellow bell peppers
- 1 red bell pepper
- 3 tablespoons extra virgin olive oil, plus more as needed
- Leaves from 2 sprigs marjoram, chopped
- ¼ cup (40 g) pine nuts
- 1 clove garlic, smashed and peeled
- 5¼ oz (150 g) robiola cheese, torn into small chunks
- 6 tablespoons (40 g) grated Pecorino Romano cheese
- Salt

Preparation Time: 30 minutes plus resting time
Cooking Time: 50 minutes
Serves: 4

Preheat the boiler.

Sift the chestnut flour directly into a large bowl. While whisking, drizzle in the milk and whisk until combined, then add the eggs and a pinch of salt and whisk to incorporate. Let the batter rest for 30 minutes in a cool place.

In the meantime, brush the bell peppers with a little oil and place them on a sheet pan. Broil, turning them to ensure they cook evenly, until lightly charred and softened, 4 to 5 minutes. Remove from the oven, transfer to a bowl, cover with plastic wrap (cling film), and let cool. Set the oven to 350°F (180°C).

Peel and seed the roasted peppers, then thinly slice the flesh and transfer it to a medium bowl. Sprinkle with the olive oil, marjoram, pine nuts, garlic, and a pinch of salt. Allow the flavors to develop for 15 minutes, then discard the garlic.

Lightly grease an 8-inch (20 cm) nonstick frying pan and heat it over medium heat. Pour in a small ladleful of batter, then lift and tilt the pan to allow the batter to spread uniformly over the surface. Cook the crêpe for 1 minute on each side, then transfer it to a plate. Repeat with the remaining batter.

Lightly grease a baking dish. Fill the crêpes with the roasted pepper mixture and the robiola cheese, then roll them up around the filling. Place them in the prepared baking dish, sprinkle the top with the pecorino, drizzle with a little oil, and bake for about 20 minutes, until golden brown. Serve hot.

Robiola is a soft fresh cheese that can be made with cow's, sheep's, or goat's milk. It can be shaped into a round or a square and has a delicate, slightly acidic taste.

Baked Pasta with Sunchokes and Spinach

Pasta gratinata con topinambur e spinaci e mandorle

- Juice of 1 lemon
- 10½ oz (300 g) sunchokes (Jerusalem artichokes)
- ¼ cup (60 ml) plus 3 tablespoons extra virgin olive oil
- 10½ oz (300 g) spinach, coarsely chopped
- ⅓ cup (50 g) raw almonds, coarsely chopped
- 2 tablespoons (30 g) vegan butter, plus more for greasing
- ⅓ cup (40 g) all-purpose (plain) flour
- 2 cups plus 2 tablespoons (500 ml) unsweetened almond milk
- Leaves from 2 sprigs thyme, chopped
- 6 tablespoons (40 g) breadcrumbs
- ¼ cup (20 g) sliced (flaked) almonds
- 11¼ oz (320 g) whole wheat maccheroni pasta
- Salt and black pepper

Preparation Time: 20 minutes
Cooking Time: 50 minutes
Serves: 4

Preheat the oven to 350°F (180°C). Butter a baking dish.

Fill a large bowl with cold water and add the lemon juice. Peel the sunchokes (Jerusalem artichokes) and cut them into small cubes, adding them to the lemon water as you go (this prevents them from browning).

In a large frying pan, heat the ¼ cup olive oil over medium-high heat. Drain the sunchokes (Jerusalem artichokes) and add them to the pan, along with a pinch of salt and a small ladleful of water. Cook for about 10 minutes. Add the spinach, raise the heat to high, and cook for another 5 minutes. Remove from the heat, season with salt and pepper, and stir in the chopped almonds.

In a medium saucepan, melt the butter over medium heat. Add the flour and cook for a few seconds, stirring continuously, to toast the flour. While whisking, slowly pour in the milk and whisk to combine. Cook the sauce for 7 to 8 minutes. Remove from the heat, season with salt, and stir in the thyme.

Bring a large pot of water to a boil.

In a medium frying pan, heat the remaining 3 tablespoons oil over medium heat. Add the breadcrumbs and toast until golden. Remove from the heat and stir in the sliced (flaked) almonds.

Salt the boiling water, add the pasta, and cook for half the time indicated on the package. Drain the pasta and return it to the pot. Add the béchamel sauce and the vegetables and stir to coat. Pour the pasta into the prepared baking dish and top with the breadcrumb mixture. Bake the pasta for about 25 minutes, until the top is golden, then serve.

The pasta can be enriched at the end of the cooking time by sprinkling it with a spoonful of wheat germ and replacing the breadcrumbs with 6 tablespoons (40 g) quick-cooking oats. Spinach has large leaves that can absorb large quantities of pesticides, so it's best to choose organic spinach.

Buckwheat Lasagna with Broccoli

Lasagne di grano saraceno con broccoli

For the pasta:
- ⅔ cup (100 g) buckwheat flour
- 1⅔ cups (200 g) "00" flour
- 3 eggs

For the filling:
- 2¼ lb (1 kg) broccoli florets
- 1 savoy cabbage, cored and chopped
- 2 tablespoons (25 g) butter
- 2 shallots, thinly sliced
- ½ cup (120 ml) ricotta cheese
- ⅔ cup (50 g) grated Parmesan cheese
- Freshly grated nutmeg
- ½ teaspoon salt
- Pepper

For the béchamel:
- 2 tablespoons (30 g) butter
- 2 tablespoons all-purpose (plain) flour
- 2 cups (475 ml) milk
- 3½ oz (100 g) Emmental cheese, diced
- Grated Parmesan cheese, to taste
- Salt and pepper

To assemble:
- Butter, for greasing
- 1 teaspoon olive oil
- Salt and pepper

Preparation Time: 30 minutes plus 30 minutes resting
Cooking Time: 1 hour
Serves: 8

Make the pasta: Sift both types of flour together directly onto a clean work surface, form them into a mound, and make a well in the center. Break the eggs into the well and use a fork to gradually combine them with the flour until a dough comes together. Knead the dough until smooth. Wrap in plastic wrap (cling film) and let rest for 30 minutes.

Make the filling: Bring a large saucepan of salted water to a boil. Add the broccoli and cook for 2 minutes, or until bright green but still crisp. Use a slotted spoon to transfer the broccoli to a colander to drain. Repeat with the cabbage.

In a large saucepan, melt the butter over medium-low heat. Add the shallots and cook gently for a few minutes, then add the cabbage and broccoli. Cover and cook, stirring occasionally, for 5 minutes, or until the vegetables have softened. Remove from the heat and let cool, then stir in the ricotta, Parmesan, nutmeg, and salt and season with pepper.

Make the béchamel: In a small saucepan, melt the butter over medium heat. Add the flour and stir, cooking until the flour has browned slightly, about 1 minute. Gradually add the milk, stirring continuously. Continue cooking the sauce until it thickens, about 10 minutes. Add the Emmental then remove from the heat and season with parmesan, salt, and pepper.

Assemble the lasagna: Roll out the pasta, cut it into noodles (sheets), and let dry for 20 minutes. Meanwhile bring a large saucepan of salted water to a boil. Add the olive oil, then add the pasta, a few pieces at a time. When the noodles rise to the surface, remove them with a slotted spoon and spread them out flat on a clean kitchen towel.

Preheat the oven to 350°F (180°C). Grease a large baking dish with butter.

Place a layer of pasta in the bottom of the prepared baking dish, cover with half the vegetables, then spread with ⅓ of the béchamel sauce. Repeat, ending with the béchamel. Bake for 20 to 25 minutes, until golden. Serve hot.

Eggplant and Ricotta Lasagna

Lasagne alle melanzane e ricotta

- Butter, for greasing
- 1 large eggplant (aubergine), sliced
- 1 tablespoon olive oil, plus more for brushing and drizzling
- 1 pound (500 g) fresh pasta for lasagna
- Scant ½ cup (50 g) pine nuts, finely chopped
- ⅔ cup (180 ml) ricotta cheese
- ½ cup (120 ml) tomato puree (passata)
- Fresh basil leaves
- Grated Parmesan cheese, for serving
- Salt

Preparation Time: 15 minutes plus 30 minutes resting
Cooking Time: 1 hour
Serves: 4

Preheat the broiler (grill) or preheat the oven to 350°F (180°C). Grease a baking dish with butter.

Put the eggplant (aubergine) slices in a colander, sprinkle with salt, and set the colander in the sink. Let the eggplant drain for 30 minutes, then rinse under cold running water and pat dry with paper towels. Put the eggplant slices on a sheet pan, brush with olive oil, and broil or bake until tender, about 10 minutes. Remove from the oven but keep the oven on.

Bring a large saucepan of salted water to a boil. Add the olive oil, then add the pasta a few noodles (sheets) at a time. When the noodles rise to the surface, remove them with a slotted spoon and spread them flat on a clean kitchen towel or parchment paper.

Layer half the lasagna noodles over the bottom of the prepared baking dish, followed by half the eggplant slices. Sprinkle with some of the pine nuts, crumble half the ricotta cheese on top, then pour over ¼ cup (60 ml) of the tomato puree (passata) and top with some basil leaves. Drizzle with a little oil. Place the remaining lasagna noodles in a layer on top and cover with the remaining ingredients. Sprinkle evenly with grated Parmesan and bake for about 40 minutes. Serve hot.

For a creamier texture, mix the ricotta cheese with a scant ½ cup (100 ml) whole milk or light (single) cream. You can also flavor the tomato puree by adding a finely chopped shallot, 3 tablespoons olive oil, a pinch of sugar, and a pinch of salt and cooking it in a small saucepan over medium-low heat for 5 to 6 minutes.

Baked Fusilli with Tomato and Mozzarella

Fusilli alla vesuviana

- 1 lb 2 oz (500 g) plum tomatoes
- 3½ oz (100 g) fior di latte (cow's-milk mozzarella) cheese, sliced
- 6 tablespoons (40 g) grated Pecorino Romano cheese
- ¼ cup (60 ml) extra virgin olive oil
- Pinch of dried oregano
- 11¼ oz (320 g) fusilli
- Salt and black pepper

Preparation Time: 10 minutes
Cooking Time: 20 minutes
Serves: 4

Preheat the oven to 400°F (200°C).

Bring a large pot of water to a boil. Add the tomatoes and blanch for a few seconds, then remove them with a slotted spoon and let cool; return the water to a boil.

Peel, seed, and coarsely chop the tomatoes. Transfer them to a large frying pan and add the mozzarella, pecorino, olive oil, oregano, and a pinch of salt. Cover and cook over medium heat while you cook the pasta.

Add a pinch of salt to the boiling water, then add the pasta and cook according to the package instructions until al dente but still quite firm.

Drain the fusilli, add it to the pan with the sauce, and stir to coat. Season with some pepper, then transfer the pasta and sauce to a baking dish. Bake for 5 to 10 minutes, then serve.

To ensure that the mozzarella does not release too much water during cooking, slice it 15 minutes before you need it and place it on paper towels to dry.

Chestnut Lasagna with Squash and Kale

Lasagne di castagne con zucca e cavolo nero

- 2 cups (200 g) chestnut flour
- 2 eggs
- ¼ cup (60 ml) plus 3 tablespoons extra virgin olive oil
- 10½ oz (300 g) peeled pumpkin, sliced ¼ inch (6 mm) thick
- 3 cloves garlic, smashed and peeled
- 10½ oz (300 g) Tuscan kale (cavolo nero)
- Scant ½ cup (50 g) all-purpose (plain) flour
- Scant 3 cups (700 ml) milk
- Pinch of freshly grated nutmeg
- 6 tablespoons (40 g) grated Parmesan cheese
- Salt and black pepper

Preparation Time: 25 minutes plus resting time
Cooking Time: 1 hour 15 minutes
Serves: 4

Preheat the oven to 350°F (180°C).

Sift the chestnut flour onto your work surface, form it into a mound, and make a well in the center. Break the eggs into the well, add 1 tablespoon of the olive oil and a pinch of salt, then use a fork to gradually incorporate the eggs and oil into the flour until the dough comes together. Knead the dough for a few minutes, then wrap it in plastic wrap (cling film) and refrigerate for at least 30 minutes.

In a large bowl, combine the pumpkin, garlic, 2 tablespoons of the oil, a pinch of salt, and some pepper and toss to coat the pumpkin. Spread the pumpkin (and the garlic) over a sheet pan, cover with foil, and bake for about 30 minutes, until the pumpkin is tender. Remove from the oven and discard the garlic; keep the oven on.

Bring a large pot of salted water to a boil. Add the kale leaves and cook for 5 minutes. Drain and let cool, then squeeze out any excess water and chop the kale.

In a medium saucepan, heat the remaining ¼ cup (60 ml) oil over medium heat. Add the all-purpose (plain) flour and cook for a few seconds. Whisking continuously, slowly pour in the milk. Still whisking, cook the sauce for 7 to 8 minutes. Whisk in the nutmeg, a pinch of salt, and some pepper, then stir in the kale. Turn the heat off and stir in the Parmesan.

Bring a large pot of water to a boil.

To prevent the béchamel sauce from forming a skin as it cools (which can turn into lumps when it is stirred into the sauce), cover the sauce with parchment paper or plastic wrap (cling film) while still warm, pressing it directly against the surface of the sauce.

On a lightly floured surface, roll out the dough into a thin sheet, then cut it into 2¾ x 6-inch (7 x 15 cm) rectangles. Salt the boiling water, add the dough rectangles, and cook for 2 to 3 minutes. Drain the noodles, then lay them flat on a sheet of parchment paper to dry.

Arrange a layer of noodles in a 9 x 13-inch (23 x 33 cm) baking dish. Top with a layer of the béchamel sauce, then a layer of the pumpkin. Repeat these layers, ending with a layer of pumpkin. Bake for about 35 minutes. Serve hot.

Vegetable Tarts & Pastries

Grains, legumes, and other protein-rich ingredients such as cheese, eggs, oil-rich seeds, tofu, and, of course, vegetables (even better if they're in season): These are the elements needed to prepare nourishing and delicious quiches, strudels, flans, and tatins, to be served as appetizers or main courses, dishes that can stand on their own as a meal, depending on the ingredients used and the portion size.

Tasty dishes to please everyone

Great classics of the Italian gastronomic tradition, savory pies represent an excellent all-purpose culinary element. Their versatility allows them to be served as a main course, an appetizer, or—and why not?—for appetizers or a quick snack. Furthermore, enjoyed both hot and cold, they can satisfy not only different tastes but also different dietary needs, especially for those following a vegetarian diet.

Proteins from the East

Tofu and tempeh, ingredients from the culinary traditions of Asia, can be used as alternative protein in savory vegetarian dishes, as they can replace eggs, milk, or cheese. These soy-based foods are cholesterol-free and low in saturated fats. Seitan, from a nutritional point of view, is just as valuable, but since it's derived from wheat, it is not suitable for people with celiac disease or gluten intolerance.

Nutritious and versatile

The nutritional value of vegetarian savory pies varies considerably depending on the ingredients used, as they can be filled in myriad ways, limited only by the imagination of the chef. Vegetables, especially fresh and in-season options, play a big role in the preparation of light and tasty recipes, of course. Savory pies are also an effective way to get younger children used to eating vegetables.

A green starter . . .

Savory pies with vegetables as their main ingredients are a source of valuable nutrients, including vitamins, fiber, and minerals. However, in the context of a balanced meal, they need to be accompanied by dishes with adequate quantities of other nutrients, especially protein. This is why they are preferably served as starters, followed, for example, by a protein-rich second course and then by a fruit salad or fruit-based dessert.

...or a main course?

Many vegetarian savory pies can be served as a single-course meal thanks to the inclusion of protein-rich ingredients such as legumes, grains, eggs, cheese, and other dairy products. In vegan dishes, eggs and dairy can be replaced by vegan protein sources, such as tofu, tempeh, or seitan, which are derived from soy or wheat.

Nutritious pastry

To improve the nutritional value of a savory pie, whole-grain flours, from wheat or other grains, can be used to prepare the dough. As these flours are not refined, they retain all the nutrients present in the grain, including fiber, vitamins, minerals, and antioxidants. Also worth trying are oil-rich seeds such as sunflower, flaxseed (linseed), pumpkin, poppy, and sesame seeds, to name but a few. When added to the dough, they are a source of vitamins, essential fatty acids, and protein.

Lots of great ideas for the table

There is more to savory pies than you might think. In practice, this definition refers to very different dishes, in both appearance and preparation style. However, all of them are suitable for vegetarian preparations.

Quiches, tarts, and pies

Quiches are egg-based dishes baked in a pastry crust. The word *quiche* derives from the German *Kuchen*, meaning "cake." In the classic quiche Lorraine, the pastry is filled with an egg-and-cream mixture, bacon, and cheese. However, quiches can be filled with vegetables, grains, and legumes. Savory tarts and pies consist of various fillings baked, like their sweet counterparts, in a pastry crust.

Tatins

Tarte tatin, an upside-down apple pie, is the sweet symbol of French pâtisserie. The savory vegetarian variant is also "upside down," as the vegetables are arranged in the baking pan first, then topped with the pastry and baked.

Strudels

Its very name, which means "whirlpool" in German, describes the appearance of this filled pastry, which is rolled to form a spiral. A traditional strudel is prepared with a basic dough made from flour, oil and water, but some recipes use puff pastry instead, with excellent results. Filled with mixed vegetables and cheese, strudels can be baked in advance and then reheated.

Flans

Known in Italy as *sformato*, a flan is similar to a soufflé, but less airy. In vegetarian flans, the base ingredients are béchamel sauce, eggs, Parmesan cheese, and vegetables. It is generally baked in a special ring-shaped pan called a flan ring.

Supporting players

Legumes, grains, seasonal vegetables, eggs and dairy products (for those who eat them)—in savory pies, it is possible to serve all the basic components of a balanced vegetarian diet.

Flavor boosters
Savory pies often use aromatic herbs, which historically were cheap ingredients easily found growing wild. It is a way of adding flavor without using too much salt. Fresh herbs offer the best flavor, but ground, dried, or frozen herbs will work as well.

Legumes
Peas, beans, chickpeas, fava (broad) beans, and lentils can be a source of vegan protein in no way inferior to that provided by meat. They are rich in fiber, which aids digestion, B vitamins, and minerals. Fresh legumes can be found in season, when their flavor, nutritional value, and appearance are all at their best, but legumes are also sold frozen, jarred or canned, or dried.

Grains
In the form of flour, grains are an essential ingredient of the dough for savory pies. Many recipes, however, also use grains in their filling. Whole grains are among the most balanced foods found in nature, as they contain carbohydrates, protein, and fats. The most widely used grains are wheat, corn, oats, barley, and rice. Quinoa, Kamut, and amaranth are equally nutritious.

Vegetables
Zucchini (courgettes), peppers, spinach, eggplants (aubergines), onions, potatoes, artichokes, asparagus: with their wealth of vitamins, minerals, and trace elements, they are the main ingredients in both traditional and more contemporary savory pies.

Eggs and dairy products
Eggs provide high-quality protein, as they are rich in essential amino acids as well as fat-soluble vitamins and minerals. The proteins in milk and cheese contain all nine essential amino acids, and dairy products are also rich in calcium. Vegans can replace these ingredients with soy- and wheat-based products such as tofu, seitan, or tempeh.

Rye Crostata with Peas and Asparagus

Crostata di farro e semi ai piselli e asparagi

- 1¾ cups (220 g) farro (emmer) flour, plus more for sprinkling
- Scant ½ cup (50 g) all-purpose (plain) flour
- 3 tablespoons black sesame seeds
- 1 tablespoon brown flaxseeds (linseeds)
- ¼ cup (60 ml) plus 3½ tablespoons extra virgin olive oil
- 4 spring onions, chopped
- 1 bunch asparagus, thinly sliced
- 1⅓ cups (200 g) shelled fresh peas
- Scant 1 cup (200 ml) soy milk
- Grated zest of ½ lemon
- 2 egg yolks
- 2½ tablespoons sunflower seeds
- Salt and black pepper

Preparation Time: 30 minutes plus resting time
Cooking Time: 1 hour
Serves: 6 to 8

In a food processor, combine the farro flour, all-purpose (plain) flour, sesame seeds, flaxseeds (linseeds), 3½ tablespoons of the olive oil, and a pinch of salt and process the mixture until crumbly. With the motor running, drizzle in ⅓ cup (75 ml) cold water and process until the dough comes together and forms a ball. Wrap the dough in plastic wrap (cling film) and refrigerate for at least 30 minutes.

Preheat the oven to 350°F (180°C) with a rack in the lower third.

In the meantime, in a heavy-bottomed frying pan, heat the remaining ¼ cup (60 ml) oil over medium heat. Add the onions and asparagus and cook for 2 to 3 minutes. Add the peas and a scant ½ cup (100 ml) water and cook for 7 to 8 minutes, until the liquid has evaporated. Sprinkle the vegetables with farro flour, drizzle in the milk, and stir.

Reduce the heat to low and cook the sauce for 5 to 6 minutes. Season with salt and pepper, then stir in the lemon zest. Remove from the heat and let the sauce cool. Add the egg yolks and stir to combine.

On a lightly floured surface, roll out two-thirds of the dough into a 2 mm-thick sheet and transfer it to a 9-inch (22 cm) round baking pan. Fill the crust with the vegetable mixture. Roll the remaining dough into a thin sheet and cut it into ¾-inch-wide (1.5 cm) strips. Arrange the strips over the filling to form an open lattice. Press the lattice strips against the bottom crust to seal, then trim the excess dough around the edges.

Brush the lattice with a little water and sprinkle with the sunflower seeds. Bake the tart in the lower third of the oven for about 40 minutes. Serve warm.

To enhance the flavor of the sesame seeds, toast them, covered, in a heavy-bottomed frying pan over medium heat until they start to crackle, then transfer to a plate and let cool. For a vegan version of the recipe, replace the egg yolks with a heaping tablespoon of millet flakes.

Mini Lentil and Chickpea Quiche

Mini quiche di ceci e lenticchie

- 1 cup plus 2 tablespoons (100 g) chickpea flour
- Scant ¾ cup (100 g) all-purpose (plain) flour
- 3 tablespoons extra virgin olive oil, plus more as needed
- 7 oz (200 g) dried red lentils, rinsed
- 1 bay leaf
- 7 oz (200 g) silken tofu or soft tofu
- 1 shallot
- 1 sprig rosemary
- 4 sage leaves
- Salt and black pepper
- Scant ½ cup (50 g) shelled pistachios
- 1¾ oz (50 g) oil-packed semi-dried or sun-dried tomatoes, drained, patted dry, and finely chopped

Preparation Time: 30 minutes
plus resting time
Cooking Time: 1 hour
Serves: 6 to 8

In a food processor, combine the chickpea flour, all-purpose (plain) flour, olive oil, a pinch of salt, and 3 tablespoons cold water and process until the dough comes together and forms a ball. Wrap the dough in plastic wrap (cling film) and refrigerate for at least 30 minutes.

Meanwhile, put the lentils and bay leaf in a medium saucepan and add cold water to cover by at least 2 inches (5 cm). Bring to a boil over high heat, reduce the heat to maintain a simmer, and cook for about 25 minutes. Drain the lentils, discard the bay leaf, and let cool.

Preheat the oven to 350°F (180°C) with a rack positioned in the bottom third.

In a blender, combine the tofu, shallot, rosemary, sage leaves, a pinch of salt, and some pepper and blend until smooth. Pour the tofu mixture into a large bowl.

Coarsely chop ¼ cup (30 g) of the pistachios and add them to the tofu mixture; finely chop the remaining pistachios.

Add the lentils and tomatoes to the tofu mixture and stir to combine; set aside.

On a lightly floured surface, roll out the dough into a thin sheet. Cut 5-inch (12 cm) rounds of dough and transfer them to individual 3-inch (8 cm) tartlet pans, pressing the dough into the corners. Remove the excess dough using a rolling pin and set the tartlet shells on a sheet pan. Prick the bottom of each tartlet shell all over with a fork, then fill them with the lentil-tofu mixture. Bake the tartlets for about 30 minutes, until the crusts are golden and the filling is set.

Serve the tartlets warm, garnished with the finely chopped pistachios.

The silken tofu can be replaced with regular tofu; blend it with 3 to 4 tablespoons soy milk to make it creamier. For a more delicately flavored crust, replace half the extra virgin olive oil with corn oil.

Spinach Quiche with Ricotta Salata

Quiche ai germogli di spinaci, primo sale e feta

- 9 oz (250 g) puff pastry dough, thawed if frozen
- All-purpose (plain) flour, for dusting
- 4 eggs
- 7 oz (200 g) ricotta salata or salted soft cheese, crumbled
- 3½ oz (100 g) feta cheese, drained and diced
- ¼ cup (35 g) pine nuts
- 7 oz (200 g) spinach, chopped
- Olive oil, for drizzling
- Salt and pepper

Preparation Time: 15 minutes
Cooking Time: 30 to 40 minutes
Serves: 6

Preheat the oven to 400°F (200°C). Line an 8-inch (20 cm) round baking pan with parchment paper.

On a lightly floured surface, roll out the dough into a round large enough to fit the prepared pan. Transfer the dough to the pan and prick it all over with a fork. Set the baking pan on a sheet pan.

In a medium bowl, beat together the eggs and ricotta, then stir in the feta. Season with pepper and lightly with salt, and pour the mixture into the prepared pan. Sprinkle with the pine nuts, add the spinach, and drizzle with olive oil. Bake for 10 minutes, then reduce the oven temperature to 350°F (180°C) and bake for another 20 to 30 minutes, until the filling is set. Remove from the oven and let cool in the pan on a wire rack.

Serve the quiche lukewarm.

Upside-Down Pumpkin and Pepper Tart

Tatin di zucca e peperoni

- 1 red bell pepper
- 1 yellow bell pepper
- Extra virgin olive oil
- 7 oz (200 g) peeled pumpkin, sliced ¼ inch (6 mm) thick
- 1½ tablespoons butter
- 2 teaspoons raw sugar
- 1 (1¼-inch/3 cm) piece fresh ginger, peeled and grated
- 3½ oz (100 g) primo sale or other semisoft sheep's-milk cheese, sliced
- ½ (17.25 oz/490 g) package frozen puff pastry (1 sheet), thawed
- 1 tablespoon chopped cilantro (fresh coriander)
- Salt

Preparation Time: 30 minutes
Cooking Time: 55 minutes
Serves: 4 to 6

Preheat the broiler.

Brush the bell peppers with a little oil and place them on a sheet pan. Broil, turning them to ensure they cook evenly, until lightly charred and softened, 4 to 5 minutes. Remove from the oven, transfer to a bowl, cover with plastic wrap (cling film), and let cool. Leave the broiler on.

Meanwhile, fill a large saucepan with an inch or two of water, set a steamer basket inside, and bring the water to a simmer. Add the pumpkin and steam for 5 minutes.

Peel and seed the roasted peppers, then cut the flesh into large strips.

Melt the butter and pour it into a 9-inch (22 cm) pie plate. Add the sugar, sprinkling it evenly over the butter, then place the pumpkin slices and the peppers on top.

Sprinkle with a pinch of salt and the grated ginger, then broil for 5 to 6 minutes, until the sugar caramelizes. Remove from the oven and let cool; set the oven to 350°F (180°C).

Arrange the sliced cheese over the vegetables, then place the puff pastry on top and press the edges down around the filling along the inside edge of the pan.

Prick the dough all over with a fork. Bake the tart for about 30 minutes, until the pastry is golden brown. Remove from the oven and let cool in the pan for 5 minutes.

Invert the tart onto a serving plate. Garnish with the cilantro and serve.

For a vegan version, ensure that the puff pastry does not contain any animal fat, and replace the butter with vegan butter and the primo sale with herbed tofu or coarsely grated smoked tofu.

Leek and Apple Quiche

Crostata con mele e porri

- 2½ cups (300 g) buckwheat flour
- 10½ tablespoons (150 g) butter, cut into very small cubes and chilled, plus 1½ tablespoons (20 g)
- 2 Fuji apples, peeled, cored, and sliced
- 1 leek, washed well and thinly sliced
- 1 bay leaf
- 2 eggs
- 3½ oz (100 g) Gruyère cheese, coarsely grated
- ½ cup (20 g) radish sprouts, coarsely chopped
- Salt and black pepper

Preparation Time: 20 minutes plus resting time
Cooking Time: 45 minutes
Serves: 4 to 6

In a food processor, combine the flour, the chilled cubes of butter, a pinch of salt, and 3 tablespoons ice water and process until the dough comes together and forms a ball. Wrap the dough in plastic wrap (cling film) and refrigerate for at least 30 minutes.

Preheat the oven to 350°F (180°C).

In a nonstick frying pan, melt the remaining 1½ tablespoons (20 g) butter over medium heat. Add the apples, leek, and bay leaf and season with salt. Cook for 7 to 8 minutes. Remove from the heat and discard the bay leaf.

Beat the eggs in a medium bowl. Add the Gruyère, radish sprouts, a pinch of salt, and a generous sprinkle of pepper and stir to combine.

On a lightly floured surface, roll out the dough into a thin sheet, then transfer it to a 9½-inch (24 cm) fluted tart pan with a removable bottom, pressing the dough into the sides and corners of the pan. Run the rolling pin over the top of the tart pan to trim any excess dough. Fill the tart shell with the apple mixture and spread it evenly with a spatula, then pour in the egg mixture. Bake the tart in the lower third of the oven for about 35 minutes, until set. Serve warm.

If you wish, you can make a vegan dough for the crust by using oil instead of butter, leaving out the cheese (or replacing it with vegan cheese), and replacing the eggs with 1 cup plus 2 tablespoons (100 g) chickpea flour mixed with 1¼ cups (300 ml) soy milk.

Zucchini and Rice Galette

Torta di zucchine e riso

- 1½ cups plus 1 tablespoon (200 g) all-purpose (plain) flour
- 3 tablespoons extra virgin olive oil
- Scant ½ cup (100 ml) white wine
- Scant ½ cup (80 g) Arborio rice
- 1 lb 2 oz (500 g) tromboncino squash or zucchini (courgette), thinly sliced into rounds
- 1 white onion, very thinly sliced
- 1¾ oz (50 g) Parmesan cheese, grated
- 1 egg
- Salt and black pepper

Preparation Time: 30 minutes plus resting time
Cooking Time: 50 minutes
Serves: 4 to 6

In a food processor, combine the flour and a pinch of salt. With the motor running, drizzle the olive oil and the wine and process until the dough comes together and forms a ball. Wrap the dough in plastic wrap (cling film) and refrigerate for at least 30 minutes.

Preheat the oven to 350°F (180°C). Lightly oil a 9-inch (22 cm) pie plate or other round baking dish.

Bring a small saucepan of water to a boil. Salt the water, add the rice, and cook for 5 to 6 minutes, then drain and let cool.

In a large bowl, combine the rice, squash, onion, Parmesan, and egg, season with salt and pepper, and stir well.

On a lightly floured surface, roll out the dough into a very thin round and transfer it the prepared pan. Add the filling and level the top with a spatula. Fold the overhanging dough over the filling, leaving the center uncovered. Bake the tart for about 45 minutes to an hour, until the crust is golden brown. Serve warm or at room temperature.

For a vegan version of this classic tart from Liguria, boil the rice for 12 minutes, drain, and let cool. Cook the onion with 3 tablespoons olive oil and 3 tablespoons water over low heat for 6 to 7 minutes. Add the squash and a pinch of salt, raise the heat to medium, and cook for 5 to 6 minutes, then mix the cooked vegetables with the rice and stir in 6 tablespoons (50 g) toasted pumpkin seeds. Omit the egg and Parmesan and continue as above.

Zucchini and Pine Nut Tart

Tarte di zucchine e pinoli

- 1½ cups plus 1 tablespoon (200 g) whole wheat (wholemeal) flour
- ¼ cup (60 ml) plus 2 tablespoons extra virgin olive oil, plus more as needed
- 6 tablespoons (50 g) pine nuts
- 1 shallot, finely chopped
- 16 squash blossoms (courgette flowers), pistils removed, coarsely chopped (keep a few whole for garnish)
- 2 zucchini (courgettes)
- 10½ oz (300 g) ricotta cheese
- 6 tablespoons (40 g) grated Parmesan cheese
- 2 eggs
- 2 sprigs marjoram
- 1 sprig thyme
- 10 basil leaves
- Pinch of freshly grated nutmeg
- 1¾ oz (50 g) sliced whole wheat (wholemeal) bread
- Salt and black pepper

For a vegan version, omit the ricotta, eggs, and Parmesan. Chop 10½ oz (300 g) tofu and sauté it with the shallot and squash blossoms (courgette flowers), then blend as directed.

Preparation Time: 30 minutes plus resting time
Cooking Time: 50 minutes
Serves: 6 to 8

In a food processor, combine the flour, a pinch of salt, and some pepper and pulse to combine. With the motor running, drizzle in ¼ cup (60 ml) of the olive oil and ¼ cup (60 ml) water and process until the dough comes together and forms a ball. Wrap the dough in plastic wrap (cling film) and refrigerate for at least 30 minutes.

Put 2 tablespoons of the pine nuts in a small bowl, add water to cover, and set aside to soak for 20 minutes, then drain.

Preheat the oven to 350°F (180°C).

In a large frying pan, combine the shallot, 2 tablespoons oil, and 2 tablespoons water and cook over medium-low heat for 4 to 5 minutes. Add the squash blossoms (courgette flowers) and season with salt. Raise the heat to high and cook for 2 minutes. Remove from the heat and let cool.

In a blender, combine the ricotta, Parmesan, eggs, marjoram, thyme, basil, remaining 3 tablespoons unsoaked pine nuts, the nutmeg, and a pinch of salt. Add the squash blossom (courgette flower) mixture and blend until well combined.

In a food processor, pulse the bread until broken down into coarse crumbs, then transfer them to a frying pan and cook over medium-low heat until lightly toasted. Let cool.

On a lightly floured surface, roll out the dough into a 2 mm thick sheet and transfer it to a nonstick 9-inch (22 cm) round baking pan, pressing the dough into the corners. Trim the excess dough and prick the bottom all over with a fork. Sprinkle with the toasted breadcrumbs, then fill with the ricotta mixture and smooth the top with the back of a spoon.

Using a vegetable peeler, slice the zucchini (courgettes) lengthwise into ribbons and arrange them over the ricotta mixture. Brush the zucchini (courgettes) with a little oil, sprinkle with a pinch of salt, and distribute the soaked pine nuts evenly over the top. Bake the tart in the lower third of the oven for about 40 minutes. Serve hot or warm.

Pumpkin Tart

Torta di zucca

- 1½ oz (20 g) dried mushrooms
- 4 tablespoons (60 ml) olive oil
- 1 onion, chopped
- 1 (2¼ lb/1 kg) pumpkin, peeled, seeded, and diced
- Butter, for greasing
- All-purpose (plain) flour, for dusting
- 1 clove garlic, peeled
- 2 eggs, lightly beaten
- 3½ oz (100 g) Parmesan cheese, grated
- Pinch of freshly grated nutmeg
- 14 oz (400 g) pie dough (shortcrust pastry dough), thawed if frozen
- 3½ oz (100 g) fontina cheese, sliced
- Salt and pepper

Preparation Time: 30 minutes
Cooking Time: 55 minutes
Serves: 4

Put the mushrooms in a small bowl, add warm water to cover, and set aside to soak for 10 minutes, then drain and squeeze out any excess liquid.

In a large saucepan, heat 2 tablespoons of the olive oil over low heat. Add the onion and cook, stirring occasionally, for 5 minutes, or until softened and translucent. Add the pumpkin, 3 to 4 tablespoons water, and a pinch of salt and cook, stirring continuously, until the pumpkin has broken down into a puree. Remove the pan from the heat.

In a small frying pan, heat the remaining 2 tablespoons oil over low heat. Add the garlic and cook, stirring frequently, for a few minutes, until golden, then remove. Add the mushrooms and cook over low heat, stirring frequently, for 15 minutes, then remove from the heat.

Meanwhile, preheat the oven to 400°F (200°C). Grease a 9-inch (22 cm) cake pan with butter, dust it with flour, and tap out any excess.

On a lightly floured surface, roll out the dough into a round large enough to fit the prepared cake pan. Transfer the dough to the pan, making sure that it comes all the way up the sides.

In a large bowl, mix together the pumpkin puree, eggs, Parmesan, mushrooms, and nutmeg and season with pepper. Spoon the pumpkin mixture into the lined pan, place the slices of fontina on top, and bake for 40 minutes. Serve warm.

Cauliflower Tart

Torta al cavolfiore

- 1 head cauliflower, cut into florets
- 13 oz (375 g) puff pastry, thawed if frozen
- 1½ tablespoons milk
- 4 eggs, lightly beaten
- Pinch of freshly grated nutmeg
- Generous ¾ cup (100 g) grated Emmental cheese
- Salt and pepper

Preparation Time: 20 minutes
Cooking Time: 45 minutes
Serves: 4

Preheat the oven to 400°F (200°C).

Bring a large saucepan of salted water to a boil. Add the cauliflower and cook for 10 minutes, then drain and let cool.

On a lightly floured surface, roll out the puff pastry into an 8 x 10-inch (20 x 25 cm) rectangle. Place it on a sheet pan and bake for 5 to 10 minutes. Remove from the oven and arrange the cauliflower florets on top. Reduce the oven temperature to 320°F (160°C).

In a medium bowl, stir together the milk, eggs, nutmeg, and cheese and season with salt and pepper. Pour this mixture over the cauliflower florets, then bake for 25 minutes. Remove from the oven and let cool, then slice and serve.

To prevent the cauliflower from releasing too much water during cooking, you can steam it instead. Divide it into small florets, place them in a steamer basket set in a saucepan of simmering water, cover, and cook for about 10 minutes, or until tender.

Artichoke and Zucchini Strudel

Torta arrotolata di carciofi e zucchini

For the strudel:
- ¼ cup (60 ml) olive oil
- 1 clove garlic, crushed
- 4 young, tender artichokes, trimmed and thinly sliced
- 2 zucchini (courgettes), diced
- About ¼ cup (50 ml) vegetable stock
- Pinch of ground mace (optional)
- ¾ cup (180 ml) ricotta cheese
- 9 oz (250 g) puff pastry, thawed if frozen
- All-purpose (plain) flour, for dusting
- 1 egg, lightly beaten
- 1 tablespoon sesame seeds
- Salt and pepper

For the sauce:
- ¼ oz (10 g) dried porcini mushrooms
- 3 tablespoons (30g) butter
- ¼ cup (30 g) flour
- 2 cups (500 ml) hot vegetable stock
- ¼ cup (15 g) finely chopped flat-leaf parsley
- Salt and pepper

Preparation Time: 40 minutes
Cooking Time: 1 hour 20 minutes
Serves: 6

Preheat the oven to 375°F (190°C). Line a large sheet pan with parchment paper.

Make the strudel: In a Dutch oven or casserole dish, heat the olive oil over medium-high heat. Add the garlic, brown it lightly, then remove it with a slotted spoon. Add the artichokes and cook over high heat for 5 minutes. Add the zucchini (courgettes), stock, and mace, season with salt and pepper, and cook for 10 minutes. Stir in the ricotta and remove from the heat.

On a lightly floured surface, roll out the pastry into a large rectangle. Spread the ricotta-vegetable mixture over it and, starting from one long side, roll up the pastry to enclose the filling.

In a small bowl, mix the egg with a little water to make an egg wash. Brush the surface of the pastry with the egg wash, sprinkle with the sesame seeds, and use a small, sharp knife to cut diagonal incisions in the top of the roll. Transfer the strudel to the prepared sheet pan, seam side down, and bake for 40 to 45 minutes. Remove from the oven and let cool until just warm.

Meanwhile, make the sauce: Put the mushrooms in a small bowl, add warm water to cover, and set aside to soak for 10 minutes, then drain them, squeeze out any excess liquid, and finely chop.

In a medium saucepan, melt the butter over medium heat. Add the flour and stir well. While whisking continuously, slowly pour in the stock, then add the mushrooms and cook, stirring occasionally, for 20 minutes. Season with salt and pepper and add the parsley.

Slice the strudel and serve the slices on individual plates, with 1 to 2 tablespoons of the sauce on the side.

Eggplant-Tomato Strudel

Strudel di melanzane e pomodori

- 1½ cups plus 1 tablespoon (200 g) all-purpose (plain) flour
- 5½ to 6½ tablespoons extra virgin olive oil
- 1 large eggplant (aubergine), sliced ¼ inch thick
- 6 plum tomatoes, sliced ½ inch thick
- 1 clove garlic, sliced
- 1 cup (80 g) fresh rye breadcrumbs
- Scant ⅔ cup (80 g) raw almonds, coarsely chopped
- Leaves from 3 sprigs thyme
- Pinch of red pepper flakes
- Salt

Preparation Time: 30 minutes
plus resting time
Cooking Time: 50 minutes
Serves: 6 to 8

Preheat the oven to 425°F (220°C). Line a roasting pan with parchment paper.

In a food processor, combine the flour and a pinch of salt. With the motor running, drizzle in 3½ tablespoons of the olive oil and a scant ½ cup (100 ml) warm water and process until the dough comes together. Wrap the dough in plastic wrap (cling film) and refrigerate for 30 minutes.

Arrange the eggplant (aubergine) and tomato slices in the prepared pan and lightly salt them. Sprinkle with the garlic and drizzle with the remaining 2 to 3 tablespoons oil. Roast for about 20 minutes, until the eggplant is tender. Remove from the oven and let cool; keep the oven on.

In a small bowl, combine the breadcrumbs, almonds, thyme, and red pepper flakes.

On a sheet of parchment paper, roll out the dough into a very thin rectangle. Arrange the roasted vegetables over the dough, leaving a 1-inch (2.5 cm) border uncovered, then sprinkle evenly with the breadcrumb mixture. Fold the long edges toward the center. Starting from one short end, roll up the dough to enclose the filling, using the parchment to help. Transfer the filled dough, still on the parchment, to a sheet pan.

Bake the strudel for about 30 minutes, until lightly browned. Serve warm or at room temperature.

This recipe can be made using prepared puff pastry, which is normally made with vegetable oil or shortening.

Fried Turnovers with Capers and Olives

Calzuncieddi

- Scant 3¼ cups (400 g) all-purpose (plain) flour
- ⅓ oz (10 g) fresh yeast, crumbled, or ½ (¼ oz/7 g) packet active dry yeast (1⅛ teaspoons)
- ¼ cup (30 g) salt-cured capers, rinsed
- ¼ cup (60 ml) extra virgin olive oil
- 1 lb 2 oz (500 g) white onions, thinly sliced
- 1 cup (150 g) pitted black olives
- 10 cherry tomatoes, chopped
- Pinch of salt
- Handful of parsley, chopped
- 3½ oz (100 g) semi-aged pecorino cheese, grated
- Peanut (groundnut) oil, for frying

Preparation Time: 25 minutes plus rising time
Cooking Time: 25 minutes
Serves: 4

In a large bowl, stir together the flour, yeast, and a scant 1 cup (200 ml) warm water, then cover and let rise in a warm place for 1 hour.

Put the capers in a small bowl, add warm water to cover, and set aside to soak for 10 minutes, then drain.

In the meantime, in a large frying pan, heat the olive oil over medium-low heat. Add the onions and cook for 1 or 2 minutes. Add the olives, tomatoes, capers, and salt and cook for about 10 minutes. Remove from the heat and let cool, then stir in the parsley and the pecorino.

Punch down the dough slightly and divide it into chunks. On a lightly floured surface, roll each chunk of dough into a thin disk with a diameter of approximately 5 inches (12 cm). Place a spoonful of the onion filling in the center of each disk, fold the dough over the filling to make a half-moon, then seal the edges with a fork.

Line a sheet pan with paper towels. Fill a high-sided frying pan with about 2 inches (5 cm) of peanut (groundnut) oil and heat over medium-high heat to 350°F (180°C). Working in batches to avoid crowding the pan, carefully add the turnovers and fry until they are puffy and golden, 3 to 4 minutes. Transfer to the paper towels to drain, then serve.

For best results when frying leavened dough, the oil temperature shouldn't be too high. This way, the dough will cook on the inside without burning and color evenly on the outside.

Fried Turnovers with Tomato and Ricotta

Panzarotti

- 1 oz (35 g) fresh yeast, crumbled
- 1 lb 2 oz (500 g) flour, preferably Italian "00," plus more for dusting
- 1 cup (250 ml) ricotta cheese
- 6 or 7 firm red cherry tomatoes, peeled and diced
- Olive oil, for frying
- Salt and pepper

Preparation Time: 3 hours 30 minutes, including rising
Cooking Time: 8 to 10 minutes
Serves: 4

In a liquid measuring cup, combine the yeast and 1 cup (250 ml) warm water and mash with a fork until smooth.

Sift the flour with a pinch of salt directly onto a clean work surface, form it into a mound, and make a well in the center. Pour the yeast mixture into the well and use your fingers to gradually incorporate the flour until a dough forms. Knead the dough well until smooth and elastic. Shape the dough into a ball, put it in a bowl, cover with a clean kitchen towel, and let rise in a warm place for 2 to 3 hours, until almost doubled in size.

On a lightly floured surface, divide the dough into 8 pieces and roll out each piece into a fairly thick sheet. Season the ricotta with salt and pepper. Spoon the ricotta into the middle of each sheet, dividing it evenly, and top with the tomatoes. Fold the dough over the filling and crimp the edges to seal.

Fill a high-sided frying pan with about 4 inches (10 cm) of olive oil and heat over medium-high heat to 350° to 375°F (180° to 190°C), or until a cube of bread browns in 30 seconds. Working in batches if necessary, add the turnovers and fry for 8 to 10 minutes, until golden brown all over. Remove with a slotted spoon, drain on paper towels, and serve immediately.

Flaky Onion and Tomato Roll

Sfogliata arrotolata alle cipolle e pomodori

- ⅓ oz (10 g) fresh yeast, crumbled, or ½ (¼ oz/7 g) packet active dry yeast (1⅛ teaspoons)
- Scant 3¼ cups (400 g) all-purpose (plain) flour, plus more for dusting
- 1 teaspoon sugar
- ½ cup (120 ml) extra virgin olive oil, divided, plus more for brushing
- Black pepper
- 1 teaspoon salt, plus more as needed
- ⅓ cup (40 g) salt-cured capers, rinsed
- 1 lb 2 oz (500 g) yellow onions, very thinly sliced
- 10 large ripe cherry tomatoes, finely chopped
- 1¼ cups (200 g) Gaeta or other black olives, pitted
- Handful of parsley, coarsely chopped
- 3½ oz (100 g) Pecorino Romano cheese, grated

Preparation Time: 40 minutes plus resting time
Cooking Time: 1 hour
Serves: 4

In a large bowl, combine the yeast and a scant 1 cup (200 ml) warm water and stir until the yeast has dissolved. Add the flour, sugar, ¼ cup (60 ml) of the olive oil, and some pepper and stir for 1 minute to combine. Add the salt and knead the dough for 10 minutes. Cover the dough and let it rise in a warm place for 2 hours.

Preheat the oven to 350°F (180°C). Line a sheet pan with parchment paper.

Put the capers in a small bowl, add warm water to cover, and set aside to soak for 10 minutes, then drain.

In a nonstick frying pan, heat the remaining ¼ cup (60 ml) oil over medium-low heat. Add the onions, tomatoes, and a pinch of salt, reduce the heat to low, and cook for about 15 minutes. Add the olives, capers, parsley, and pecorino and cook until any remaining liquid has evaporated. Remove from the heat and let cool.

On a lightly floured surface, roll out the dough into a thin square. Place a line of the cooled filling along one side, then fold the dough over the filling to cover it. Add another line of filling alongside the fold and fold again. Continue until the filling has been used up and there is no dough left to fold.

Flatten the filled roll of dough and twist it into a spiral. Place it on the prepared pan, brush the surface with oil, and bake for about 40 minutes, until golden brown. Let cool, then slice and serve.

For an alternative filling, in a medium bowl, stir together 7 oz (200 g) ricotta salata and 2 beaten eggs. Cut 7 oz (200 g) mozzarella cheese and 3½ oz (100 g) caciocavallo cheese into small cubes, stir them into the ricotta mixture, and fill the dough as directed.

Radicchio Pie

Pizza di verdure con radicchio

- ⅓ oz (10 g) fresh yeast, crumbled, or ½ (¼ oz/7 g) packet active dry yeast (1⅛ teaspoons)
- Scant 3¼ cups (400 g) all-purpose (plain) flour, plus more for dusting
- 1 teaspoon sugar
- ½ cup (120 ml) extra virgin olive oil
- Black pepper
- 1 teaspoon salt
- 1 heaping tablespoon salt-cured capers, rinsed
- 1 clove garlic, smashed and peeled
- 1¾ lb (800 g) radicchio, sliced into strips
- 12 Gaeta or other black olives, pitted
- 1 egg, beaten

Preparation Time: 30 minutes plus resting time
Cooking Time: 40 minutes
Serves: 4

In a large bowl, combine the yeast and a scant 1 cup (200 ml) warm water and stir until the yeast has dissolved. Add the flour, sugar, ¼ cup (60 ml) of the olive oil, and some pepper and stir for 1 minute to combine. Add the salt and knead the dough for 10 minutes. Cover the dough and let it rise in a warm place for 2 hours.

Preheat the oven to 350°F (180°C).

Put the capers in a small bowl, add warm water to cover, and set aside to soak for 10 minutes, then drain.

In a large frying pan, heat the remaining ¼ cup (60 ml) oil over medium-low heat. Add the garlic and cook, stirring, until golden, then use a slotted spoon to remove and discard the garlic.

Raise the heat to medium-high, add the radicchio, and season with a little salt. Cook for 5 to 6 minutes, then add the capers and olives. Remove from the heat and let cool.

Punch down the dough and divide it in half. On a lightly floured surface, roll each half into a thin sheet. Use one of the sheets to line a 10-inch (26 cm) round baking dish, then fill it with the cooled radicchio mixture. Top with the second sheet of dough and crimp the edges to seal. Brush the dough with the egg and bake for about 30 minutes. Let cool completely before slicing and serving.

When preparing this pie, you can replace the radicchio with 2 heads escarole or frisée lettuce, or the garlic with 3 sliced spring onions (no need to discard).

Onion and Potato Slab Pie

Sfogliata di patate e cipollotti

- 7 oz (200 g) tempeh, cut into cubes
- 2 tablespoons soy sauce
- 1 (1¼-inch/3 cm) piece fresh ginger, peeled and grated
- 14 oz (400 g) red potatoes
- ¼ cup (60 ml) peanut (groundnut) oil
- 2 spring onions, sliced
- ⅓ cup (40 g) coarsely chopped walnuts
- Leaves from 2 sprigs thyme
- 1 (17.25 oz/490 g) package frozen puff pastry (2 sheets), thawed
- Salt and black pepper

Preparation Time: 20 minutes
Cooking Time: 1 hour
Serves: 4

Preheat the oven to 350°F (180°C). Line a 9 x 13-inch (23 x 33 cm) baking pan with parchment paper.

In a medium bowl, combine the tempeh, soy sauce, and ginger, and let it marinate for 30 minutes.

Peel the potatoes, cut them into cubes, and place them in a bowl of cold water.

In a large nonstick frying pan, heat the oil over medium-high heat. Add the tempeh with its marinade and cook for 3 to 4 minutes. Drain the potatoes and add them to the pan. Add the onions and reduce the heat to low. Cover and cook for 10 minutes, stirring from time to time. Remove from the heat and let cool, then add the walnuts and thyme and stir to combine.

Place one sheet of the puff pastry in the prepared pan, then pour in the tempeh-potato filling. Cut the other sheet of puff pastry into strips and place them crosswise over the filling, slightly overlapping them. Roll the edges of the pastry to seal, trim any the excess pastry, and bake the tart for about 40 minutes, until golden brown.

To make tempeh, fresh soybeans are cooked, then fermented, and finally pressed into blocks. It is very high in protein and is easier to digest than tofu and other unfermented soy products. It is also rich in calcium, iron, B vitamins, lecithin, and fiber. It holds its shape when sliced or cubed and can be dredged in flour and fried, steamed, grilled, or sautéed with vegetables. Prepared puff pastry is usually made with vegetable oil or shortening and is therefore safe to use in vegan recipes; check the label to make sure before purchasing.

Fava and Chestnut Pie

Torta di San Pietro con fave e castagne

- 7 oz (200 g) dried fava (broad) beans
- 7 oz (200 g) dried chestnuts
- 2 cups (200 g) rye flour
- Scant ¾ cup (100 g) all-purpose (plain) flour
- ⅓ oz (10 g) fresh yeast, crumbled, or ½ (¼ oz/7 g) packet active dry yeast (1⅛ teaspoons)
- 2 tablespoons extra virgin olive oil
- 1 lb 2 oz (500 g) white potatoes
- ⅓ cup (80 g) butter
- 2 cloves garlic
- 1 sprig rosemary
- 2 sprigs thyme
- Scant ½ cup (100 ml) milk
- Pinch of freshly grated nutmeg
- Salt

Preparation Time: 30 minutes
plus resting time
Cooking Time: 1 hour 45 minutes
Serves: 6

Put the fava (broad) beans and the chestnuts in separate large bowls, add cold water to cover by several inches, and set aside to soak for 12 hours.

In a large bowl, stir together the rye flour, all-purpose (plain) flour, yeast, olive oil, ⅔ cup (150 ml) warm water, and a pinch of salt. Cover the dough and let it rise for 2 hours.

Drain the chestnuts and place them in a large saucepan. Drain the beans, remove their skins, and add them to the pan with the chestnuts. Add cold water to cover by several inches. Bring the water to a boil and cook for 30 minutes.

In the meantime, peel and coarsely chop the potatoes. When the beans and chestnuts have cooked for 30 minutes, add the potatoes to the pot and cook for another 30 minutes. Drain and transfer the mixture to a large bowl. Mash with a potato masher.

Preheat the oven to 350°F (180°C). Line an 8-inch (20 cm) round baking pan with parchment paper.

In a small frying pan, melt the butter over medium-low heat. Add the garlic, rosemary, and thyme and remove from the heat. Let the butter cool, then discard the garlic and herbs and add the butter to the mashed vegetables. Add the milk, nutmeg, and a pinch of salt and stir to combine.

Divide the dough in half. On a lightly floured surface, roll out half the dough into a ⅛-inch-thick (3 to 4 mm) sheet, then transfer it to the prepared pan. Pour in the filling and level the top with a spatula. Roll out the remaining dough into a thin sheet and place it over the filling. Crimp the edges to seal, prick the top all over with a fork, and bake the pie on the lower rack for about 35 minutes, until the top is golden.

For a vegan version of this savory pie, replace the butter with vegan butter or use 3½ tablespoons extra virgin olive oil mixed with 3½ tablespoons peanut (groundnut) oil, and replace the milk with soy milk.

Artichoke Pie

Torta verde di carciofi

- 4 cups (500 g) all-purpose (plain) flour
- ½ cup (120 ml) extra virgin olive oil
- Juice of 1 lemon
- 6 artichokes
- 1 small yellow onion, finely chopped
- Handful of parsley
- Leaves from 3 sprigs marjoram, chopped
- ½ cup (50 g) grated Parmesan cheese
- 6 eggs
- Salt and black pepper

Preparation Time: 30 minutes plus resting time
Cooking Time: 1 hour 5 minutes
Serves: 6

Preheat the oven to 350°F (180°C). Line an 8-inch (20 cm) springform pan with parchment paper.

In a large bowl, stir together the flour, ¼ cup (60 ml) of the olive oil, a pinch of salt, and about 1 cup (250 ml) water, then shape the dough into a ball (add a bit more water if the dough isn't coming together). Wrap the dough in plastic wrap (cling film) and refrigerate for at least 30 minutes.

Fill a large bowl with cool water and add the lemon juice. Trim the artichokes, cut them into wedges, and cut the fuzzy choke from the center, dropping the wedges into the bowl of lemon water as you go (this prevents them from browning).

In a large saucepan, heat the remaining ¼ cup (60 ml) oil over medium heat. Add the onion and cook for 4 to 5 minutes. Drain the artichokes, add them to the pan, and season with salt. Cover and cook for 15 minutes, or until the artichokes are soft, then uncovered and cook until any remaining liquid has evaporated. Remove from the heat, stir in the parsley and marjoram, and let cool.

Divide the dough into 12 equal balls. On a lightly floured surface, roll six balls of the dough into very thin sheets, stacking them on top of each other as you go.

Transfer the stack of dough sheets to the prepared pan, gently pressing it down into the corners of the pan and allowing the excess dough to overhang the sides. Fill with the artichoke mixture and sprinkle with half the Parmesan. Make six hollows in the filling and break an egg into each one. Sprinkle with a little salt, some pepper, and the remaining Parmesan.

For a vegan version, replace the eggs with 3½ oz (100 g) roasted seitan, chopped, and the Parmesan with ¾ cup (80 g) coarsely grated rice cheese.

Roll the remaining six balls of dough into very thin sheets, stack them on top of each other, and place the stack over the filling. Trim any excess dough and roll the edge over to form a little cord. Bake the tart in the lower third of the oven for about 45 minutes, until lightly browned. Serve warm or at room temperature.

Beet Torte

Torta pasqualina

- Butter, for greasing
- 1⅓ cups (320 g) ricotta cheese
- 2 tablespoons grated Parmesan cheese
- 2 tablespoons breadcrumbs
- 8 eggs, 4 lightly beaten
- ¼ cup (60 ml) light (single) cream
- 2 cups (300 g) chopped cooked beets (beetroot)
- 1 sprig marjoram, chopped
- 14 oz (400 g) puff pastry, thawed if frozen
- Olive oil, for brushing
- All-purpose (plain) flour, for dusting
- Salt and pepper

Preparation Time: 1 hour
Cooking Time: 1 hour
Serves: 8 to 10

Preheat the oven to 400°F (200°C).

Put the ricotta in a fine-mesh sieve set over a medium bowl. Using a rubber spatula, push the ricotta through the sieve. Add the Parmesan, breadcrumbs, the 4 beaten eggs, and the cream. Season with salt and pepper. Add the beets (beetroot) and the marjoram and stir well to combine.

On a lightly floured surface, divide the pastry in half and roll out one half into a 10-inch (25 cm) disk, about ¼ inch (0.5 cm) thick. Use the pastry to line a 7-inch (18 cm) cake pan, creating a rim with the pastry around the edge, and brush with olive oil. Pour in half the beet mixture. Make four wells in the beet mixture and crack an egg into each of them. Season with salt and pepper. Pour over the remaining beet mixture and smooth out the top with a wet knife.

Roll out the remaining pastry into an 8-inch (20 cm) disk, about ¼ inch (.5 cm) thick. Place the pastry over the filling, pressing down well around the edges of the pan, and fold over the edges of the pastry to seal. Prick the pastry with a fork and bake for about 30 minutes. Cover the pastry with aluminum foil and bake for another 30 minutes. Remove from the oven and let rest for about 10 minutes.

Transfer the torte to a serving dish and serve warm or at room temperature.

Swiss Chard and Potato Pie

Pasticcio di bietole e patate

- 2¼ lb (1 kg) Swiss chard, stemmed
- 2 tablespoons olive oil, plus more for brushing
- 1 chile, seeded and finely chopped
- 1 clove garlic, peeled
- 4 potatoes, peeled and cut into wedges
- 4 hard-boiled eggs, peeled and cut into small pieces
- 3 oz (80 g) smoked mozzarella or provolone cheese, coarsely grated
- 2 to 3 tablespoons fresh breadcrumbs
- Salt and pepper

Preparation Time: 1 hour
Cooking Time: 20 minutes
Serves: 6

Bring a large pot of salted water to a boil. Add the chard and blanch for 2 to 3 minutes, then drain, reserving the cooking liquid. Coarsely chop the chard and set aside.

In a large pan, heat the olive oil over low heat. Add the chile and garlic and cook, stirring occasionally, for a few minutes, until the garlic is lightly browned. Remove the garlic with a slotted spoon. Add the chard and potatoes to the pan, and pour in the reserved cooking liquid to cover. Season with salt and pepper, and cook for about 40 minutes, adding more liquid, if necessary, to keep the potatoes submerged.

Meanwhile, preheat the oven to 375°F (190°C). Brush a 9-inch (23 cm) baking dish with oil.

Drain the chard-potato mixture in a colander, then transfer to a large bowl. Stir in the hard-boiled eggs, cheese, and breadcrumbs. Transfer the mixture to the prepared baking dish and bake for 15 to 20 minutes. Remove from the oven and let stand for 5 minutes before serving.

Ricotta and Sweet Potato Tart

Torta di ricotta e patata dolce

- Olive oil
- 4½ cups (1 kg) ricotta cheese
- 2⅓ cups (200 g) grated Parmesan cheese
- 2 eggs
- 3½ cups (100 g) arugula (rocket)
- 2 tablespoons chopped flat-leaf parsley
- 2 oz (50 g) fresh sage leaves
- 1 sweet potato, thinly sliced
- 2 tablespoons (30 g) butter
- Salt and pepper

Preparation Time: 25 minutes
Cooking Time: 25 to 30 minutes
Serves: 8

Preheat the oven to 325°F (160°C). Brush a 9½-inch (24 cm) square baking pan with olive oil.

In a food processor, combine the ricotta, Parmesan, and eggs and process until well combined. Add the arugula (rocket), parsley, and half the sage and process until well combined.

Pour the cheese mixture into the prepared pan and arrange the sweet potato slices on top. Season with salt and pepper, and drizzle with a little oil. Bake for 20 to 25 minutes.

Meanwhile, in a small saucepan, melt the butter over low heat. Add the remaining sage leaves and cook for 30 to 60 seconds.

Remove the tart from the oven, sprinkle with the buttered sage leaves, and let cool until just warm before serving.

The tart can be prepared in advance. Just before serving, cover it with a sheet of aluminum foil and heat it over a saucepan of boiling water.

Amaranth Cake with Caponata

Flan di amaranto con caponata

- 1 cup (200 g) amaranth, rinsed
- 3½ oz (100 g) sheep's-milk ricotta cheese
- 6 tablespoons (40 g) grated Parmesan cheese
- 6 to 8 basil leaves, shredded, plus a few whole leaves for garnish
- 3 tablespoons extra virgin olive oil, plus more for greasing
- 1 purple eggplant (aubergine), cut into small cubes
- 1 celery heart, sliced
- 1 small red onion, such as Tropea or torpedo, thinly sliced into rounds
- ⅔ cup (100 g) cherry tomatoes, halved
- 12 Taggiasca or Niçoise olives, crushed and pitted
- Salt

Preparation Time: 25 minutes
plus resting time
Cooking Time: 1 hour 25 minutes
Serves: 4

 (GF) (CT)

In a large saucepan, combine the amaranth and 3 cups (720 ml) water, cover, and cook over low heat for about 40 minutes. Turn off the heat and let rest for 10 minutes.

Meanwhile, preheat the oven to 350°F (180°C). Lightly oil an 8-inch (20 cm) casserole dish.

Drain the amaranth and transfer it to a large bowl. Add the ricotta, Parmesan, and half the shredded basil. Season with salt and stir well to combine. Press the mixture over the bottom of the prepared casserole dish and bake for 20 minutes.

Meanwhile, in a large frying pan, heat the olive oil over medium-high heat. Add the eggplant (aubergine), celery heart, and onion and season with salt. Cook for 7 to 8 minutes, until the vegetables are soft. Add the tomatoes and olives and cook for 5 minutes more. Add the remaining shredded basil, then remove from the heat.

Top the amaranth crust with the vegetables and bake for 10 minutes.

Garnish with a few whole basil leaves and serve.

Even though amaranth is considered a grain, it is not part of the grain family, Gramineae, but instead belongs to the Amaranthaceae family, so it can be eaten by people who are intolerant to gluten. For a vegan dish, cook 1 cup (200 g) dried split red lentils in boiling water for 15 minutes, then drain; add the lentils to the amaranth in place of the ricotta and Parmesan cheeses and continue as directed. Serve garnished with a sprinkle of vegan Parmesan or gomasio.

Chickpea and Onion Flatbread

Fainé, torta di ceci e cipollotti

- 5½ cups (500 g) chickpea flour
- ¼ cup (60 ml) extra virgin olive oil, plus more as needed
- 4 spring onions, sliced
- 1 tablespoon fennel seeds, coarsely ground
- Salt and black pepper

Preparation Time: 10 minutes plus resting time
Cooking Time: 35 minutes
Serves: 4

Sift the chickpea flour directly into a large bowl. While whisking to avoid lumps, drizzle in 4¼ cups (1 l) water and whisk until all the flour is incorporated. Cover the bowl and let the batter rest at room temperature overnight.

The next day, preheat the oven to 450°F (230°C). Lightly oil a 12-inch (30 cm) round baking pan.

In a large frying pan, heat the olive oil over medium heat. Add the onions and a pinch of salt and cook until softened. Remove from the heat and let cool.

Skim off any foam that has formed on top of the batter and stir in the onions and a pinch of salt. Pour the batter into the prepared pan, sprinkle it with the fennel seeds, and drizzle with a little olive oil. Bake for about 25 minutes, until golden brown.

Serve warm, garnished with a generous sprinkle of pepper.

For a crunchy addition to the recipe, sprinkle the top of the batter with 5 tablespoons (40 g) mixed pumpkin and sunflower seeds before baking.

Truffled Polenta Cake

Pizza di farina gialla con tartufi

- 3 cups (750 ml) milk
- ¾ cup plus 1 tablespoon (150 g) fine cornmeal
- 1¾ oz (50 g) Parmesan cheese, grated
- Scant ½ cup (100 ml) extra virgin olive oil
- 5 eggs
- 1 egg yolk
- 1 oz (30 g) black truffle, cleaned and coarsely grated
- Salt and black pepper

Preparation Time: 20 minutes plus resting time
Cooking Time: 1 hour 15 minutes
Serves: 4

In a medium saucepan, heat the milk over medium heat until just before it starts to boil. Add a pinch of salt, then, while stirring, pour in the cornmeal. Reduce the heat to low and cook the polenta for 40 minutes.

Pour the polenta into a large bowl. Add the Parmesan and 3½ tablespoons of the olive oil and stir to combine. Set the polenta aside to cool.

Preheat the oven to 350°F (180°C). Line an 8-inch (20 cm) springform pan with parchment paper.

Separate the eggs and put the whites in a clean large bowl. Add all the yolks (including the additional one) to the cooled polenta and stir to incorporate. Stir in the truffle and a generous sprinkle of pepper.

Using a handheld mixer or a whisk, whip the egg whites until they hold firm peaks, then gently fold them into the polenta.

Pour the polenta into the prepared pan and bake for about 35 minutes. Remove from the oven and let the polenta cake cool in the pan for 10 minutes. Remove the springform ring, transfer the polenta cake to a serving plate, and serve.

The best black truffles are from Norcia and are available from December to March. Truffles from Scorzone, available from June to September, have a more delicate flavor.

Grains, Gratins, & Stuffed Vegetables

If nature has gifted us many varieties of vegetables, the dishes we can prepare with them are even more numerous. Tasty au gratin dishes, risottos, or stuffed preparations are other ways to make the most of our precious produce.

A complete dish

In combination with vegetables, cheese, legumes, or other protein-rich ingredients such as tofu, tempeh, and seitan, rice can become a complete meal, able to supply all the nutrients a body needs: carbohydrates, vitamins, fiber, minerals, and protein. As for other grains, the winning combination is with legumes, such as in traditional dishes like rice and peas: together, these two ingredients guarantee a combination of high-quality vegan protein that is in no way inferior to protein of animal origin.

For lunch or dinner

Nutritionists advise eating a 2¾ oz (80 g) portion of rice or pasta daily, up to a maximum of eight portions per week. A rice dish is an excellent idea for dinner, in particular. Recent studies have shown that compared to other carbohydrate-rich foods, such as pasta and bread, eating rice leads to an increase in tryptophan, which in turn stimulates the production of serotonin, a hormone that, among other things, aids restful sleep.

Cooking to preserve vitamins

Vegetables should not be cooked for too long or at too high a temperature so as to retain their vitamin content. One way to cook them is by steaming, which does not alter their nutritional properties and retains their natural flavor without the addition of any fats. A good alternative is to use a pressure cooker: it is fast and requires little water, so fewer water-soluble vitamins are lost (compared to when the vegetables are boiled, for example).

Gluten-free carbohydrates

Rice has a carbohydrate content of over 90 percent and proteins with a good nutritional value. It is easy to digest and contributes to healthy gut flora. It is also gluten-free. Rich in potassium and B vitamins but low in sodium, rice helps manage hypertension and fights stress and fatigue.

Different cooking times

While whole-grain rice is preferable for its nutritional content, white rice cooks faster, in 15 to 20 minutes versus 45 to 50 (although cooking whole-grain rice in a pressure cooker can reduce its cooking time to 25 minutes). For those with limited time, quick-cooking or "instant" rice is also available: parboiling and then dehydrating the rice creates micro cracks in the grain, which allows boiling water to penetrate faster.

Lots of great ideas for the table

Rice and vegetables can be cooked in a variety of dishes that vary widely both in appearance and in the way in which they are prepared.

Risotto

A typical dish in Italian cuisine, risotto comes in numerous variations. The rice grains are first toasted and then cooked in stock, which is added a little at a time. When the rice absorbs the stock, it releases starch, which creates risotto's classic creamy consistency. Once cooked to al dente, the risotto is removed from the heat and butter or cheese is stirred in until melted. The risotto is then left to rest.

Boiled or steamed

The simplest way of cooking rice is in abundant boiling water (up to ten times the volume of the rice), with the saucepan uncovered. When the rice is al dente, it is drained, cooled under cold running water, then drained again and fluffed with a fork. Steaming (in a pressure cooker or steamer basket) preserves the nutritional properties of the rice, but requires an additional step: the rice must be rinsed to remove the starch before cooking.

Rice pilaf

A preparation of Middle Eastern origin, pilafs are served mainly as a side dish. The rice is first toasted, then cooked in double its volume of stock (with other ingredients added for flavor). The rice is then baked for 18 to 20 minutes. Once cooked, rice pilaf looks quite fluffy and needs to be left to rest for 2 minutes before serving.

Timbales, croquettes, and gratins

Timbales are baked in deep baking dishes, then unmolded onto a serving dish. Croquettes are prepared using boiled rice mixed with eggs, Parmesan, spices, and herbs, and fried. Gratins are finished in the oven at a high temperature to form their typical crunchy crust; this cooking method enhances the flavor of many rice recipes.

Stuffed or rolled vegetables

Stuffed vegetables are a great classic, especially in Italian cuisine. Zucchini (courgettes), tomatoes, peppers, and onions (to name but a few) can be stuffed with fillings prepared with other vegetables, grains, or cheese, and can satisfy the most demanding of palates. *Involtini*, or "little parcels," are a tasty variation: the filling is placed on a thin slice or leaf of the vegetable, which is then rolled up or folded to enclose the filling.

Stir-fries, loaves, and au gratin dishes

Vegetables can be sautéed or stir-fried in a frying pan with oil, salt, spices, or aromatic herbs. They can be used as the main ingredient in vegetable loaves and meatballs, or contribute to the success of crunchy golden au gratin dishes.

The ingredients to always have on hand

Though most vegetables can be found fresh all year round thanks to refrigeration and speedy shipping, it is still best to use vegetables that are in season (and, if possible, grown locally). Eating in season naturally varies our diet, and local, in-season fresh vegetables have more nutrients than greenhouse-grown produce. They also cost less and often have a lower environmental toll.

Spring When recovering your energy after the cold winter, spring vegetables like asparagus (which has detoxifying properties and very few calories), artichokes (a great source of fiber and minerals), onions (which have detoxifying and decongestant qualities), and spinach (its production is concentrated in autumn and winter but the spring sun increases its antioxidant qualities) can be very beneficial.

Summer Make way for vegetables that supplement the liquid your body loses in the summer heat. These include tomatoes (they contain lots of water, and lycopene, a powerful antioxidant), peppers (they have one of the highest concentrations of vitamin C of any vegetable), eggplants (aubergines, rich in fiber), and zucchini (courgettes, which contain vitamins A, C, and E, and folic acid to counteract skin aging).

Autumn In this season, nature offers us, among other things, vegetables such as pumpkins (very easy to digest and an excellent source of fiber, potassium, selenium, and antioxidants), leeks (a source of prebiotics, which feed the good bacteria in your gut), and beets (they contain magnesium, iron, and chlorophyll, and support the digestive system).

Winter The cold weather requires dishes that heat the body and satisfy the palate, rich recipes that include vegetables like broccoli (rich in antioxidants that are beneficial to the heart, liver, and skin), cabbage (with a calcium content higher than that of milk), and cauliflower (the vitamin C it supplies helps the immune system fight seasonal ailments), alongside grains, legumes, and cheese.

Best unrefined

White rice is obtained through a refining process that strips the grains of many nutrients. It is therefore best to use unrefined whole-grain rice, rich in fiber and with up to four times the minerals and vitamins. Whole-grain rice is not, however, suitable for all recipes. A good compromise is partially refined rice (known in Italy as *riso semintegrale*).

Black rice	Black rice has been known in China for centuries, but it used to be reserved exclusively for the imperial court, as it was very rare and expensive. Its deep, dark color comes from a layer of antioxidant pigments, also found in blueberries and grapes.
Venere rice	Venere rice, an ebony-colored whole-grain rice with the aroma of freshly baked bread, evokes exotic landscapes but is in fact Italian. Introduced in 1997 in Vercelli, it is today cultivated by a few select agricultural companies in Piedmont and Sardinia.
Common, semi-fine, fine, and superfine rice	Common rice has small and round grains, which cook in 12 to 13 minutes; it is suitable for use in timbales, croquettes, and soups; Italian varieties include Originario, Balilla, and Americano. Semi-fine rice has medium grains, cooks in 13 to 15 minutes, and is suitable for timbales or boiling; varieties include Vialone Nano, Maratelli, and Padano. Fine rice cooks in 14 to 16 minutes, has tapered grains, and is suitable for use in risotto, salads, and side dishes; varieties include Ribe and Razzotto. Superfine rice has large grains that are ready in 16 to 18 minutes and is ideal for risotto or dishes such as paella, where the grains need to be fluffy; varieties include Carnaroli, Arborio, Baldo, and Roma.
Brown rice and semi-refined rice	Compared to refined white rice, which undergoes bleaching and polishing, brown rice is richer in nutrients, including fiber, vitamins, mineral salts, protein, and fat. Suitable for risotto and croquettes, semi-refined rice is obtained by only partially removing the germ and husk. Semi-refined rice retains a good portion of its nutrients and has the advantage of a reduced cooking time.

Wild Rice Balls

Polpettine di riso Venere

- 1½ cups (300 g) black rice, rinsed and drained
- 2 scallions, whites and greens separated and finely chopped
- 7 oz (200 g) frozen shelled edamame
- 1 (¾-inch/2 cm) piece fresh ginger, peeled and grated
- 5 to 6 tablespoons (75 to 90 ml) peanut (groundnut) oil
- ¼ cup (40 g) flaxseeds (linseeds)
- ⅓ cup (40 g) black sesame seeds
- 3 tablespoons soy sauce
- 1 tablespoon rice vinegar
- 1 small fresh hot chile, very thinly sliced
- Salt

Preparation Time: 20 minutes
Cooking Time: 1 hour 5 minutes
Serves: 4

Put the rice in a large saucepan, add cold water to cover, and bring the water to a boil. Cook for 45 minutes, adding salt halfway through the cooking time.

Bring a large pot of salted water to a boil. Add the scallion whites and the edamame and simmer for 10 minutes. Drain them, transfer to a large bowl, and purée with a hand blender. Season with salt and stir in the ginger.

Drain the rice and stir it into the edamame purée. Let cool, then shape the mixture into walnut-size balls.

In a large nonstick frying pan, heat the oil over medium-high heat.

Combine the sesame seeds and flaxseeds (linseeds) in a shallow bowl. Roll the rice balls in the seed mixture to coat. Add them to the hot oil and fry for 4 to 5 minutes, then transfer to paper towels to drain.

In a small bowl, stir together the soy sauce, vinegar, chile, and scallion greens.

Serve the rice balls hot, with the sauce.

Edamame, or green soybeans, is a good source of protein. When served with rice, which is high in carbohydrates, they make a meal with a complete nutritional profile. Edamame is also rich in vitamins C and E, magnesium, potassium, iron, and phosphorus.

Rice Pilaf with Roasted Carrots and Asparagus

Riso pilaf con carote e asparagi arrosto

- About 3½ cups (800 ml) vegetable stock
- ¼ cup (60 ml) plus 3 tablespoons extra virgin olive oil
- 1 yellow onion
- 2 whole cloves
- 1½ cups (300 g) jasmine rice, rinsed
- 4 carrots, quartered lengthwise
- 1 bunch asparagus, tough ends trimmed
- 2 tablespoons soy sauce
- 5 tablespoons (40 g) slivered almonds
- Salt

Preparation Time: 20 minutes
Cooking Time: 35 minutes
Serves: 4

Preheat the oven to 350°F (180°C).

In a small saucepan, bring the stock to a boil.

In an oven-safe medium saucepan with a lid, heat ¼ cup (60 ml) of the olive oil over medium heat. Stud the onion with the cloves and brown it gently in the oil. Add the rice and toast, stirring continuously, for 1 minute.

Pour the stock over the rice and return it to a boil. Cover the saucepan, transfer it to the oven, and bake for 20 minutes.

In the meantime, line a roasting pan with parchment paper. Bring a large pot of salted water to a boil. Add the carrots and cook for 5 minutes, then use tongs to transfer them to the prepared pan. Add the asparagus to the boiling water and cook for 2 minutes, then drain and transfer to the pan with the carrots. Drizzle the vegetables with the remaining 3 tablespoons oil and the soy sauce, then sprinkle with the almonds. Bake for 20 minutes.

Uncover the rice and discard the onion. Using a ring mold, form the rice into small cakes on individual plates, and serve with the vegetables alongside.

This rice pilaf is a side dish originally from Turkey. It can be prepared with basmati rice in place of the jasmine rice.

Rice with Mushrooms and Tomatoes

Riso asciutto con pomodori e funghi

- 12¼ oz (350 g) plum tomatoes
- 3 tablespoons (40 g) butter
- 1 small yellow onion, finely chopped
- 1 clove garlic, finely chopped
- 4 basil leaves
- 10½ oz (300 g) porcini mushrooms, sliced ¼ inch (6 mm) thick
- 1½ cups (300 g) Vialone Nano or other medium-grain rice
- Handful of parsley, finely chopped
- 6 tablespoons (40 g) grated Parmesan cheese
- Salt and black pepper

Preparation Time: 20 minutes
Cooking Time: 40 minutes
Serves: 4

Bring a large pot of water to a boil. Add the tomatoes and blanch for 30 seconds, then drain them and let cool. Peel and seed the tomatoes and cut their flesh into small cubes.

In a large saucepan, melt 2 tablespoons (30 g) of the butter over medium-low heat. Add the onion and the garlic and cook for a few minutes, until softened. Add the tomatoes and the basil and reduce the heat to low. Cover and cook for 20 minutes.

Add the mushrooms to the pan with the tomatoes. Season with salt and pepper and cook for 15 minutes more.

Cook the rice according to the package directions until al dente, then add the remaining 1 tablespoon (10 g) butter, the parsley, and the Parmesan.

Transfer the rice to a serving dish and serve with the mushrooms and tomatoes alongside.

If fresh porcini mushrooms aren't available, soak 1 oz (30 g) dried porcini mushroom in a bowl of warm water for 10 minutes. Lift them out of the water (leaving any grit behind in the bowl), slice them, if necessary, and add them to the pan with the tomatoes as directed.

Rice with Cabbage and Beans

Riso alla valtellinese con verza e fagioli

- 1 small savoy cabbage, cored and thinly sliced
- 1½ cups (300 g) Arborio rice
- 3½ cups (600 g) cooked fresh borlotti beans
- 3 tablespoons (40 g) butter
- 8 sage leaves
- 6 tablespoons (40 g) grated Parmesan cheese
- Salt and black pepper

Preparation Time: 20 minutes
Cooking Time: 20 minutes
Serves: 4

Bring a large pot of salted water to a boil. Add the cabbage and cook for 2 to 3 minutes, then drain.

Fill the same pot with water, salt the water, and bring to a boil. Add the cabbage and the rice and cook for 15 to 20 minutes, until the rice is al dente, adding the beans for the last 2 to 3 minutes of cooking to heat them through.

In the meantime, in a small frying pan, melt the butter over medium heat. Add the sage and cook until crisp, 30 to 60 seconds.

Drain the rice, beans, and cabbage and transfer to a serving dish. Pour over the sage butter, then sprinkle with the Parmesan and some pepper. Serve.

Tomato Risotto with Spring Vegetables

Risotto alla paesana con verdure e legumi freschi

- 14 oz (400 g) plum tomatoes
- 1⅓ cups (200 g) shelled fresh fava (broad) beans
- ¼ cup (60 ml) extra virgin olive oil
- 1 zucchini (courgette), finely chopped
- 1 carrot, finely chopped
- 1 stalk celery, finely chopped
- 1 yellow onion, finely chopped
- 1⅓ cups (200 g) shelled fresh peas
- 4 or 5 basil leaves, chopped
- Leaves from 1 bunch parsley, chopped
- 1½ cups (300 g) Carnaroli or other medium-grain rice
- 6 tablespoons (40 g) grated Parmesan cheese
- Salt

Preparation Time: 20 minutes
Cooking Time: 50 minutes
Serves: 4

Bring a large pot of water to a boil. Add the tomatoes and blanch for 30 seconds, then transfer them with a slotted spoon to a colander to drain and cool. Add the fava (broad) beans to the boiling water and cook for 2 to 3 minutes, then drain them and let cool.

Peel and seed the tomatoes and cut the flesh into small cubes. Remove the beans from their skins and set aside in a bowl.

In a medium saucepan, bring 4½ cups (1.1 l) salted water to a boil, then reduce the heat to maintain a strong simmer.

In a large saucepan, heat the olive oil over medium-high heat. Add the zucchini (courgette), carrot, celery, and onion and cook for 2 to 3 minutes. Add the tomatoes, beans, peas, basil, and parsley, reduce the heat to low, and cook for 15 minutes.

Add the rice to the pot with the vegetables and stir to combine. Add a ladleful of the hot water and cook, stirring, until it has been absorbed. Continue in this manner, adding water and cooking until each addition has been absorbed before adding the next, for 15 minutes. Season with salt and cook, adding the water as before, until the rice is al dente, another 10 to 15 minutes. Add the Parmesan and stir. Remove from the heat and let the risotto rest for a couple of minutes, then serve.

Radicchio Risotto with Orange

Risotto con radicchio e arancia

- 4¼ cups (1 l) vegetable stock
- ¼ cup (60 ml) extra virgin olive oil
- 1 shallot, finely chopped
- 1¼ cups (250 g) parboiled short-grain rice, rinsed and drained
- 2 heads Tardivo or Treviso radicchio, thinly sliced
- 3½ oz (100 g) silken tofu
- Grated zest of ½ orange
- 1 or 2 garlic scapes, cut on an angle into long, thin strips
- Salt and black pepper

Preparation Time: 20 minutes
Cooking Time: 50 minutes
Serves: 4

In a medium saucepan, bring the stock to a boil over high heat, then reduce the heat to maintain a simmer.
In a large saucepan, heat the olive oil over medium-low heat. Add the shallot and 2 to 3 tablespoons of the hot stock and cook until soft. Add the rice and cook, stirring, for 3 to 4 minutes to toast it. Add a ladleful of the stock and cook, stirring, until it has been absorbed. Continue in this manner, adding stock and cooking until each addition has been absorbed before adding the next, for 30 minutes.

Stir in the radicchio and season with salt. Cook for another 5 minutes, then remove from the heat.

Add the tofu, orange zest, and a generous sprinkle of pepper and stir. Arrange the rice on serving plates, garnish it with the garlic scapes, and serve hot.

White rice has had its hull and bran layers removed. For this reason, it is can be tolerated by people who suffer from colitis.

Vegetable Fried Rice

Basmati saltato nel wok con verdure

- 1½ cups (300 g) basmati rice
- ¼ cup plus 2 tablespoons extra virgin olive oil
- 1 (1½-inch/4 cm) piece fresh ginger, peeled and cut into thin matchsticks
- 2 long skinny red peppers
- 1 cup (100 g) soybean sprouts
- 7 oz (200 g) green beans, thinly sliced on an angle
- 3½ oz (100 g) snow peas (mangetouts), very thinly sliced
- A few springs of cilantro (fresh coriander), coarsely chopped
- ⅓ cup (50 g) unsalted toasted peanuts
- Salt

Preparation Time: 20 minutes
Cooking Time: 25 minutes
Serves: 4

Bring a large pot of salted water to a boil. Add the rice and cook for 5 to 6 minutes, then drain and transfer to a medium bowl. Stir in 2 tablespoons of the olive oil and set aside.

In a wok or large frying pan, heat the remaining ¼ cup (60 ml) oil over medium-high heat. Add the ginger and cook, stirring, for a few seconds. Add the peppers, bean sprouts, green beans, and snow peas (mangetouts). Let the flavors develop, then add a ladleful of boiling water and season with salt. Cook for another 5 minutes. Add the rice and cook, stirring continuously, for 4 to 5 minutes.

Transfer the fried rice to a serving dish, add the cilantro (fresh coriander) and peanuts, and serve.

Basmati rice is usually cooked by absorbing the cooking water. It needs to be rinsed thoroughly, placed in a saucepan with enough water to cover it to the depth of a finger, and brought to a boil. Cook over low heat, uncovered, for 10 minutes.

Fava Bean Risotto with Pecorino

Risotto con le fave mantecato al pecorino

- 2 cups (300 g) shelled fresh fava (broad) beans
- 4¼ cups (1 l) vegetable stock
- ¼ cup (60 ml) plus 2 tablespoons extra virgin olive oil
- 3 spring onions, thinly sliced
- 1¼ cups (250 g) Carnaroli or other medium-grain rice
- Scant ½ cup (100 ml) white wine
- 1 oz (30 g) Pecorino Romano cheese, grated
- 1 oz (30 g) Pecorino Toscano Fresco cheese, grated
- Salt and black pepper

Preparation Time: 20 minutes
Cooking Time: 25 minutes
Serves: 4

Bring a large pot of water to a boil. Add the fava (broad) beans and blanch for 1 minute, then drain and let cool. Remove the beans from their skins.

In a medium saucepan, bring the stock to a boil, then reduce the heat to maintain a strong simmer.

In a large saucepan, heat ¼ cup (60 ml) of the olive oil over medium-low heat. Add the beans and onions and cook for 6 to 7 minutes. Season with salt, then transfer to a bowl with a slotted spoon and set aside.

Add the rice to the oil remaining in the pan and toast, stirring continuously, for 1 minute.

Add the wine, raise the heat to medium, and cook, stirring, until it has evaporated. Add a ladleful of the hot stock and cook, stirring, until it has been absorbed. Continue in this manner, adding stock and cooking until each addition has been absorbed before adding the next, for 15 minutes. Add the beans and onions and cook, adding stock as before, until the rice is al dente (tender but with some bite remaining) and the beans are tender, another 10 to 15 minutes. Remove from the heat.

Add the cheeses, the remaining 2 tablespoons oil, and some pepper and stir for 1 minute. Cover the pan and let the risotto rest for 2 to 3 minutes, then serve.

Toasting the rice ensures more uniform cooking of the grains and prevents it from overcooking, allowing the rice to remain al dente.

Green Risotto with Peas

Riso verde con i piselli

- 5 cups (1.2 l) vegetable stock
- ½ cup (120 ml) extra virgin olive oil
- 1 small white onion, finely chopped
- 1 lb 2 oz (500 g) peas in their pods, shelled
- 1½ cups (300 g) Carnaroli or other medium-grain rice
- ⅓ cup (30 g) grated Parmesan cheese
- Handful of parsley leaves, chopped
- Salt and black pepper

Preparation Time: 10 minutes
Cooking Time: 35 minutes
Serves: 4

In a medium saucepan, bring the stock to a boil.

In a large saucepan, heat 3 tablespoons of the olive oil over medium heat. Add the onion and a small ladleful of water and cook until the onion is transparent, 5 to 6 minutes. Add the peas and a scant 1 cup (200 ml) of the hot stock. Reduce the heat to low, cover the pot with the lid ajar, and cook for 10 minutes, or until the peas are tender. Raise the heat to medium-high and cook until any remaining liquid has evaporated, then turn off the heat.

In a separate medium saucepan, heat 2 tablespoons of the oil over medium heat. Add the rice and toast, stirring continuously, for 2 to 3 minutes. Add a ladleful of the hot stock and cook, stirring, until it has been absorbed. Continue in this manner, adding stock and cooking until each addition has been absorbed before adding the next, for 20 to 25 minutes, until the rice is al dente (tender but with some bite remaining). Add the peas, season with salt, and stir. Remove the saucepan from the heat and add the Parmesan and the remaining 3 tablespoons oil. Stir for a few seconds, then cover and let the rice rest for 2 minutes before serving.

Garnish with the parsley and some pepper, and serve.

The cooking time for the peas will vary depending on their size, from 5 minutes for small and very tender peas, up to 10 to 12 minutes for larger ones. For a vegan version of the dish, replace the Parmesan cheese with 2 tablespoons finely chopped toasted almonds.

Quinoa Torte

Tortino di quinoa

- 2½ cups (600 ml) vegetable stock
- 4 tablespoons (60 ml) extra virgin olive oil, plus more as needed
- 1½ cups (250 g) quinoa, rinsed
- 1 small head puntarelle (Catalogna chicory), thinly sliced
- 3 carrots: 2 cut into very small cubes, 1 kept whole
- 1 clove garlic
- 5 tablespoons (40 g) raw almonds, finely chopped
- 1 egg
- 1 purple carrot
- ¼ cup (20 g) sliced (flaked) almonds
- Salt

Preparation Time: 20 minutes
Cooking Time: 1 hour
Serves: 4

Preheat the oven to 350°F (180°C). Line a 7-inch (18 cm) round baking dish with parchment paper.

In a small saucepan, bring the stock to a simmer over medium-high heat.

In a medium saucepan, heat 2 tablespoons of the olive oil over medium heat. Add the quinoa and toast it, stirring continuously, for 30 seconds. Pour in the hot stock, reduce the heat to low, and cook for about 20 minutes, until all the stock has been absorbed.

Bring a large pot of salted water to a boil. Add the puntarelle and cook for 2 to 3 minutes. Using tongs or a slotted spoon, transfer the puntarelle to a colander to drain. Add the cubed carrots to the boiling water and cook for 5 minutes, then drain.

In a large frying pan, heat the remaining 2 tablespoons oil over medium heat. Add the garlic, puntarelle, and cubed carrots and cook for 3 to 4 minutes. Discard the garlic and season with salt.

In a large bowl, stir together the quinoa, vegetables, chopped almonds, and egg until well combined. Pour the quinoa mixture into the prepared pan, level the top with a spatula, and bake for about 30 minutes.

Meanwhile, using a vegetable peeler, slice the remaining whole carrot and the purple carrot into ribbons.

Invert the quinoa tart onto a serving plate and garnish it with the carrot ribbons and the sliced (flaked) almonds. Drizzle with a little oil and sprinkle with a pinch of salt, then serve.

Quinoa is the seed of a plant that belongs to the same family as spinach and beets, not wheat, and is therefore suitable for gluten-intolerant people. It is high in protein and unsaturated fat. For a vegan version of this dish, omit the egg; in a small frying pan, heat 2 tablespoons olive oil over medium heat. Add 6 tablespoons (40 g) breadcrumbs and toast until golden, then stir them into the quinoa mixture and bake as directed.

Baked Wild Rice with Parsnip

Gratin di riso selvaggio con pastinaca

- 1¾ cups (300 g) wild rice, rinsed and drained
- ¼ cup (60 ml) soy sauce
- 2 tablespoons gomasio
- ¼ cup (60 ml) peanut (groundnut) oil, plus more as needed
- 1 red onion, very thinly sliced
- 14 oz (400 g) parsnips, peeled and cut into small wedges
- 4 sage leaves
- Salt
- 2 cups (300 g) cooked mung beans
- 1 cup (100 g) grated vegan cheese

Preparation Time: 25 minutes
Cooking Time: 1 hour 25 minutes
Serves: 4

Put the rice in a large saucepan with three times its volume of water. Bring it to a boil over high heat, then reduce the heat to low, cover, and cook for 45 minutes. Add the soy sauce and the gomasio, stir, and turn the heat off.

Preheat the oven to 350°F (180°C).

In a large nonstick frying pan, heat the oil over medium heat. Add the onion, parsnips, sage, and a pinch of salt. Add a ladleful of boiling water and reduce the heat to low. Cover and cook for 20 minutes. Discard the sage, stir in the beans, and turn off the heat.

Oil a baking dish. Pour in half the rice and level it with a spatula. Cover the rice with half the parsnip mixture, then add the remaining rice and level the top. Finish with the remaining parsnip mixture. Sprinkle with the cheese, drizzle with a little oil, and bake for about 20 minutes. Serve hot.

Wild rice comes from four species of aquatic plants belonging to the genus *Zizania*, and is unrelated to "true" rice (genus *Oryza*). It contains more protein and fiber than *Oryza* rices.

Rice Gratin with Brussels Sprouts and Walnuts

Gratin di riso con cavolini e noci

- 1 lb 2 oz (500 g) Brussels sprouts
- 1½ cups (300 g) Arborio rice
- ¼ cup (60 ml) extra virgin olive oil, plus more as needed
- ¼ cup (40 g) rice flour
- 2 cups plus 2 tablespoons (500 ml) rice milk
- Scant ½ cup (50 g) walnuts
- 1¾ oz (50 g) Parmesan cheese, grated
- Handful of parsley, coarsely chopped
- Salt and black pepper

Preparation Time: 20 minutes
Cooking Time: 55 minutes
Serves: 4

Preheat the oven to 350°F (180°C). Lightly oil a baking dish.

Bring a large pot of salted water to a boil. Cut a deep cross into the bottom of each Brussels sprout, add them to the boiling water, and cook for 6 to 7 minutes, then drain them. Cut 6 of the sprouts into wedges and set aside; transfer the rest to a food processor and purée.

Bring a medium pot of salted water to a boil. Add the rice and cook for 10 minutes, then drain and cool under cold running water.

In a medium saucepan, heat the olive oil over medium heat. Add the rice flour and toast, stirring continuously, for 30 seconds. While whisking, slowly pour in the milk and whisk to combine. Cook the sauce for 7 to 8 minutes.

Coarsely chop half the walnuts and set aside. Finely chop the remaining walnuts and add them to the sauce. Add the sprout purée, a third of the Parmesan, some pepper, and a pinch of salt and stir to combine.

Add the rice and stir to incorporate. Pour the mixture into the prepared baking dish and spread it evenly. Arrange the Brussels sprout wedges on top and sprinkle with the coarsely chopped walnuts and the remaining Parmesan. Bake for 25 minutes, or until browned.

Sprinkle the gratin with the parsley and serve.

Arborio rice, used for risotto, has large grains whose volume significantly increases during cooking. It can be replaced with parboiled rice.

Seedy Basmati Rice

Riso pilaf con semi e germogli

- 5 tablespoons (75 ml) peanut (groundnut) oil
- 1 small yellow onion, peeled and halved
- 1½ cups (300 g) brown basmati rice
- 2½ cups (600 ml) vegetable stock
- 2 tablespoons toasted sesame oil
- 6 tablespoons (50 g) pumpkin seeds, toasted
- ⅓ cup (50 g) sunflower seeds
- ¼ cup (40 g) golden flaxseeds (linseeds)
- 4 sage leaves, finely chopped, plus more for garnish
- Leaves from 4 sprigs thyme, finely chopped, plus more for garnish
- Leaves from 1 sprig rosemary, finely chopped, plus more for garnish
- Salt
- 1 cup (50 g) bean sprouts
- 3 tablespoons soy sauce
- 1 tablespoon wheat germ

Preparation Time: 10 minutes
Cooking Time: 30 minutes
Serves: 4

Preheat the oven to 350°F (180°C).

In an oven-safe large saucepan with a lid, heat 3 tablespoons of the peanut (groundnut) oil over medium heat. Add the onion and the rice and cook, stirring, for 1 minute to toast it. Pour the stock into the saucepan and bring it to a boil. Cover the pan, transfer it to the oven, and bake the rice for 25 minutes. Remove from the oven and discard the onion.

In a large nonstick frying pan, heat the sesame oil and remaining 2 tablespoons peanut (groundnut) oil over medium heat. Add the pumpkin seeds, sunflower seeds, flaxseeds, sage, thyme, and rosemary and cook for 2 to 3 minutes to deepen their flavor.

Add the rice, raise the heat to high, and cook, stirring, for 1 minute. Remove from the heat and season with salt.

In a small bowl, combine the bean sprouts, soy sauce, and wheat germ.

Arrange the rice on serving plates, garnish with the herbs and sprouts, and serve.

Wheat germ is rich in carbohydrates, protein, and soluble fiber (unlike the fiber found in wheat bran, which is insoluble). It is also an excellent source of omega-3 fatty acids.

Potato-Leek Gratin

Tortino di patate e porri

- 4½ lb (2 kg) potatoes
- 5 tablespoons (65 g) butter, plus more for greasing
- 2 tablespoons olive oil
- 2 leeks, finely chopped
- 2 onions, thinly sliced
- ¼ cup (10 g) fresh breadcrumbs
- 11 oz (300 g) mascarpone cheese
- 1 egg, lightly beaten
- Salt and pepper

Preparation Time: 20 minutes
Cooking Time: 1 hour
Serves: 8

Put the potatoes in a large pan, add water to cover and a pinch of salt, and bring to a boil. Cook for 25 minutes, or until tender. Drain the potatoes and let cool slightly, then peel them, transfer the flesh to a large bowl, and mash.

In a medium frying pan, heat about 2 tablespoons (25 g) of the butter and the olive oil over low heat. Add the leeks and onions and cook, stirring occasionally, for 5 minutes, or until softened and translucent. Season lightly with salt and remove from the heat.

Preheat the oven to 350°F (180°C). Grease a baking dish with butter and sprinkle with the breadcrumbs.

Bring a small saucepan of water just to a simmer. Put the remaining 3 tablespoons butter in a heatproof bowl and set it over the simmering water to melt.

Add the leek-onion mixture, mascarpone, and melted butter to the bowl with the potatoes and season with salt and pepper. Spoon the mixture into the prepared baking dish and gently smooth the top. Brush the surface with the egg and bake for 20 minutes, or until the top is golden brown. Serve immediately.

Swiss Chard Gratin

Bietole gratinate

- Butter, for greasing
- 2¼ lb (1 kg) Swiss chard
- 3 tablespoons (45 g) butter
- ⅓ cup (50 g) all-purpose (plain) flour
- 2¼ cups (560 ml) milk
- Salt
- 3 oz (80 g) Parmesan cheese, grated

Preparation Time: 25 minutes
Cooking Time: 15 minutes
Serves: 4

Preheat the oven to 350°F (180°C). Grease a baking dish with butter.

Separate the chard leaves from the stems using kitchen scissors or a sharp knife (reserve the leaves for another use, such as making soup.)

Bring a large pot of lightly salted water to a boil. Add the chard stems and cook for 10 to 15 minutes, until tender, then drain well and cut them into small pieces.

In a small saucepan, melt the butter over medium heat. Add the flour and stir well, cooking until the flour has browned very slightly, about 1 minute. Gradually add the milk, stirring continuously. Continue cooking the sauce while stirring until it thickens, about 10 minutes. Remove from the heat and season with salt.

Spread a layer of the chard stalks over the bottom of the prepared baking dish, then top with a layer of the béchamel sauce and then a layer of Parmesan. Repeat, ending with a layer of Parmesan. Bake for about 15 minutes. Serve immediately.

Broccoli, Kale, and Cauliflower Gratin

Gratin di cavolfiore, broccoletti e cavolo nero

- 1 medium cauliflower, cut into florets
- 14 oz (400 g) broccoli, cut into florets
- 1 bunch Tuscan kale (cavolo nero), leaves stemmed
- 6 tablespoons (90 ml) extra virgin olive oil, plus more for greasing
- 3 tablespoons rice flour
- 1⅔ cups (400 ml) unsweetened rice milk
- Pinch of freshly grated nutmeg
- ⅓ cup (50 g) coarsely chopped raw almonds
- Scant ⅓ cup (30 g) breadcrumbs
- Salt and black pepper

Preparation Time: 20 minutes
Cooking Time: 45 minutes
Serves: 4

 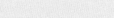

Preheat the oven to 350°F (180°C). Lightly oil a baking dish.

Bring a large pot of salted water to a boil. Add the cauliflower and cook for 5 minutes, then use a spider (skimmer) to transfer it to a colander to drain and cool. Repeat with the broccoli, transferring it to a separate colander to drain. Add the kale leaves to the boiling water and cook for 6 to 7 minutes, then drain and run under cold running water to cool. Squeeze out any excess water and chop the kale.

In a small saucepan, heat 3 tablespoons of the olive oil over medium heat. Add the rice flour and toast, stirring continuously, for a few seconds. While whisking, slowly drizzle in the rice milk and whisk until combined. Reduce the heat to low and cook the béchamel sauce for 7 to 8 minutes. Season with the nutmeg and some salt, then pour the béchamel sauce into a bowl.

Add the cauliflower to the béchamel and purée with a hand blender until smooth. Add the kale and almonds, season with salt and pepper, and stir to combine.

In a small bowl, mix the breadcrumbs with the remaining 3 tablespoons oil.

Pour the cauliflower-béchamel mixture into the prepared baking dish. Arrange the broccoli on top and sprinkle with the breadcrumbs, then bake for about 30 minutes, until golden brown.

For a vegetarian (but not vegan) version, enrich the béchamel sauce with 6 tablespoons (40 g) grated Parmesan cheese and mix the breadcrumbs with 3 tablespoons more grated Parmesan. The breadcrumbs can also be replaced with 2 heaping tablespoons quick-cooking oats or crumbled cornflakes.

Rice Timbale with Zucchini and Peppers

Timballo di riso con zucchine e peperoni

- 2 red bell peppers
- 1½ cups (300 g) Vialone Nano or other medium-grain rice
- ¼ cup (60 ml) extra virgin olive oil, plus more as needed
- 1 lb 2 oz (500 g) zucchini (courgettes), coarsely grated
- ½ cup (50 g) grated Parmesan cheese
- 3½ oz (100 g) provolone dolce cheese, grated
- Leaves from 3 sprigs marjoram
- Leaves from 3 sprigs thyme
- 3 sprigs wild fennel or fennel fronds
- Leaves from 3 sprigs oregano
- 2 eggs
- Juice of 1 lemon
- 4 squash blossoms (courgette flowers), pistils removed
- Salt and black pepper

Preparation Time: 25 minutes
Cooking Time: 1 hour
Serves: 4

Preheat the broiler. Line an 8-inch (20 cm) springform pan with parchment paper.

Brush the bell peppers with a little oil and place them on a sheet pan. Broil, turning them to ensure they cook evenly, until lightly charred and softened, 4 to 5 minutes. Remove from the oven, transfer to a bowl, cover with plastic wrap (cling film), and let cool. Set the oven to 350°F (180°C).

Bring a medium pot of salted water to a boil. Add the rice and cook for 10 minutes, then drain and let cool.

In a large nonstick frying pan, heat the ¼ cup (60 ml) olive oil over medium-high heat. Add the zucchini (courgettes) and a pinch of salt and cook for 3 to 4 minutes.

In a blender, process the Parmesan, provolone, marjoram, thyme, fennel, oregano, eggs, and lemon juice until well combined. Season with salt and pepper and pour into a large bowl. Add the cooled rice and stir to combine.

Peel and seed the roasted peppers, then coarsely chop the flesh.

Spread one-third of the rice mixture over the prepared pan, then top with half the zucchini (courgettes). Add half the remaining rice, then the roasted peppers. Top with the remaining zucchini (courgettes) and finish with the remaining rice. Bake the timbale for about 30 minutes. Let cool in the pan for a few minutes, then remove the springform ring and set the timbale on a serving dish.

Garnish with the squash blossoms (courgette flowers) and serve.

Vialone Nano is a medium-grain semi-fine rice variety, in the same category as Padano, Italico, and Lido. It can also be used for risotto.

Rice and Eggplant Casserole

Timballo di riso e melanzane alla palermitana

- 10½ oz (300 g) plum tomatoes
- 2 white onions
- ½ cup (120 ml) extra virgin olive oil
- 4 or 5 basil leaves
- 2¾ cups (650 ml) vegetable stock
- 1½ cups (300 g) medium-grain rice, such as Padano
- 1¾ oz (50 g) caciocavallo cheese, grated
- Peanut (groundnut) oil, for frying
- All-purpose (plain) flour, for dusting
- 3 round eggplants (aubergines), sliced lengthwise ¼ inch (6 mm) thick
- Salt

If you use long eggplants (aubergines), place them in a colander after slicing them, sprinkle them with salt, and leave them for an hour to remove the bitterness. Rinse and dry them, then fry as directed.

Preparation Time: 20 minutes
Cooking Time: 50 minutes
Serves: 4

 GF

Preheat the oven to 350°F (180°C).

Bring a large pot of salted water to a boil. Add the tomatoes and blanch for 30 seconds, then transfer to a colander with a slotted spoon to drain and cool. Add the onions to the boiling water and cook for 10 minutes.

Peel and seed the tomatoes and cut the flesh into small cubes. Drain the onions and let cool. Thinly slice the onions.

In a large saucepan, heat ¼ cup (60 ml) of the olive oil over medium-low heat. Add half the onions and cook for 3 to 4 minutes. Add the tomatoes and the basil, season with salt, and reduce the heat to low. Cover and cook for 15 minutes.

In a small saucepan, bring the stock to a boil.

In an oven-safe medium saucepan with a lid, heat the remaining ¼ cup (60 ml) oil over medium-low heat. Add the remaining onion and cook for a few minutes. Add the rice and cook for 1 minute to toast it. Pour the boiling stock into the pan, stir, and return the stock to a boil. Cover the pan, transfer it to the oven, and bake for 15 minutes. Remove from the oven and stir in half the caciocavallo. Raise the oven temperature to 400°F (200°C).

In the meantime, fill a frying pan with about 1 inch (2.5 cm) of peanut (groundnut) oil and heat over medium-high heat. Put some flour in a shallow bowl. Working in batches, dredge the eggplant (aubergine) slices in the flour, then add them to the hot oil and fry until golden brown, 2 to 3 minutes per side. Transfer them to paper towels to drain.

Line the bottom of a baking dish with a few of the eggplant slices. Top with a layer of the tomatoes and then a layer of rice. Continue with these layers, ending with a layer of eggplant. Sprinkle the remaining caciocavallo over the top and bake the timbale for about 15 minutes, then serve.

Artichoke, Potato, and Rice Casserole

Tiella di riso, patate e carciofi

- Extra virgin olive oil
- Juice of 1 lemon
- 4 artichokes
- 1 lb 2 oz (500 g) potatoes, peeled and very thinly sliced
- 1 ½ cups (300 g) medium-grain rice, such as Padano
- 6 tablespoons (40 g) grated Pecorino Romano cheese
- Handful of parsley, chopped
- 1 clove garlic, chopped
- Salt

Preparation Time: 20 minutes
Cooking Time: 30 minutes
Serves: 4

Preheat the oven to 350°F (180°C). Lightly oil a 9½-inch (24 cm) round baking dish.

Fill a large bowl with cool water and add the lemon juice. Trim the artichokes, cut them into wedges, and cut the fuzzy choke from the center, then thinly slice them, dropping them into the bowl of lemon water as you go (this prevents them from browning).

Arrange a layer of the potatoes over the bottom of the prepared baking dish. Drain the artichokes, then continue layering with part of the rice, the pecorino, parsley, and garlic, and continue alternating layers of rice and vegetables.

Pour 3 cups (700 ml) water into the baking dish, season with salt, and cover the dish with foil. Bake the casserole for about 45 minutes, then serve.

Cooking the rice for the preparation of this casserole is tricky. Alternatively, you can use parboiled rice cooked in boiling salted water for 5 minutes.

Tomato Strata

Tortino rustico di pomodori

- Butter, for greasing
- 3 tablespoons olive oil
- 3 spring onions, finely chopped
- 12 thin slices whole wheat (wholemeal) bread, crusts removed
- 1 lb 2 oz (500 g) tomatoes, sliced
- Pinch of dried oregano
- 1 egg
- ⅔ cup (160 ml) milk
- 2 oz (50 g) pecorino cheese, very thinly sliced
- Salt and pepper

Preparation Time: 10 minutes
Cooking Time: 40 minutes
Serves: 6

Preheat the oven to 350°F (180°C). Grease a rectangular baking pan with butter.

In a medium frying pan, heat the olive oil over low heat. Add the spring onions and cook, stirring occasionally, for 5 minutes. Lightly season with salt and remove from the heat.

Arrange half the bread over the bottom of the prepared pan and spoon the spring onions on top. Place the tomato slices on top, sprinkle with the oregano, and cover with the remaining bread.

In a small bowl, beat the egg with the milk and season with salt and pepper. Pour the egg mixture over the bread, cover with the pecorino, and bake for 30 minutes, or until the cheese has melted and turned golden brown. Let cool slightly, then turn out onto a serving dish and serve.

Polenta with Kale and Beans

Infarinata

- 1½ cups (300 g) dried borlotti beans
- 1 clove garlic, smashed and peeled
- 2 sage leaves
- 1 small bunch Tuscan kale (cavolo nero), leaves stemmed
- 1 medium potato
- ¼ cup (60 ml) extra virgin olive oil, plus more as needed
- 1 stalk celery, tough strings removed, finely chopped
- 1 carrot, finely chopped
- ¾ cup (150 g) cornmeal
- Salt and black pepper

Preparation Time: 20 minutes plus soaking time
Cooking Time: 2 hours 45 minutes
Serves: 4

Soak the beans in warm water to cover for 8 to 10 hours, then drain and rinse them. Transfer them to a large saucepan and add cold water to cover, the garlic, and the sage. Cover and cook over very low heat for about 2 hours, until the beans are tender.

In the meantime, bring a large pot of salted water to a boil. Add the kale and cook for 5 minutes, then drain and let cool. Squeeze out any excess water and coarsely chop the kale.

Peel the potato and cut it into small cubes.

In a large saucepan, heat the olive oil over medium heat. Add the celery and carrot and cook, stirring, for 4 to 5 minutes. Add the kale, potato, and the beans with their cooking liquid and season with salt. While stirring, pour in the cornmeal all at once. Reduce the heat to low and cook for 45 minutes, adding more hot water if the polenta is sticking or scorching. Taste and season with salt.

Serve drizzled with a little oil and sprinkled with some pepper.

If you like the intense taste of Tuscan kale, skip the blanching step and simply coarsely chop the raw kale, then add it as directed.

Roasted Cardoons with Tomatoes and Pecorino

Cardi al forno con pomodoro e pecorino

- 3 cups (500 g) canned whole peeled tomatoes, chopped
- 1 small yellow onion, finely chopped
- Juice of 1 lemon
- 1¾ lb (800 g) hunchback cardoons or celery
- Peanut (groundnut) oil, for frying
- 2 eggs
- All-purpose (plain) flour
- 3½ oz (100 g) fresh pecorino cheese, sliced
- 6 tablespoons (40 g) grated Parmesan cheese
- Salt and black pepper

Preparation Time: 20 minutes
Cooking Time: 40 minutes
Serves: 4

Preheat the oven to 350°F (180°C).

In a medium saucepan, combine the tomatoes, onion, and a pinch of salt. Bring to a simmer over medium-high heat, reduce the heat to maintain a simmer, and cook for 20 minutes.

Meanwhile, bring a large pot of salted water to a boil. Fill a large bowl with cool water and add the lemon juice. Trim the cardoons and cut them into little sticks, dropping them into the bowl of lemon water as you go. Drain them and cook them in the boiling water for 10 minutes, then drain again and pat dry.

Fill a high-sided frying pan with about 2 inches (5 cm) of peanut (groundnut) oil and heat over medium-high heat to 350°F (180°C).

In a shallow bowl, beat the eggs with a pinch of salt and some pepper. Put some flour in a separate shallow bowl. Roll the cardoons in the flour to coat, then dip them in the eggs, letting any excess drip off. Carefully add them to the hot oil and fry until golden, 1 to 2 minutes. Use a slotted spoon to transfer them to paper towels to absorb excess oil.

In a baking dish, alternate layers of the cardoons, sliced pecorino, tomato sauce, and Parmesan, then bake for about 20 minutes, until the cheese has melted and the cardoons are tender. Serve immediately.

Hunchback cardoons are the most prized variety of cardoon. They get their name because the plants are partially covered with soil as they grow to protect them from the cold and keep them white, so eventually the stalks curve upward toward the light. Cardoons are rich in calcium, potassium, and sodium, and can also be eaten raw; first remove the tough strings running along the stalks. If you can't find cardoons, you can substitute celery or fennel.

Stuffed Artichokes with Quinoa and Mushrooms

Carciofi ripieni con quinoa rossa e funghi

- 6 to 7 tablespoons (90 to 105 ml) extra virgin olive oil
- 1¼ cups (200 g) red quinoa, rinsed
- ¾ oz (20 g) dried porcini mushrooms
- Zest and juice of 1 lemon
- 4 globe artichokes
- 6 tablespoons (40 g) grated Parmesan cheese
- 4 oil-packed sun-dried tomatoes, drained and finely chopped
- Leaves from 1 bunch parsley, chopped
- 1 clove garlic, finely chopped
- Salt
- 3 tablespoons breadcrumbs

Preparation Time: 25 minutes plus resting time
Cooking Time: 50 minutes
Serves: 4

Preheat the oven to 350°F (180°C). Line a sheet pan with parchment paper.

In a medium saucepan, heat 2 tablespoons of the olive oil over medium heat. Add the quinoa and toast, stirring continuously, for 1 minute, then add 2½ cups (625 ml) hot water and bring it to a boil. Reduce the heat to low, cover, and cook for 15 minutes. Let the quinoa stand, covered, for 5 minutes.

Put the dried mushrooms in a small bowl, add warm water to cover, and set aside to soak for 10 minutes, then drain and chop them.

Bring a large pot of salted water to a boil. Fill a large bowl with cool water and add the lemon juice. Remove the stems from the artichokes and cut their bottoms level so they stand flat, then remove the tougher outer leaves. Cut across the top of the artichoke to remove the top ¾ inch (1.5 cm), then spread the leaves so you can see the hairy choke at the center and remove it with a melon baller. Place the artichokes in the lemon water as you prep them.

Drain the artichokes, add them to the boiling water, and cook for 6 to 7 minutes. Drain them again and set them upside down on a clean dish towel to cool.

Fluff the quinoa and stir in the reserved mushrooms, ⅓ cup (30 g) of the Parmesan, the sun-dried tomatoes, parsley, lemon zest, garlic, 2 tablespoons of the oil, and a pinch of salt.

Rinsing the quinoa well is important to get rid of saponin, a natural coating on the grains that has a slightly bitter, soapy taste. You can use the artichoke stems by cutting away the fibrous outer part, then thinly slicing the centers and adding them to a risotto.

Wrap each artichoke in a piece of parchment paper and tie it with kitchen twine. Stuff the artichokes with the quinoa mixture. In a small bowl, stir together the breadcrumbs and the remaining Parmesan and sprinkle the mixture over the quinoa filling. Place the artichokes on the prepared pan, drizzle with the remaining 2 to 3 tablespoons oil, and bake for 25 minutes.

Trio of Stuffed Vegetables with Avocado and Cheese

Tris di Involtini di verdure all'avocado, robiola e ceci

- 3 tablespoons raisins
- 2 long eggplants (aubergines), sliced lengthwise ¼ inch (0.5 cm) thick
- 2 tablespoons extra virgin olive oil, plus more as needed
- 2 carrots
- 2 zucchini (courgettes), sliced lengthwise ¼ inch (0.5 cm) thick
- ⅔ cup (100 g) cooked chickpeas
- Juice of 1 lemon
- 1 tablespoon gomasio
- 1 avocado, halved and pitted
- Pinch of cayenne pepper
- 1 tablespoon wheat germ
- 3½ oz (100 g) goat's-milk robiola cheese
- Leaves from 2 sprigs thyme
- ¼ cup (10 g) mixed sprouts
- Salt and black pepper

Preparation Time: 40 minutes plus soaking time
Cooking Time: 10 minutes
Serves: 4

Put the raisins in a small bowl, add warm water to cover, and set aside to soak for 10 minutes, then drain and pat dry.

Preheat the broiler.

Put the eggplant (aubergine) slices on a sheet pan in a single layer and brush them with a little oil. Broil for 6 to 7 minutes, turning them as necessary, until they are tender and golden brown.

Meanwhile, bring a large pot of salted water to a boil. Using a mandoline or a vegetable peeler, slice the carrots lengthwise into thin ribbons. Add the carrots to the boiling water and cook for 30 seconds.

Heat a grill pan over medium-high heat. Add the zucchini (courgettes) and cook for 30 seconds on each side.

Place the chickpeas in a clean kitchen towel and rub gently to remove their skins; discard the skins and transfer the chickpeas to a food processor. Add the olive oil, half the lemon juice, and the gomasio and process until well combined and smooth. Transfer the chickpea purée to a small bowl and wash the food processor bowl.

Peel the avocado and drop the flesh in the food processor. Add the cayenne, a few drops of lemon juice, the wheat germ, and a pinch of salt and process until smooth.

In a small bowl, stir together the robiola cheese, raisins, thyme, and a generous sprinkle of pepper.

Spread the chickpea purée over the eggplant slices, the avocado purée over the zucchini (courgette) slices, and the robiola mixture over the carrot ribbons, then roll up the vegetables lengthwise around the filling. (Secure the rolls with toothpicks, if you need to.)

Place the rolls on a serving platter, sprinkle with the mixed sprouts, and serve.

Long eggplants (aubergines) can be a little bitter. To eliminate this bitter note, sprinkle their flesh with coarse salt and let them rest for 30 minutes, then rinse them and dry them with paper towels. In all the recipes in this book, it is advised to use unbleached unrefined sea salt, which is rich in trace minerals.

Herby Stuffed Tomatoes

Gratin di pomodori alle erbe

- Extra virgin olive oil
- ½ cup (50 g) breadcrumbs
- 6 tablespoons (40 g) grated pecorino cheese
- Handful of parsley leaves, finely chopped
- Leaves from 1 small bunch basil, finely chopped
- 4 mint leaves, finely chopped
- 4 large tomatoes on the vine
- Salt and black pepper

Preparation Time: 15 minutes
Cooking Time: 20 minutes
Serves: 6

Preheat the oven to 400°F (200°C). Lightly oil a sheet pan.

In a small bowl, stir together the breadcrumbs, pecorino, parsley, basil, mint, a pinch of salt, and some pepper.

Cut the tops off the tomatoes, set the tops aside, and seed the tomatoes. Sprinkle with some salt, then stuff the tomatoes with the breadcrumb mixture. Transfer them to the prepared pan, drizzle them with a little oil, and replace the tops. Bake for 15 to 20 minutes, then serve warm or at room temperature.

Use fully ripe tomatoes. If they seem a bit too acidic, sprinkle the insides of the tomatoes with a pinch of raw sugar. These tomatoes can also be cut into small pieces and added, with their cooking liquid, to cooked short whole wheat pasta shapes.

Stuffed Cabbage with Buckwheat and Pumpkin

Fagottini di verza con grano saraceno e zucca

- ½ cup (120 ml) extra virgin olive oil
- 1½ cups (250 g) buckwheat, rinsed
- 7 oz (200 g) peeled pumpkin, cut into small cubes
- 1 clove garlic, finely chopped
- Handful of parsley leaves, chopped
- ⅔ cup (80 g) chopped walnuts
- Scant 1 cup (200 ml) vegetable stock
- 1 small savoy cabbage
- 1 small red onion, very thinly sliced
- Salt and black pepper

Preparation Time: 20 minutes
Cooking Time: 1 hour
Serves: 4

In a medium saucepan, heat 2 tablespoons of the olive oil over medium heat. Add the buckwheat and toast, stirring continuously, for 2 to 3 minutes. Add 2½ cups (600 ml) boiling water, reduce the heat to low, and cook for 20 minutes.

In a large frying pan, heat 2 tablespoons of the oil over medium heat. Add the pumpkin, garlic, a pinch of salt, and a scant ½ cup (100 ml) boiling water. Cook until the pumpkin is tender, then transfer it to a medium bowl. Mash the pumpkin with a fork and add the buckwheat, parsley, walnuts, a pinch of salt, and some pepper. Stir well to combine.

In a small saucepan, bring the stock to a boil.

Bring a large pot of salted water to a boil. Discard the outer leaves from the cabbage. Pull off 12 leaves, put them in the boiling water, and blanch for 2 minutes, then drain them and cut out the tough central ribs.

Spread the cabbage leaves out on your work surface (work in batches, if necessary). Divide the buckwheat mixture among the cabbage leaves, placing it in the center of the leaves and folding the leaves over the filling to make small parcels.

In a large nonstick frying pan, heat the remaining ¼ cup (60 ml) oil. Add the onion and 2 tablespoons of the hot stock. Arrange the stuffed cabbage leaves in the saucepan, then add the remaining stock. Cover and cook for 25 minutes, until the cabbage leaves are translucent and the filling is heated through, then serve.

Buckwheat is a good source of potassium and magnesium, which can help to lower cholesterol levels and blood pressure. This recipe can be enriched with 3½ oz (100 g) seitan; coarsely chopped it and add it to the pumpkin while it is cooking.

Escarole Stuffed with Olives and Capers

Indivia ripiena di olive e capperi

- 1½ cloves garlic
- 2 heads escarole, washed
- 3 tablespoons olive oil, plus more for brushing
- 1 cup (50 g) fresh breadcrumbs
- 3 oz (80 g) green olives, pitted and sliced
- Scant ¼ cup (25 g) capers, drained and rinsed
- 1 sprig parsley, chopped
- Salt and pepper

Preparation Time: 10 minutes
Cooking Time: 45 minutes
Serves: 4

Preheat the oven to 350°F (180°C). Brush a baking dish with olive oil.

Chop the whole garlic clove. Put the escarole heads, with some water from washing still clinging to their leaves, in a large frying pan with 2 tablespoons of the olive oil and the chopped garlic. Season with salt and pepper. Cover and cook over low heat for about 15 minutes.

In a medium frying pan, heat the remaining 1 tablespoon oil over medium-low heat. Add the breadcrumbs and remaining garlic and cook, stirring frequently, until the breadcrumbs are golden. Remove the garlic and stir in the olives, capers, and parsley.

Gently pull open the escarole heads and stuff them with almost all the breadcrumb mixture, then press them back into their original shape. Place the stuffed escarole heads in the prepared baking dish and sprinkle with the remaining breadcrumbs. Bake for about 20 minutes. Serve warm.

Millet-Stuffed Tomatoes and Zucchini

Pomodori e zucchine ripieni di miglio

- 2 tablespoons extra virgin olive oil, plus more as needed
- 1 cup (200 g) millet, rinsed thoroughly
- 4 tomatoes on the vine
- 1 spring onion, sliced
- 5 or 6 basil leaves, thinly sliced
- 6 tablespoons (40 g) grated Parmesan cheese
- 3 large zucchini (courgettes)
- 1¾ oz (50 g) ricotta cheese
- Leaves from 2 sprigs marjoram, chopped
- Salt and black pepper

Preparation Time: 25 minutes plus resting time
Cooking Time: 1 hour
Serves: 4

Preheat the oven to 350°F (180°C). Line a sheet pan with parchment paper.

In a large saucepan, heat 1 tablespoon of the olive oil over medium heat. Add the millet and toast, stirring continuously, for 2 minutes. Add 2 cups (500 ml) boiling water, reduce the heat to low, cover, and cook the millet for 20 minutes. Let it stand, covered, for 10 minutes, then fluff it with a fork and divide it between two medium bowls.

Slice the tops off the tomatoes; set the tops aside. Using a melon baller, scoop out some of the flesh from each tomato, creating a cup, and coarsely chop the flesh. Set the tomatoes and the chopped flesh aside.

In a small frying pan, heat the remaining 1 tablespoon oil over medium-low heat. Add the spring onion and the chopped tomato. Season with salt and cook for 5 to 6 minutes. Add the onion-tomato mixture to one bowl of the millet. Add the basil and the Parmesan, and stir to combine.

Bring a large pot of salted water to a boil. Add the zucchini (courgettes) and cook for 5 minutes, then drain them and let cool slightly. Slice the zucchini (courgettes) crosswise into 1¼- to 1½-inch-wide (3 to 4 cm) pieces and hollow them out with the melon baller, leaving approximately ½ inch (1 cm) of flesh at the bottom. Chop the flesh you scoop out and add it to the second bowl of millet. Add the ricotta, marjoram, a pinch of salt, and some pepper and stir to combine.

Stuff the tomatoes with the tomato-millet mixture and the zucchini (courgettes) with the ricotta-millet mixture, then place the vegetables on the prepared pan and drizzle them with a little oil. Bake for about 30 minutes, then serve warm or hot.

Of all cereal grains, millet has the highest protein content, and it is also gluten-free. It needs to be rinsed thoroughly before cooking to remove any impurities. Toasting the millet ensures even cooking.

Zucchini and Halloumi Gratin

Parmigiana di zucchine con formaggio halloumi

- Peanut (groundnut) oil, for frying
- 2¼ lb (1 kg) zucchini (courgettes)
- All-purpose (plain) flour
- 10½ oz (300 g) plum tomatoes
- 7 oz (200 g) halloumi cheese, thickly sliced
- Leaves from 1 small bunch basil, thinly sliced
- 4 or 5 mint leaves, thinly sliced
- Salt

Preparation Time: 20 minutes
Cooking Time: 45 minutes
Serves: 4

Preheat the oven to 350°F (180°C).

Fill a large high-sided frying pan with about 2 inches (5 cm) of peanut (groundnut) oil and heat over medium-high heat to 350°F (180°C).

Use a mandoline to thinly slice the zucchini (courgettes) into ribbons. Dust the ribbons with flour, then place them in a large colander and shake them to remove any excess. Working in batches, add the zucchini (courgette) slices to the hot oil and fry until they start to turn golden. Use a spider (skimmer) to transfer them to paper towels to absorb excess oil. Repeat to fry the remaining slices.

Bring a large pot of water to a boil. Add the tomatoes and blanch them for 30 seconds, then drain them and let cool slightly. Slice the tomatoes ¼ inch (0.5 cm) thick.

In a baking dish, alternate layers of the zucchini (courgettes), halloumi, basil and mint, and tomatoes, sprinkling each layer with a pinch of salt. Bake the parmigiana for about 25 minutes. Serve hot or warm.

Halloumi is a cheese produced in Cyprus, made with goat's and sheep's milk, with a salty taste. It can be replaced with the same quantity of vegan cheese and, for a lighter dish, the zucchini (courgettes) can be grilled instead of fried, in which case there is no need to dust them in flour.

Stuffed Squash Blossoms

Fiori di zucca ripieni

- 1 lb 2 oz (500 g) white-fleshed potatoes
- ¾ cup (70 g) grated Parmesan cheese
- 2 eggs
- 1 small clove garlic, pressed through a garlic press
- 5 or 6 basil leaves, thinly sliced
- Pinch of freshly grated nutmeg
- 16 squash blossoms (courgette flowers), pistils removed
- Extra virgin olive oil
- Salt

Preparation Time: 20 minutes
Cooking Time: 1 hour
Serves: 4

Put the potatoes in a large saucepan, add cold water to cover, and bring to a boil. Reduce the heat to maintain a simmer and cook for 40 minutes, until the potatoes are tender and easily pierced with a fork. Drain them and let cool.

Preheat the oven to 350°F (180°C). Line a sheet pan with parchment paper.

Peel the potatoes, transfer the flesh to a large bowl, and mash it with a potato masher. Add ½ cup (50 g) of the Parmesan, the eggs, garlic, basil, nutmeg, and a pinch of salt to the potatoes and stir well to combine. Transfer the potato mixture to a disposable piping bag.

Fill the squash blossoms (courgette flowers) with the potato mixture, placing them on the prepared pan as you go. Drizzle them with a little olive oil, sprinkle them with the remaining Parmesan, and bake them for 20 minutes, until golden.

For a vegan version of this dish, chop 10½ oz (300 g) tofu and place it in a large bowl. Grate 1 zucchini (courgette) and squeeze it to remove excess water, then add it to the bowl with the tofu. Stir in ¼ cup (40 g) chopped toasted pine nuts, 3 tablespoons olive oil, the chopped leaves from 1 sprig marjoram, and salt to taste. Fill the flowers with this mixture. Bake them for 25 minutes and serve them sprinkled with 1 teaspoon nutritional yeast (yeast flakes).

Sweet-and-Sour Stuffed Peppers

Involtini di peperoni in agrodolce

- 3 red bell peppers
- ¼ cup (60 ml) plus 3 to 4 tablespoons extra virgin olive oil, plus more as needed
- 2 cups (100 g) fresh breadcrumbs
- Handful of parsley leaves
- 2 cloves garlic, smashed and peeled
- 1½ oz (40 g) Pecorino Romano cheese, grated
- 3½ oz (100 g) primo sale or other semisoft sheep's-milk cheese, sliced
- Scant ½ cup (100 ml) white wine vinegar
- 1 teaspoon sugar
- Salt and black pepper

Preparation Time: 20 minutes
Cooking Time: 40 minutes
Serves: 4

Preheat the broiler.

Brush the bell peppers with a little oil and place them on a sheet pan. Broil, turning them to ensure they cook evenly, until lightly charred and softened, 4 to 5 minutes. Remove from the oven, transfer to a bowl, cover with plastic wrap (cling film), and let cool. Peel and seed the peppers, then cut the flesh into large, long pieces.

In a food processor, combine the breadcrumbs, parsley, 1 garlic clove, the pecorino, 3 to 4 tablespoons of the olive oil, a pinch of salt, and some black pepper. Pulse until well combined.

Lay the roasted pepper pieces flat on your work surface. Sprinkle them with some of the breadcrumb mixture, then arrange a piece of the primo sale cheese on each piece of pepper and roll up the peppers around the cheese. Put the remaining breadcrumb mixture in a shallow dish and dredge the rolls in the mixture to coat.

In a large frying pan, heat the remaining ¼ cup (60 ml) oil with the remaining garlic. Add the pepper rolls and cook until they are golden. Turn off the heat and transfer the rolls to a serving dish.

In a small saucepan, combine the vinegar and the sugar and heat over low heat, stirring, until the sugar has dissolved.

Drizzle the vinegar over the pepper rolls and let cool before serving.

For a vegan version, process the breadcrumbs with 1¼ cups (200 g) cooked cannellini beans, the garlic, the parsley, and the olive oil, then continue as directed.

Sweets & Desserts

An ideal way to finish a meal or to enjoy a sweet snack, desserts are often assumed to have limited nutritional value and too many calories (though with good reason), and are treated as occasional indulgences. But here are guidelines for irresistible, nutritionally balanced, and incredibly light desserts.

Simple sweet things

Desserts are generally considered the enemy, but this is not always true. It's entirely possible to create delicious, nutritionally balanced desserts without too many calories.

Instead of milk and eggs

Those who have eliminated animal products from their diet can prepare tasty (and lighter) desserts by replacing 1 egg with 1/2 banana, mashed, or 2 tablespoons cornstarch (cornflour). Agar-agar, a powdered thickening agent derived from seaweed, can be used in puddings and gelled desserts. Nondairy milks like soy milk (easy to digest and protein-rich), rice milk, and oat milk can be used in place of cow's milk.

Whole-grain flours

Many dessert recipes call for all-purpose (plain) flour, the most refined type. Using whole-grain or partially refined flours or alternative flours such as farro, buckwheat, rice, chestnut, quinoa, or amaranth can vary the flavors and ensure a wider range of nutritional elements.

Delicious and healthy

It is not necessary to entirely eliminate sugar from desserts—it is sufficient not to use it to excess. A valid alternative to refined white sugar is unrefined raw sugar, which contains more vitamins and minerals. Natural sweeteners can be used in place of sugar; these include honey, agave syrup (with a glycemic value lower than that of sugar), barley malt extract, and brown rice syrup. Stevia, extracted from a South American plant, has a high sweetening power and almost no calories; just be sure to buy all-natural stevia, not a stevia-based sugar substitute.

Fats

Butter is often synonymous with pastry making. It can, however, be replaced in baked goods with extra virgin olive oil, which does not contain any cholesterol and is a source of "good" fats; use 6 tablespoons (90 ml) olive oil to replace ½ cup (1 stick/115 g) butter. Other alternatives are vegan butter, coconut oil, and nondairy yogurt.

Rising, naturally

Some commercially available yeasts contain animal-sourced ingredients, such as the stabilizer E470a, which will be identified on the label. For this reason, vegans (and some nonvegans) prefer to use cream of tartar, a natural leavener derived from a by-product of the winemaking process, or baking soda (bicarbonate of soda), which must be mixed with lemon juice or vinegar to activate.

Lots of great ideas for the table

From fruit-based preparations to small pastries, the choice of vegetarian desserts is varied.

Little sweet treats

The word *dessert* is derived from the French *desservir*, meaning "clear the table." Originally, it was used to describe any course served at the end of a meal, including a cheese course. Today, however, it refers to a sweet dish.

Cakes and muffins

Cakes are the baked dessert par excellence. They are best if prepared with whole wheat (wholemeal) flour or alternative flours, which offer different textures and flavors as well as being healthier options. Typical of American culinary tradition, muffins are small cakes of varying sweetness baked in paper cups, and can include fruit or chocolate.

Fruit desserts

There are a variety of baked fruit desserts, including crostata, a tart with a pastry base filled with jam and topped with strips of pastry; crumbles, a layered dessert consisting of a flour, butter, and sugar mixture sprinkled over a layer of cooked fruit; and the classic strudel, made with a very thin pastry crust and filled with apples flavored with cinnamon or other seasonal fruit.

Fresh fruit

Fruit desserts are tasty and light, starting with fruit salad, which becomes a veritable dessert if accompanied by ice cream, heavy cream, or whipped cream. Fruit gelatin can be made by setting fruit juice with agar-agar, a vegan substitute for gelatin (an animal product), derived from seaweed. Fresh fruit can also be immersed in melted sugar and caramelized.

Cookies (biscuits)

Cookies (biscuits) are classic small pastries. They are made with a stiff batter or dough, arranged on sheet pans lined with parchment paper, and baked until golden. Bars are made with grains, and are prepared in one large block, then cut into individual bars. They come in two varieties: oven-baked, and no-bake, which are refrigerated until firm.

The ingredients to always have on hand

In addition to the basic flours, sweeteners, fats, and leavening agents, having other products on hand can make it easy to put together an interesting and delicious dessert without much hassle.

Fruits and preserves

These can make the best of a seasonal bounty and give an extra touch to vegetarian desserts.

Vanilla, cinnamon, and anise seeds

Some people think spices work best in savory recipes. However, spices are also used in the preparation of delicious desserts. Vanilla extract and vanilla bean seeds can be used to flavor cakes, creams, ice creams, puddings, and other desserts. Cinnamon is also commonly used in desserts, and anise seeds, which have a licorice flavor, can be used to flavor cookies (biscuits) like the Italian *anicini* and other traditional preparations like fruitcake.

Other spices

Originally from Asia, ginger, turmeric, and cardamom are obtained from rhizomes, left to dry, and then finely ground. They are excellent for flavoring cakes, creams, and cookies (biscuits) and can be used in place of cinnamon for a different warming flavor. Cloves are also worth a mention: they are traditionally used to flavor tarts, jams, and chestnut-based desserts.

Small seeds, great virtues

Seeds can be used to impart a crunchy note to cakes, mousses, and ice cream, and they are also concentrated sources of nutrition. Sesame seeds are very high in alcium, which makes them an excellent alternative to dairy products to strengthen bones and teeth. Hemp seeds contain iron, phosphorus, and omega-3 fatty acids, as well as all nine essential amino acids. Poppy seeds have similar qualities and also contain phytosterols, which help to reduce cholesterol levels. The presence of beta-carotene makes pumpkin seeds valuable for eye health, while sunflower seeds have significant antibacterial properties. Lastly, flaxseeds (linseeds) can help prevent cardiovascular disease and, compared to other types of seeds, have a lower calorie content.

Whole-Grain Cake with Almond Butter

Torta di farro integrale farcita con burro di mandorle

- 1 (13.5 oz/400 ml) can full-fat coconut milk
- ½ cup (100 g) coconut butter, plus more for greasing
- ¼ cup (30 g) all-purpose (plain) flour, plus more for dusting
- ½ cup plus 1 tablespoon (120 g) raw sugar
- Pinch of salt
- 3 eggs
- Scant ⅓ cup (50 g) whole wheat (wholemeal) farro flour
- ¾ cup (80 g) almond meal/flour (ground almonds)
- 1 level teaspoon baking powder, sifted
- Scant ½ cup (100 g) almond butter
- 5 tablespoons (40 g) coarsely chopped raw almonds

Preparation Time: 20 minutes
Cooking Time: 30 minutes
Serves: 4

(DF)

Refrigerate the unopened can of coconut milk overnight.

Preheat the oven to 350°F (180°C). Lightly grease a 7-inch (18 cm) springform pan and dust it with flour, tapping out any excess (or line it with parchment paper).

In a small saucepan, melt the coconut butter over very low heat, then pour it into a large bowl and let cool slightly. Add the sugar and a pinch of salt and whisk for 3 to 4 minutes. Add the eggs one at a time, whisking until each is combined before adding the next.

In a medium bowl, combine the whole wheat (wholemeal) flour, all-purpose (plain) flour, almond meal/flour (ground almonds), and baking powder. Add the flour mixture to the coconut butter mixture and stir to combine. Pour the batter into the prepared pan.

Bake the cake for about 30 minutes, then remove it from the oven and let cool in the pan on a wire rack.

Remove the springform ring from the pan and transfer the cake to a cutting board. Cut it in half horizontally, then set one layer cut side up on a serving plate. Spread the almond butter over the cut side of the cake layer and top with the second cake layer, cut side down.

Open the chilled can of coconut milk and scoop the solid white portion into a large bowl (discard the clearish liquid or refrigerate for another use). Using a handheld mixer, whip the cream until it holds firm peaks, then use an offset spatula to spread it all over the cake, covering it completely. Press the almonds against the sides of the cake and serve.

The almond butter can be made at home: spread ¾ cup (100 g) blanched almonds over a small sheet pan and toast in a preheated 125°F (50°C) oven for 5 minutes, then remove from the oven and let cool. Transfer the almonds to a food processor and process until smooth. Transfer the almond butter to a jar and store in the refrigerator for up to 2 weeks.

Orange Bundt Cake with Fruit Salad

Ciambella all'arancia con insalata di frutta

- ½ cup (120 ml) extra virgin olive oil plus more for greasing
- Scant 2½ cups (300 g) all-purpose (plain) flour
- 2 teaspoons (8 g) baking powder
- 3 eggs
- ⅔ cup (120 g) natural brown sugar
- Zest and juice of 1 orange
- 1 cup (250 ml) milk
- Pinch of salt
- 4 slices pineapple, cored and cut into small triangles
- 2 kiwi fruits, peeled, halved, and sliced
- 1 banana, sliced on an angle
- 4¼ oz (120 g) raspberries
- 2 tablespoons honey
- Pinch of cinnamon
- Mint leaves, for garnish

Preparation Time: 20 minutes plus resting time
Cooking Time: 45 minutes
Serves: 6 to 8

Preheat the oven to 350°F (180°C). Lightly oil and flour a bundt (ring) pan.

Sift the flour and the baking powder directly into a large bowl. Break the eggs into a separate medium bowl, add the sugar, and whisk to combine. Add the orange zest, the oil, milk, and salt and whisk to combine. Pour the egg mixture into the flour mixture and stir to combine.

Pour the batter into the prepared pan. Bake the cake for about 45 minutes. Remove from the oven and let cool for a bit, then turn it out onto a wire rack to cool.

In a medium bowl, combine the pineapple, kiwis, banana, and raspberries. Drizzle the fruit with the orange juice and the honey, then sprinkle with the cinnamon and let stand for 10 minutes.

Transfer the cake to a serving plate. Drain the fruit, reserving the juice, and arrange the fruit in the hole in the cake. Drizzle the cake with the fruit juice and serve right away, garnished with a few mint leaves.

For the vegan version, in a food processor, combine 2 cups (250 g) all-purpose (plain) flour, ¼ cup (30 g) cornstarch, ½ teaspoon cream of tartar, a scant ½ cup (80 g) raw sugar, 1½ cups (350 ml) almond milk, 3½ tablespoons (50 ml) corn oil, the grated zest of ½ orange, and a pinch of salt and process until well combined, then bake for 35 minutes.

Bread and Fruit Cake

Miascia, torta di pane e frutta di tremezzo

- 5¼ oz (150 g) stale bread, coarsely chopped
- Scant 1 cup (200 ml) milk, warmed
- ¼ cup (30 g) raisins
- ¼ cup (50 g) sugar
- 1 egg
- Zest and juice of 1 lemon
- 1 tablespoon all-purpose (plain) flour
- 1 tablespoon fine cornmeal
- 1 small bunch white grapes
- 1 Golden Delicious apple, peeled, cored, and cut into small cubes
- 1 pear, peeled, cored, and cut into small cubes
- Pinch of salt
- Leaves from 1 sprig rosemary
- 3 tablespoons (40 g) butter, very thinly sliced or grated

Preparation Time: 20 minutes plus resting time
Cooking Time: 1 hour
Serves: 6 to 8

Put the bread in a large bowl, pour the warmed milk over it, and let it soften for 1 hour.

Preheat the oven to 350°F (180°C). Line a 9½-inch (24 cm) round baking dish with parchment paper.

Put the raisins in a small bowl, add warm water to cover, and soak for 20 minutes, then drain them and pat dry.

Add the sugar, egg, lemon zest, raisins, all-purpose (plain) flour, cornmeal, grapes, apple, pear, and salt to the bread mixture and stir to combine.

Pour the mixture into the prepared baking dish, sprinkle the top with the rosemary and butter, then bake it for about 1 hour, until golden brown. Serve the cake warm.

You can add 2 tablespoons pumpkin seeds or chopped walnuts to the mixture. For a vegan version, replace the cornmeal with 1 tablespoon all-purpose (plain) flour, and replace the egg with 1 tablespoon chia seeds, soaked in warm water for 15 minutes (no need to drain).

Seeded Spice Cake

Torta speziata con semi

- 10½ oz (300 g) dried dates, pitted
- 3½ oz (100 g) dried apricots
- 2 green cardamom pods
- Scant ½ cup (100 ml) sesame oil
- 1 teaspoon ground ginger
- 1 teaspoon ground cinnamon
- Pinch of salt
- 1 cup (120 g) whole wheat (wholemeal) flour
- 1 level teaspoon baking soda (bicarbonate of soda)
- Juice of ½ lemon
- 5 tablespoons (40 g) pumpkin seeds, toasted, plus more for garnish
- 2½ tablespoons sunflower seeds, plus more for garnish
- Powdered (icing) sugar, for dusting

Preparation Time: 20 minutes
Cooking Time: 1 hour
Serves: 6 to 8

Preheat the oven to 350°F (180°C). Line a 7-inch (18 cm) springform pan with parchment paper.

In a medium saucepan, combine the dates and the apricots and add enough water to just cover the fruit. Cook over medium heat for 10 minutes, then turn off the heat and let cool.

Open the cardamom pods and tip the seeds into a mortar, then crush them with a pestle.

In a food processor, combine the rehydrated fruit and its cooking liquid, oil, cardamom seeds, ginger, cinnamon, and salt, then process until the mixture becomes a smooth paste. Add the flour, baking soda (bicarbonate of soda), and lemon juice, then process again.

Transfer the batter to a bowl, add the pumpkin and sunflower seeds, and stir to combine. Pour the batter into the prepared pan and garnish with additional pumpkin and sunflower seeds. Bake the cake for 45 to 50 minutes. Let cool, then dust the top with a little powdered (icing) sugar and serve.

As well as being rich in iron, vitamins, and minerals, dates are naturally sweet and can be used instead of sugar to sweeten cakes and other sweet preparations.

Honey-Quinoa Cake

Torta di mele e quinoa

- 2 Reinette or other firm cooking apples, peeled, cored, and finely diced
- ⅔ cup (130 g) raw sugar
- Zest of ½ lemon
- Juice of 1 lemon
- ⅔ cup (120 g) quinoa
- 1 cup plus 1 tablespoons (130 g) whole wheat (wholemeal) flour
- 1 teaspoon baking powder
- Pinch of salt
- 1 Golden Delicious apple

Preparation Time: 20 minutes
Cooking Time: 55 minutes
Serves: 8

Preheat the oven to 350°F (180°C). Line an 8-inch (20 cm) round pan with parchment paper.

In a small saucepan, combine the apples, 2 tablespoons of the sugar, the lemon zest, half the lemon juice, and 2 tablespoons water. Cover and cook over low heat for about 10 minutes, until the apples are tender. Raise the heat to medium and cook until any remaining liquid has evaporated, then remove from the heat and let cool slightly. Purée the mixture directly in the pot with a hand blender until smooth.

In a medium saucepan, toast the quinoa over medium heat for a few minutes, then add 1⅓ cups (330 ml) water. Reduce the heat to low, cover, and cook for 20 minutes. Fluff it with a fork and let cool.

In a large bowl, combine the flour, the remaining sugar, the baking powder, and the salt. Add the apple purée and the quinoa and stir to combine.

Pour the batter into the prepared pan. Peel the Golden Delicious apple, core it, and very thinly slice it, then arrange the slices on the top of the batter and drizzle with the remaining lemon juice. Bake the tart for about 30 minutes. Let cool before serving.

Whole-grain flour retains the external coating of the wheat grain and its germ, which are rich in fiber, proteins, B vitamins, and minerals. Only buy organic whole wheat (wholemeal) flour, because conventional wheat retains all the chemical substances used during cultivation.

Almond-and-Honey Cookies

Fiadoni alla trentina

- ¾ cup (100 g) finely chopped blanched almonds
- 2 tablespoons breadcrumbs
- 1 teaspoons ground cinnamon
- Pinch of ground cloves
- ½ cup plus 2 tablespoons (150 g) acacia honey
- 2 tablespoons brandy
- 2 cups (250 g) all-purpose (plain) flour, plus more for dusting
- 2 teaspoons (8 g) baking powder
- 6 tablespoons (80 g) sugar
- Zest of 1 lemon
- 7 tablespoons (100 g) butter, cut into small cubes
- Scant ½ cup (100 ml) milk
- Pinch of salt
- 1 egg, lightly beaten
- ½ cup (100 g) white sprinkles

Preparation Time: 25 minutes
Cooking Time: 15 minutes
Serves: 6 to 8

Preheat the oven to 350°F (180°C). Line a sheet pan with parchment paper.

In a medium bowl, combine the almonds, breadcrumbs, cinnamon, cloves, honey, and brandy, then stir until the mixture is well combined.

In a food processor, combine the flour, baking powder, sugar, lemon zest, butter, milk, and salt and process until a dough forms. Turn the dough out onto a lightly floured working surface and roll it out to ⅛ inch (2 to 3 mm) thick. Cut the dough into 4-inch (10 cm) squares.

Fill the dough squares with the almond filling, fold them into triangles and press the edges to seal, then place them on the prepared pan. Brush them with the lightly beaten egg and garnish with the sprinkles. Bake for about 15 minutes, until golden brown. Let cool completely before serving.

For a vegan version, prepare the dough with a scant ½ cup (100 ml) oil instead of the butter, almond milk instead of the cow's milk, maple syrup instead of the honey, and leave out the egg and sprinkles and garnish the fiadoni with powdered (icing) sugar instead.

Chocolate Granola Bars

Barrette di cereal alle prugne e cioccolato crudo

- 2 teaspoons loose Lapsang Souchong tea
- 5¼ oz (150 g) pitted dried prunes
- 7 oz (200 g) raw chocolate, finely chopped
- ⅔ cup (100 g) sesame seeds, lightly toasted
- 6 cups (100 g) puffed quinoa
- 3 cups (50 g) puffed brown rice

Preparation Time: 20 minutes plus resting time
Cooking Time: 10 minutes
Serves: 6 to 8

In a small saucepan, bring 1¼ cups (300 ml) water to a boil, then turn the heat off, add the tea, and let it infuse for 5 minutes. Strain the tea and return it to the pot. Add the prunes and let soak for 4 hours. Drain them, pat dry, and transfer to a food processor. Process the prunes into a smooth paste.

Set a heatproof bowl over a saucepan of simmering water (be sure the bottom of the bowl does not touch the water). Put the chocolate in the bowl and let it melt, then add it to the food processor with the puréed prunes and process for a few seconds to combine. Transfer the chocolate mixture to a large bowl and add the sesame seeds, puffed quinoa, and puffed rice. Stir to coat the seeds and puffed grains with the chocolate mixture.

Line a 9-inch (22 cm) square baking pan with parchment paper. Scrape the mixture into the pan with a spatula, packing it down and leveling the top. Score lines into the top (you'll use these to cut the block into bars), then cover and freeze for 40 minutes.

Turn the block out onto a cutting board and cut it into individual bars along the scored lines. Store the bars in an airtight container in the refrigerator.

Raw chocolate retains all its nutritional qualities. In fact, it is rich in magnesium, antioxidants, and tryptophan, which are lost when the cocoa beans are roasted. If you can't find raw chocolate, the same quantity of regular chocolate can be used instead.

Fruitcake

Pan speziale o certosino

- ½ cup (100 g) raisins
- ½ cup (130 g) acacia honey
- 6 tablespoons (80 g) sugar
- 1 teaspoon baking soda (bicarbonate of soda)
- 1 level teaspoon anise seeds
- 2 cups (250 g) all-purpose (plain) flour
- ¾ cup (100 g) blanched almonds
- ¾ cup (100 g) pine nuts
- 3½ oz (100 g) candied citron and orange peel
- 3½ oz (100 g) chocolate, coarsely chopped
- Pinch of salt

Preparation Time: 20 minutes plus soaking time
Cooking Time: 45 minutes
Serves: 8

Preheat the oven to 350°F (180°C). Line a 9-inch (22 cm) springform pan with parchment paper.

Put the raisins in a small bowl, add warm water to cover, and set aside to soak for 10 minutes, then drain them and pat dry with paper towels.

In a small bowl, stir together the honey, sugar, baking soda (bicarbonate of soda), and anise seeds. Pour in a scant 1 cup (200 ml) boiling water, then add the flour and mix the ingredients together using a spatula. Add the raisins, almonds, pine nuts, candied fruit, chocolate, and salt, then stir to combine.

Pour the mixture into the prepared pan and bake for about 45 minutes. Let cool, then wrap it in plastic wrap (cling film) and allow it to mellow for a few days before serving.

This dessert has a long life, and can be stored in a cupboard, well wrapped, for about 1 month. Its top can be decorated with additional almonds and pieces of candied fruit, if desired.

Sour Cherry Tart

Crostata di visciole

- 2 cups (250 g) all-purpose (plain) flour, plus more for dusting
- ¾ cup (100 g) powdered (icing) sugar
- ½ cup (1 stick/120 g) butter, cut into cubes
- Zest of 1 lemon
- 1 egg
- 1 egg yolk
- 14 oz (400 g) sour cherries, pitted
- ¾ cup (150 g) granulated sugar
- 1 teaspoon ground cinnamon
- Pinch of salt

Preparation Time: 20 minutes plus resting time
Cooking Time: 55 minutes
Serves: 8

Preheat the oven to 350°F (180°C). Position a rack in the lower third of the oven.

In a food processor, combine the flour, powdered (icing) sugar, butter, lemon zest, and a pinch of salt and process until the mixture is crumbly. Add the egg and the egg yolk and process again until the dough comes together and forms a ball. Wrap the dough in plastic wrap (cling film) and refrigerate for 30 minutes.

In the meantime, in a medium saucepan, combine the sour cherries, granulated sugar, and cinnamon and cook over medium heat for about 20 minutes, until the mixture thickens. Allow it to cool.

On a lightly floured surface, roll out two-thirds of the dough into a round ⅛ inch (2 to 3 mm) thick and transfer it to an 8-inch (20 cm) round tart pan with a removable bottom, gently pressing the dough into the corners of the pan to fit. Roll your rolling pin over the top of the pan, pressing gently, to trim excess dough.

Prick the bottom of the tart shell with a fork, then pour the sour cherries into the tart shell. Roll out the remaining dough and cut it into ¼ inch wide (.5 cm) strips. Arrange them over the filling, pressing the edges against the bottom crust to seal, and trim any excess dough. Bake the tart on the lower rack for about 35 minutes. Let cool completely before serving.

This tart tastes better if eaten the day after it is prepared. An excellent diuretic infusion can be prepared with ¾ oz (20 g) sour cherry pits and 1⅔ cups (400 ml) water: bring the water to a boil, pour it over the pits, cover the container, and let cool. After 20 minutes, strain the liquid and, if desired, sweeten it with a little honey.

Peach-Blackberry Crostata

Tarte di avena con pesche e more

- 2¼ cups (200 g) oat flour
- Scant ¾ cup (100 g) all-purpose (plain) flour, plus more for dusting
- Scant ½ cup (90 g) natural brown sugar
- Pinch of salt
- Zest and juice of 1 lemon
- ½ cup (1 stick/120 g) butter, cut into small cubes and chilled
- 6 peaches, halved, pitted, and cut into wedges
- 5¼ oz (150 g) blackberries
- Scant ½ cup (40 g) rolled oats

Preparation Time: 20 minutes plus resting time
Cooking Time: 35 minutes
Serves: 4

In a food processor, combine the oat flour, all-purpose (plain) flour, ¼ cup (45 g) of the sugar, the salt, and the lemon zest and pulse briefly to combine. Add the butter and pulse until the mixture becomes crumbly. Add a scant ½ cup (100 ml) cold water and process until the dough forms a ball. Wrap the dough in plastic wrap (cling film) and refrigerate for 30 minutes.

Preheat the oven to 350°F (180°C). Line a sheet pan with parchment paper.

In a large bowl, combine the peaches, blackberries, lemon juice, and remaining sugar and toss to combine.

On a lightly floured surface, roll out the dough into a round ⅛ inch (2 to 3 mm) thick and place it on the prepared sheet pan. Sprinkle the rolled oats over the dough, leaving a 2½- to 3-inch (7 to 8 cm) border uncovered. Arrange the fruit on top of the oats and fold the dough over the filling, leaving the filling exposed in the center. Bake the crostata for about 35 minutes, until the crust is golden brown, then remove from the oven and let cool before serving.

The rolled oats can be replaced with about ⅓ cup (40 g) unseasoned breadcrumbs, toasted in a nonstick frying pan, or ⅓ cup (40 g) cookie (biscuit) crumbs. For a vegan version, replace the butter with the same weight of vegan butter.

Banana-Pistachio Muffins

Muffins di banana e pistacchi con amaranto

- Scant 1 cup (120 g) shelled pistachios
- Scant 1½ cups (180 g) all-purpose (plain) flour
- ½ cup (60 g) amaranth flour
- 2 teaspoons baking soda (bicarbonate of soda)
- ½ cup (100 g) raw sugar
- 1 teaspoon ground cinnamon
- ½ teaspoon freshly grated nutmeg
- Pinch of salt
- 3 bananas, chopped into chunks
- Juice of 1 lemon
- 1 tablespoon apple cider vinegar
- Scant ½ cup (100 ml) sesame oil

Preparation Time: 20 minutes
Cooking Time: 40 minutes
Serves: 8

Preheat the oven to 350°F (180°C). Line a 12-cup muffin tin with paper liners.

Bring a medium pot of water to a boil. Add the pistachios and blanch for 1 minute, then drain them. Place them in a clean kitchen towel and rub gently to remove their skins; discard the skins. Transfer two-thirds of the pistachios to a food processor and pulse to finely chop them, then transfer to a large bowl. Coarsely chop the remaining pistachios and set them aside for garnish.

Add the all-purpose (plain) flour, amaranth flour, baking soda (bicarbonate of soda), sugar, cinnamon, nutmeg, and salt to the bowl with the finely chopped pistachios.

In the food processor, combine the bananas, lemon juice, vinegar, and oil and process until smooth and well combined. Pour the banana mixture into the bowl with the flour mixture and stir to combine.

Pour the batter into the prepared pan, then sprinkle the tops with the coarsely chopped pistachios. Bake the muffins for about 35 minutes, until a toothpick inserted into the center of a muffin comes out clean.

Amaranth is not a "true" grain and it does not contain gluten. For a gluten-free version of this cake, replace the all-purpose (plain) flour with gluten-free flour.

Mango-Papaya Tiramisu

Tiramisù al mango e papaia

- 1 (13.5 oz/400 ml) can full-fat coconut milk, plus a scant 1 cup (220 ml) coconut milk
- 1 cup plus 1 tablespoon (130 g) self-rising flour, sifted
- 1 teaspoon yeast
- ½ cup (100 g) granulated sugar
- Pinch of salt
- 3½ tablespoons corn oil
- 1 teaspoon apple cider vinegar
- 1 vanilla pod, split lengthwise and seeds scraped
- ⅓ cup (40 g) powdered (icing) sugar
- 1⅔ cups (400 ml) passion fruit juice
- 1 mango, pitted, peeled, and thinly sliced
- 1 papaya, peeled, seeded, and thinly sliced

Preparation Time: 20 minutes
Cooking Time: 30 minutes
Serves: 6

Refrigerate the unopened can of coconut milk overnight.

Preheat the oven to 350°F (180°C). Line an 8-inch (20 cm) square pan with parchment paper.

In a medium bowl, combine the flour, yeast, granulated sugar, and salt.

In a small saucepan, warm the scant 1 cup (220 ml) coconut milk over medium-low heat. Remove from the heat and whisk in the oil, vinegar, and vanilla seeds.

Pour the coconut milk mixture over the flour mixture and combine with a spatula to prevent lumps forming. Pour the batter into the prepared pan and bake for about 30 minutes. Let cool in the pan, then turn it out onto a cutting board and cut it into 4 by ½-inch (10 by 1 cm) rectangles.

Open the chilled can of coconut milk and scoop the solid white portion into a large bowl (discard the clearish liquid or refrigerate for another use). Add the powdered (icing) sugar and whip with a handheld mixer until it holds soft peaks.

Arrange a layer of the cake rectangles in an 8 x 4-inch (20 x 10 cm) loaf pan and drizzle them with some of the passion fruit juice. Cover with a layer of mango and papaya slices, then top with some of the whipped coconut cream. Continue this layering until all the ingredients have been used up. Cover and refrigerate the tiramisu for 4 hours, then serve.

When chilled, the coconut milk solids separate from the coconut water in the can, making it easy to scoop the solid portion out to use for whipped coconut cream. The coconut water can be used in smoothies.

Cashew-Milk Cheesecake

Cheesecake vegano alle pesche

- 2½ cups (300 g) cashews
- 1 cup (120 g) raw almonds
- 6 dried dates, pitted
- Zest and juice of 1 lemon
- Scant 1 cup (200 ml) sweetened almond milk
- 2½ tablespoons peanut butter
- 3½ tablespoons coconut oil
- Pinch of salt
- 2 yellow peaches, halved, pitted, and cut into small wedges

Preparation Time: 20 minutes plus resting time
Cooking Time: 1 hour
Serves: 8

Line a 7-inch (18 cm) springform pan with parchment paper.

Soak the cashews in cold water to cover for 30 minutes.

In a food processor, combine the almonds, dates, and lemon zest and process until well combined. Press the mixture over the bottom of the prepared pan.

Drain the cashews and transfer them to the food processor. Add the lemon juice, almond milk, peanut butter, coconut oil, and salt and process until smooth and well combined.

Pour the cashew mixture into the pan over the almond-date crust, level the top with a spatula, cover, and refrigerate for at least 4 hours, or until set. Remove the springform ring, discard the parchment, and set the cheesecake on a serving plate. Top with the peaches and serve.

Coconut oil is obtained from the meat of coconuts. It is solid at room temperature and has a very high smoke point, so it can also be used for frying.

Avocado-Honey Parfait

Crema di yogurt al miele e avocado

- ¾ cup (100 g) shelled hazelnuts
- 1 cup (250 ml) plain full-fat yogurt
- 3½ tablespoons honey
- 1 avocado

Preparation Time: 25 minutes
Cooking Time: 10 minutes
Serves: 4

Preheat the oven to 325°F (160°C).

Spread the hazelnuts over a rimmed sheet pan and toast in the oven for 10 minutes. Transfer them to a clean kitchen towel and rub gently to remove their skins; discard the skins and transfer the hazelnuts to a food processor. Pulse until finely chopped.

In a medium bowl, mix together the yogurt and honey. Halve, pit, and peel the avocado. Dice the flesh and immediately add it to the yogurt mixture to prevent discoloration. Stir gently to combine.

Transfer the mixture to a glass serving bowl and sprinkle with the hazelnuts. Chill until ready to serve.

Rice Pudding with Fruit Compote

Composta di frutta su crema di riso

- 4 teaspoons loose jasmine tea
- 7 oz (200 g) dried apricots
- 3½ oz (100 g) pitted prunes
- 2 cups (500 ml) unsweetened almond milk
- 1 vanilla pod, split lengthwise and seeds scraped out
- Pinch of salt
- ¼ cup (50 g) rice
- 2½ tablespoons honey

Preparation Time: 10 minutes
Cooking Time: 45 minutes
Serves: 4

In a small saucepan, bring 1⅔ cups (400 ml) water to a boil, then add the tea and let it infuse for 5 minutes. Strain the tea and return it to the pot. Bring it back to just under a boil, then add the apricots and prunes. Reduce the heat to low and cook for 10 minutes. Turn off the heat and let the compote cool.

In a small saucepan, combine the milk, vanilla pod and seeds, and a pinch of salt and bring the milk just to a boil.

Add the rice, reduce the heat to low, and cook, stirring often, for about 30 minutes. Turn the heat off and discard the vanilla pod. Add the honey, then blend directly in the pot using a hand blender. Let cool completely.

Drain any excess liquid from the fruit compote.

Divide the rice pudding among four bowls, arrange the fruit compote on top, and serve.

The almond milk can be replaced with oat, rice, or soy milk, if preferred.

The rice pudding can be flavored with a 1½-inch (4 cm) cinnamon stick and the crushed seeds of 4 green cardamom pods.

Chestnut Pudding

Teste di moro

- 10½ oz (300 g) dried chestnuts
- 4¼ cups (1 l) milk
- 1 bay leaf
- Pinch of salt
- 6 tablespoons (40 g) unsweetened cocoa powder, sifted
- Scant 1 cup (200 ml) brandy
- ½ cup (100 g) granulated sugar
- Scant 1 cup (200 ml) heavy (whipping) cream
- ⅓ cup (40 g) powdered (icing) sugar

Preparation Time: 20 minutes plus soaking time
Cooking Time: 40 minutes
Serves: 6

Soak the chestnuts in cold water to cover overnight, then drain them and place them in a small saucepan. Add the milk, bay leaf, and salt. Cover with the lid ajar and cook the chestnuts over low heat for 40 minutes, or until they are cooked through. Discard the bay leaf.

Drain the chestnuts and pass them through a food mill into a medium bowl. Add the cocoa powder, brandy, and granulated sugar and stir to combine. Shape the mixture into 6 balls and place them in individual serving bowls.

In a large bowl using a whisk or handheld mixer, whip the cream with the powdered (icing) sugar until it holds medium peaks.

Top the chestnut pudding with the whipped cream and serve.

Chestnuts do not contain gluten, so this dessert can be eaten by people who suffer from celiac disease or gluten intolerance. Chestnuts are also rich in vitamin B and phosphorus. The dried chestnuts can be replaced with 1 lb 5 oz (600 g) cooked chestnuts.

Berries with Granola and Almond Cream

Frutti di bosco con granola e crema di mandorle

- ¾ cup (100 g) blanched almonds
- 2¾ cups (250 g) rolled oats
- Scant ½ cup (50 g) coconut flour
- ⅓ cup (50 g) raw almonds
- 6 tablespoons (50 g) pumpkin seeds
- 3½ tablespoons sunflower seeds
- 3 tablespoons flaxseeds (linseeds)
- 1 tablespoon ground cinnamon
- Pinch of salt
- 2 tablespoons coconut oil
- Scant ½ cup (100 ml) maple syrup
- ⅓ cup (50 g) raisins
- ¼ cup (60 ml) brown rice syrup
- Scant 1 cup (200 ml) unsweetened almond milk
- 10½ oz (300 g) mixed wild berries

Preparation Time: 20 minutes plus soaking time
Cooking Time: 25 minutes
Serves: 4 (granola serves 8)

Soak the blanched almonds in cold water to cover for about 1 hour.

Preheat the oven to 350°F (180°C). Line a sheet pan with parchment paper.

In a large bowl, combine the oats, coconut flour, raw almonds, pumpkin seeds, sunflower seeds, flaxseeds, cinnamon, and salt, and mix.

In a large spouted measuring cup, combine the coconut oil, maple syrup, and 2 tablespoons water and blend with a hand blender until the mixture is well combined. Pour the coconut oil mixture over the oat mixture and stir until well combined, then spread the mixture over the prepared pan.

Bake the granola for about 25 minutes, stirring every 10 minutes, then remove from the oven, add the raisins, and let cool, then break up any large chunks.

Drain the soaked almonds and transfer them to a food processor. Process until puréed and smooth. Add the brown rice syrup and the almond milk and process for a few more seconds.

Pour the almond mixture into individual serving bowls and arrange the berries on the top, then garnish with some of the granola. Store the remaining granola in an airtight container at room temperature.

Hazelnuts, chopped walnuts, and chopped dried dates or apricots can be added to the granola.

Honey-Almond Nougat

Turronis, Torroncini con miele e mandorle

- 1½ cups (200 g) blanched almonds
- ¾ cup plus 2 tablespoons (200 g) acacia honey
- 1 egg white
- Zest of 1 lemon

Preparation Time: 20 minutes
Cooking Time: 2 hours
Serves: 8

Preheat the oven to 250°F (120°C). Line a sheet pan with parchment paper.

Place the almonds on the pan and toast them in the oven for 15 minutes, until they are golden. Let cool.

In a small saucepan, combine the honey and egg white and cook over very low heat, stirring often, for about 2 hours, until the mixture thickens.

Add the toasted almonds and lemon zest to the saucepan and stir to coat them with the honey mixture. Pour the mixture onto the parchment-lined sheet pan, spreading it to a depth of approximately ½ inch (1 cm). Let cool, cut it into pieces, and serve. Store the nougat in an airtight container at room temperature.

Make your own almond milk using skin-on almonds: in a food processor, combine ¾ cup (100 g) almonds and ⅔ cup (150 ml) water and process until the mixture is fine and the almonds are evenly ground. Pour the mixture into a small colander lined with cheesecloth and let drain for 1 hour, then gather the edges of the cheesecloth and twist to squeeze all the liquid out of the almond pulp. Stir about 3½ cups (850 ml) water into the resulting almond milk, bottle it, and store in the refrigerator for 2 to 3 days. Shake before using.

Spiced Figs

Fichi alle spezie

- 1 teaspoon ground cinnamon
- 1 teaspoon ground coriander
- 1 teaspoon ground ginger
- 2 whole cloves
- 3½ oz (100 g) superfine (caster) sugar
- Zest of 1 orange, removed with a vegetable peeler and cut into thin strips
- 12 ripe figs

Preparation Time: 2 hours
Cooking Time: 20 minutes
Serves: 6

In a medium saucepan, combine the cinnamon, coriander, ginger, cloves, sugar, and orange zest and mix well. Pour in 2 cups (500 ml) water and bring to a boil, stirring until the sugar has dissolved, then boil, without stirring, for 10 minutes.

Add the figs to the pan and cook for 3 to 4 minutes; do not bring the syrup back to a boil. Remove the pan from the heat and let the figs cool in the syrup.

Drain the figs, reserving the syrup, and put them in a serving bowl. Return the syrup to the pan and bring to a simmer over medium heat; simmer until reduced by half. Remove and discard the cloves.

Pour the syrup over the figs. Let cool before serving.

Coriander is a plant from the same family as anise and cumin. The fresh leaves (known in some parts of the world as cilantro) are used in cooking, and the seeds are ground and used as a spice.

Frozen Berry Soufflés

Souffle gelato di lamponi e fragole

- 7 oz (200 g) raspberries, plus more for garnish
- 7 oz (200 g) strawberries, hulled
- ¾ cup plus 2 tablespoons (175 g) superfine (caster) sugar
- 3 tsp agar-agar
- 2 cups (500 ml) heavy (whipping) cream
- 2 tablespoons strawberry liqueur or other fruit liqueur
- Grated zest of ½ lemon

Preparation Time: 3 hours 20 minutes (including freezing)
Serves: 6

Cut 6 1½-inch-wide (4 cm) strips of parchment paper long enough to fit the inner circumference of 6 individual soufflé dishes. Use adhesive tape to affix the paper to the rims of the dishes.

In a blender, combine the raspberries, strawberries, sugar, and agar-agar and blend until smooth and frothy. Pour the mixture into a bowl and set aside.

In a large bowl, using a handheld mixer or a whisk, whip the cream until it holds stiff peaks.

Add the liqueur and lemon zest to the berry mixture, then carefully fold in the whipped cream, taking care not to knock air out of the mixture.

Pour the mixture into the lined soufflé dishes and freeze for 2 hours.

To serve, remove the paper from the dishes and garnish the soufflés with raspberries.

Recipe Lists & Index

Recipe List

Snacks & Small Plates

Marinated Eggplant 16
Trio of Dips: Eggplant, Pea, and Robiola Cheese 18
Sprouted Chickpea Hummus 19
Cannellini and Black Bean Hummus 20
Trio of Dips: Red Lentil, Fava Bean, and Chickpea 22
Bruschettas with Kale, Tomato, and White Beans 23
Watercress Tartines 24
Sunflower and Poppyseed Crackers 26
Seeded Crackers with Shallots 27
Mini Semolina Custards 28
Fava and Chia Pâté 30
Kale and Red Onion Flan 31
Tomato Tartlets 32
Fried Squash Blossoms with Tofu and Capers 34
Tomato Rice Fritters 35
Fried Veggie Chips 36
Medley of Fried Snacks 38
Rice Balls 40
Artichoke And Fennel Fritters 41
Cauliflower Custard with Broccoli and Walnuts 42
Zucchini and Goat Cheese Frittata 44
Vegetable and Quinoa Tartare 45
Onion Bundt Cake 46

Breads & Pizzas

Potato Flatbread with Salad 54
Sourdough Farro Bread 56
Soda Bread with Seeds and Raisins 58
Cornmeal-Millet Rolls 59
Walnut, Fig, and Raisin Rolls 60
Raisin and Rosemary Rolls 62
Whole-Grain Olive Focaccia 63
Ferrara Breadsticks 64
Hemp Sandwich Bread with Thyme and Pumpkin Seeds 66
Easter Cheese Bread 68
Onion Focaccia 69
Herb-Stuffed Bread 70
Buckwheat Pizza with Green Beans and Tomatoes 72
Basic Bread Dough 74
Tomato Pizza 75
Oat Flour Pizza with Mushroom-Stuffed Crusts 76
White Pizza 78
Potato Pizza 79
Puglian Focaccia 80
Kamut Calzone with Asparagus and Egg 82

Salads & Vegetable Sides

Fennel and Artichoke Salad 92
Green Salad with Three Dressings 94
Composed Vegetable Salad with Tarragon Vinaigrette 95
Roasted Vegetable Salad 96
Baby Zucchini Salad 98
Fennel and Pink Grapefruit 99
Avocado Salad 100
Spinach and Mushroom Salad 102
Asparagus and Herb Salad 103
Winter Salad with Mustard Dressing 104
Farmhouse Salad 106
Warm Couscous Salad with Tomatoes and Peppers 107
Farro Salad with Poached Eggs 108
Rice Salad with Artichokes and Fennel 110
Pasta Salad with Peas and Mint Pesto 111
Harvest Salad Sandwiches 112
Farro Salad with Olives and Tomatoes 114
Rice Salad with Black Olives 116
Bread Salad with Cucumbers and Tomatoes 117
Sprouted Lentil Salad with Three Dressings 118
Millet Salad with Beets and Romanesco 120
Pasta Salad with Tomato and Avocado 121
Warm Black Rice Salad with Tofu 122
Black Chickpea Salad with Apple and Sunchoke 124
Sautéed Chicories with Fava Purée 125
Sauteed Spring Vegetables 126
White Beans and Tomato with Toast 128
Sautéed Vegetables with Sprouts and Seeds 129
Vegetable Stir-Fry 130
Spring Ratatouille 132
Roasted Balsamic Tomatoes 134
Green Beans with Tomato 135
Warm Asparagus Salad 136

Soups & Stews

Summer Vegetable Soup 144
Cream of Asparagus Soup 146
Tomato and Sweet Pepper Soup 147
Beet and Fennel Gazpacho 148
Green Creamed Soup 150
Pea and Lettuce Soup 151
Carrot and Paprika Soup 152
Carrot Soup with Zucchini Salsa 154
Chickpea Soup with Tagliatelle 155
Winter Vegetable Soup 156
Millet and Buckwheat Soup 157
Kale-and-Potato Bread Soup 158
Bread and Potato Stew with Arugula 160
Barley and Porcini Soup 161
Cornmeal and Vegetable Soup 162
Genovese Minestrone 164
Chard and Chickpea Soup with Tofu 165
Tofu and Vegetable Soup 166
Fresh Pasta and Beans in Tomato Broth 168

Cabbage Soup with Pasta and all the Beans 169
Pumpkin Stew with Adzuki Beans 170
Vegetable Stew with Peppers and Tomatoes 172
Tomato and Mushroom Stew 173

**Pasta, Dumplings
& Crêpes**

Whole Wheat Tagliatelle with Avocado Pesto 182
Farro Spaghetti with Vegetables and Fresh Herbs 184
Pici with Walnut Pesto 185
Pasta with Cauliflower and Pine Nuts 186
Pappardelle with Walnuts 188
Spaghetti with Fava-Tomato Sauce 189
Pasta with Favas and Peas 190
Pasta with Parsley and Breadcrumbs 192
Saffron Gnocchi 193
Pumpkin Gnocchi with Almond-Sage Pesto 194
Gnocchi with Cocoa and Raisins 196
Sweet Spiced Tortelli 197
Kamut Gnocchi with Fava Purée 198
Baked Farro Gnocchi with Cauliflower 200
Buckwheat Cannelloni with Eggplant 201
Oat, Spinach, and Ricotta Dumplings 202
Bread Dumplings in Broth 204
Ricotta and Greens Dumplings 206
Bread Gnocchi with Zucchini Salsa 207
Chickpea Ravioli with Tomato Sauce 208
Buckwheat Crêpe Cake with Chard and Artichokes 210
Ravioli with Ricotta, Spinach, and Marjoram 212
Crêpes with Green Peas 213
Rye Crêpe Noodles with Celeriac 214
Pasta Bundles with Ratatouille 216
Crêpes with Spinach and Ricotta 217
Baked Crêpes with Tomato and Eggplant 218
Chestnut Crêpes with Sweet Peppers and Robiola Cheese 220
Baked Pasta with Sunchokes and Spinach 221
Buckwheat Lasagna with Broccoli 222
Eggplant and Ricotta Lasagna 224
Baked Fusilli with Tomato and Mozzarella 225
Chestnut Lasagna with Squash and Kale 226

**Vegetable Tarts &
Pastries**

Rye Crostata with Peas and Asparagus 234
Mini Lentil and Chickpea Quiche 236
Spinach Quiche with Ricotta Salata 237
Upside-Down Pumpkin and Pepper Tart 238
Leek and Apple Quiche 240
Zucchini and Rice Galette 241
Zucchini and Pine Nut Tart 242
Pumpkin Tart 244
Cauliflower Tart 246
Artichoke and Zucchini Strudel 247
Eggplant-Tomato Strudel 248
Fried Turnovers with Capers and Olives 250
Fried Turnovers with Tomato and Ricotta 251

Flaky Onion and Tomato Roll 252
Radicchio Pie 254
Onion and Potato Slab Pie 256
Fava and Chestnut Pie 257
Artichoke Pie 258
Beet Torte 260
Swiss Chard and Potato Pie 262
Ricotta and Sweet Potato Tart 263
Amaranth Cake with Caponata 264
Chickpea and Onion Flatbread 266
Truffled Polenta Cake 267

Grains, Gratins & Stuffed Vegetables

Wild Rice Balls 276
Rice Pilaf with Roasted Carrots and Asparagus 278
Rice with Mushrooms and Tomatoes 279
Rice with Cabbage and Beans 280
Tomato Risotto with Spring Vegetables 282
Radicchio Risotto with Orange 283
Vegetable Fried Rice 284
Fava Bean Risotto with Pecorino 286
Green Risotto with Peas 287
Quinoa Torte 288
Baked Wild Rice with Parsnip 290
Rice Gratin with Brussels Sprouts and Walnuts 291
Seedy Basmati Rice 292
Potato-Leek Gratin 294
Swiss Chard Gratin 295
Broccoli, Kale, and Cauliflower Gratin 296
Rice Timbale with Zucchini and Peppers 298
Rice and Eggplant Casserole 300
Artichoke, Potato, and Rice Casserole 301
Tomato Strata 302
Polenta with Kale and Beans 304
Roasted Cardoons with Tomatoes and Pecorino 305
Stuffed Artichokes with Quinoa and Mushrooms 306
Trio of Stuffed Vegetables with Avocado and Cheese 308
Herby Stuffed Tomatoes 309
Stuffed Cabbage with Buckwheat and Pumpkin 310
Escarole Stuffed with Olives and Capers 312
Millet-Stuffed Tomatoes and Zucchini 313
Zucchini and Halloumi Gratin 314
Stuffed Squash Blossoms 316
Sweet-and-Sour Stuffed Peppers 317

Sweets & Desserts

Whole-Grain Cake with Almond Butter 324
Orange Bundt Cake with Fruit Salad 326
Bread and Fruit Cake 327
Seeded Spice Cake 328
Honey-Quinoa Cake 330
Almond-and-Honey Cookies 331
Chocolate Granola Bars 332
Fruitcake 334

Sour Cherry Tart 335
Peach-Blackberry Crostata 336
Banana-Pistachio Muffins 338
Mango-Papaya Tiramisu 339
Cashew-Milk Cheesecake 340
Avocado-Honey Parfait 342
Rice Pudding with Fruit Compote 344
Chestnut Pudding 345
Berries with Granola and Almond Cream 346
Honey-Almond Nougat 348
Spiced Figs 349
Frozen Berry Soufflés 350

Recipe List by Icon

(DF) **Dairy Free**

Asparagus and Herb Salad 103
Avocado Salad 100
Baked Farro Gnocchi with Cauliflower 200
Baked Pasta with Sunchokes and Spinach 221
Baked Wild Rice with Parsnip 290
Banana-Pistachio Muffins 338
Barley and Porcini Soup 161
Basic Bread Dough 74
Beet Gazpacho 148
Berries with Granola and Almond Cream 346
Black Chickpea Salad with Apple and Sunchoke 124
Bread and Potato Stew with Arugula 160
Broccoli, Kale, and Cauliflower Gratin 296
Bruschettas with Kale, Tomato, and White Beans 23
Cannellini and Black Bean Hummus 20
Carrot Soup with Zucchini Salsa 152
Chard and Chickpea Soup with Tofu 165
Chickpea and Onion Flatbread 266
Chickpea Soup with Tagliatelle 155
Chocolate Granola Bars 332
Composed Vegetable Salad with Tarragon Vinaigrette 95
Cornmeal and Vegetable Soup 162
Cornmeal-Millet Rolls 59
Crêpes with Green Peas 213
Eggplant-Tomato Strudel 248
Escarole Stuffed with Olives and Capers 312
Farro Salad with Poached Eggs 108
Farro Spaghetti with Vegetables and Fresh Herbs 184
Fennel and Artichoke Salad 92
Fennel and Pink Grapefruit 99
Fresh Pasta and Beans in Tomato Broth 168
Fried Squash Blossoms with Tofu and Capers 34
Fried Veggie Chips 36
Green Beans with Tomato 135
Harvest Salad Sandwiches 112
Hemp Sandwich Bread with Thyme and Pumpkin Seeds 66
Honey-Almond Nougat 348
Honey-Quinoa Cake 330
Kale and Red Onion Flan 31
Fava and Chia Pâté 30
Kamut Gnocchi with Fava Purée 198
Pasta Salad with Peas and Mint Pesto 111
Mango-Papaya Tiramisu 339
Marinated Eggplant 16
Millet and Buckwheat Soup 157
Millet Salad with Beets and Romanesco 120

Mini Lentil and Chickpea Quiche 236
Oat Flour Pizza with Mushroom-Stuffed Crusts 76
Onion and Potato Slab Pie 256
Pasta Salad with Tomato and Avocado 121
Pasta with Favas and Peas 190
Pasta with Parsley and Breadcrumbs 192
Polenta with Kale and Beans 304
Potato Flatbread with Salad 54
Puglian Focaccia 80
Pumpkin Gnocchi with Almond-Sage Pesto 194
Pumpkin Stew with Adzuki Beans 170
Quinoa Torte 288
Radicchio Pie 254
Radicchio Risotto with Orange 283
Raisin and Rosemary Rolls 62
Ravioli with Ricotta, Spinach, and Marjoram 212
Rice Pilaf with Roasted Carrots and Asparagus 278
Rice Pudding with Fruit Compote 344
Rice Salad with Black Olives 116
Roasted Balsamic Tomatoes 134
Roasted Vegetable Salad 96
Sautéed Chicories with Fava Purée 125
Sauteed Spring Vegetables 126
Sautéed Vegetables with Sprouts and Seeds 129
Seeded Crackers with Shallots 27
Seeded Spice Cake 328
Seedy Basmati Rice 392
Sourdough Farro Bread 56
Spiced Figs 349
Spinach and Mushroom Salad 102
Spring Ratatouille 132
Sprouted Chickpea Hummus 19
Sprouted Lentil Salad with Three Dressings 118
Stuffed Cabbage with Buckwheat and Pumpkin 310
Summer Vegetable Soup 144
Tofu and Vegetable Soup 166
Tomato and Mushroom Stew 173
Tomato Pizza 75
Vegetable and Quinoa Tartare 45
Vegetable Fried Rice 274
Vegetable Stew with Peppers and Tomatoes 172
Vegetable Stir-Fry 130
Warm Asparagus Salad 136
Warm Black Rice Salad with Tofu 122
Warm Couscous Salad with Tomatoes and Peppers 107
Watercress Tartines 24
Whole Wheat Tagliatelle with Avocado Pesto 182
Whole-Grain Cake with Almond Butter 324
Whole-Grain Olive Focaccia 63
Wild Rice Balls 276
Winter Salad with Mustard Dressing 104

(GF) **Gluten Free**

Amaranth and Ricotta Cake with Caponata 264
Artichoke, Potato, and Rice Casserole 301
Asparagus and Herb Salad 103
Avocado-Honey Parfait 342
Avocado Salad 100
Baby Zucchini Salad 98
Berries with Granola and Almond Cream 346
Black Chickpea Salad with Apple and Sunchoke 124
Cannellini and Black Bean Hummus 20
Chard and Chickpea Soup with Tofu 165
Chestnut Crepes with Sweet Peppers and Robiola Cheese 220
Chestnut Pudding 345
Chickpea and Onion Flatbread 266
Chocolate Granola Bars 332
Composed Vegetable Salad with Tarragon Vinaigrette 95
Cornmeal and Vegetable Soup 162
Cornmeal-Millet Rolls 59
Fava and Chia Pâté 30
Fava Bean Risotto with Pecorino 286
Fennel and Artichoke Salad 92
Fennel and Pink Grapefruit 99
Frozen Berry Soufflés 350
Green Beans with Tomato 135
Green Risotto with Peas 287
Honey-Almond Nougat 348
Kale and Red Onion Flan 31
Marinated Eggplant 16
Millet and Buckwheat Soup 157
Millet Salad with Beets and Romanesco 120
Millet-Stuffed Tomatoes and Zucchini 313
Pasta Salad with Tomato and Avocado 121
Pea and Lettuce Soup 151
Polenta with Kale and Beans 304
Pumpkin Stew with Adzuki Beans 170
Quinoa Torte 288
Radicchio Risotto with Orange 283
Rice and Eggplant Casserole 300
Rice Pudding with Fruit Compote 344
Rice Salad with Artichokes and Fennel 110
Rice Salad with Black Olives 116
Rice Timbale with Zucchini and Peppers 298
Rice with Cabbage and Beans 280
Rice with Mushrooms and Tomatoes 279
Ricotta and Sweet Potato Tart 263
Roasted Balsamic Tomatoes 134
Roasted Vegetable Salad 96
Rye Crostata with Asparagus and Peas 234
Sautéed Chicories with Fava Purée 125
Sauteed Spring Vegetables 126
Sautéed Vegetables with Sprouts and Seeds 129
Spiced Figs 349
Spinach and Mushroom Salad 102
Spring Ratatouille 132
Stuffed Cabbage with Buckwheat and Pumpkin 310

Stuffed Squash Blossoms 316
Summer Vegetable Soup 144
Tomato and Sweet Pepper Soup 147
Tomato Risotto with Spring Vegetables 282
Trio of Dips: Eggplant, Pea, and Robiola Cheese 18
Truffled Polenta Cake 267
Vegetable and Quinoa Tartare 45
Vegetable Fried Rice 284
Vegetable Stew with Peppers and Tomatoes 172
Vegetable Stir-Fry 130
Warm Black Rice Salad with Tofu 122
Winter Salad with Mustard Dressing 104
Zucchini and Goat Cheese Frittata 44

(VG) **Vegan**

Asparagus and Herb Salad 103
Avocado Salad 100
Baked Farro Gnocchi with Cauliflower 200
Baked Pasta with Sunchokes and Spinach 221
Baked Wild Rice with Parsnip 290
Banana-Pistachio Muffins 338
Barley and Porcini Soup 161
Basic Bread Dough 74
Beet and Fennel Gazpacho 148
Berries with Granola and Almond Cream 346
Black Chickpea Salad with Apple and Sunchoke 124
Bread Salad with Cucumbers and Tomatoes 117
Bread and Potato Stew with Arugula 160
Broccoli, Kale, and Cauliflower Gratin 296
Bruschettas with Kale, Tomato, and White Beans 23
Cannellini and Black Bean Hummus 20
Carrot Soup with Zucchini Salsa 154
Cashew-Milk Cheesecake 340
Chard and Chickpea Soup with Tofu 165
Chickpea and Onion Flatbread 266
Chickpea Soup with Tagliatelle 155
Chocolate Granola Bars 332
Cornmeal and Vegetable Soup 162
Cornmeal-Millet Rolls 59
Crepes with Green Peas 213
Eggplant-Tomato Strudel 248
Escarole Stuffed with Olives and Capers 312
Farro Spaghetti with Vegetables 184
Fava and Chia Pâté 30
Fennel and Artichoke Salad 92
Fennel and Pink Grapefruit 99
Fried Veggie Chips 36
Green Beans with Tomato 135
Harvest Salad Sandwiches 112
Honey-Quinoa Cake 330
Kamut Gnocchi with Fava Purée 198
Mango-Papaya Tiramisu 339
Marinated Eggplant 16
Millet and Buckwheat Soup 157

Millet Salad with Beets and Romanesco 120
Mini Lentil and Chickpea Quiche 236
Oat Flour Pizza with Mushroom-Stuffed Crusts 76
Onion and Potato Slab Pie 256
Pasta Salad with Peas and Mint Pesto 111
Pasta with Favas and Peas 190
Pasta with Parsley and Breadcrumbs 192
Polenta with Kale and Beans 304
Pumpkin Gnocchi with Almond Pesto 194
Pumpkin Stew with Adzuki Beans 170
Radicchio Risotto with Orange 283
Raisin and Rosemary Rolls 62
Ravioli with Ricotta, Spinach, and Marjoram 212
Rice Pilaf with Roasted Carrots and Asparagus 278
Rice Pudding with Fruit Compote 344
Rice Salad with Black Olives 116
Roasted Balsamic Tomatoes 134
Roasted Vegetable Salad 94
Sautéed Chicories with Fava Purée 125
Sauteed Spring Vegetables 126
Sautéed Vegetables with Sprouts and Seeds 129
Seeded Crackers with Shallots 27
Seeded Spice Cake 328
Seedy Basmati Rice 292
Sourdough Farro Bread 56
Spinach and Mushroom Salad 102
Spring Ratatouille 132
Sprouted Chickpea Hummus 19
Sprouted Lentil Salad with Three Dressings 118
Stuffed Cabbage with Buckwheat and Pumpkin 310
Summer Vegetable Soup 144
Tofu and Vegetable Soup 166
Tomato and Mushroom Stew 173
Tomato Pizza 75
Vegetable and Quinoa Tartare 45
Vegetable Fried Rice 284
Vegetable Stew with Peppers and Tomatoes 172
Vegetable Stir-Fry 130
Warm Black Rice Salad with Tofu 122
Warm Couscous Salad with Tomatoes and Peppers 107
Whole Wheat Tagliatelle with Avocado Pesto 182
Wild Rice Balls 276

(CT) **Contemporary Tastes**

Amaranth and Ricotta Cake with Caponata 264
Baked Farro Gnocchi with Cauliflower 200
Baked Wild Rice with Parsnip 290
Banana-Pistachio Muffins 338
Beet and Fennel Gazpacho 198
Berries with Granola and Almond Cream 346
Black Chickpea Salad with Apple and Sunchoke 124
Cannellini and Black Bean Hummus 20
Chard and Chickpea Soup with Tofu 165
Chestnut Crepes with Sweet Peppers and Robiola Cheese 220

Cornmeal-Millet Rolls 59
Fried Squash Blossoms with Tofu and Capers 34
Fried Veggie Chips 36
Hemp Sandwich Bread with Thyme and Pumpkin Seeds 66
Kale and Red Onion Flan 31
Kamut Gnocchi with Fava Purée 198
Leek and Apple Quiche 240
Mango-Papaya Tiramisu 339
Millet Salad with Beets and Romanesco 120
Oat Flour Pizza with Mushroom-Stuffed Crusts 76
Onion and Potato Slab Pie 256
Pasta Salad with Tomato and Avocado 121
Pumpkin Stew with Adzuki Beans 170
Quinoa Torte 288
Radicchio Risotto with Orange 283
Ravioli with Ricotta, Spinach, and Marjoram 212
Rye Crepe Noodles with Celeriac 214
Sautéed Vegetables with Sprouts and Seeds 129
Seeded Crackers with Shallots 27
Seeded Spice Cake 328
Seedy Basmati Rice 292
Sprouted Chickpea Hummus 19
Sprouted Lentil Salad 118
Tofu and Vegetable Soup 166
Tomato and Mushroom Stew 173
Trio of Dips: Red Lentil, Fava Bean, and Chickpea 22
Vegetable Fried Rice 384
Vegetable Stir-Fry 130
Warm Black Rice Salad with Tofu 122
Wild Rice Balls 276

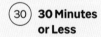

**30 Minutes
or Less**

Avocado Salad 100
Baked Fusilli with Tomato and Mozzarella 225
Beet and Fennel Gazpacho 148
Cannellini and Black Bean Hummus 20
Fennel and Artichoke Salad 92
Fennel and Pink Grapefruit 92
Fried Veggie Chips 36
Green Salad with Three Dressings 94
Harvest Salad Sandwiches 112
Pappardelle with Walnuts 188
Pasta with Cauliflower and Pine Nuts 186
Pasta with Parsley and Breadcrumbs 192
Pici with Walnut Pesto 185
Spinach and Mushroom Salad 102
Sprouted Chickpea Hummus 19
Tofu and Vegetable Soup 166
Trio of Dips: Red Lentil, Fava Bean, and Chickpea 22
Watercress Tartines 24
Whole Wheat Tagliatelle with Avocado Pesto 182
Winter Salad with Mustard Dressing 104

(5) **5 Ingredients or Less**

Avocado-Honey Parfait 342
Baby Zucchini Salad 98
Barley and Porcini Soup 161
Basic Bread Dough 74
Bread Stew with Potato and Arugula 160
Cannellini and Black Bean Hummus 20
Chickpea and Onion Flatbread 266
Ferrara Breadsticks 64
Fresh Pasta and Beans in Tomato Broth 168
Fried Turnovers with Tomato and Ricotta 251
Fried Veggie Chips 36
Honey-Almond Nougat 348
Pappardelle with Walnuts 188
Pici with Walnut Pesto 185
Potato Flatbread with Salad 54
Potato Pizza 79
Roasted Balsamic Tomatoes 134
Saffron Gnocchi 193
Sourdough Farro Bread 56
Spaghetti with Fava-Tomato Sauce 189
Spinach and Mushroom Salad 102
Swiss Chard Gratin 295
Watercress Tartines 24
White Pizza 78

Index

Note: Page references in bold indicate photographs.

A

agar-agar, 30, 320
almonds
    Almond-and-Honey Cookies, 331
    Berries with Granola and Almond Cream, 346, **347**
    butter, 324
    Cashew-Milk Cheesecake, 340, **341**
    Fruitcake, 334
    Honey-Almond Nougat, 348
    milk, 348
    Pumpkin Gnocchi with Almond-Sage Pesto, 194, **195**
    Whole-Grain Cake with Almond Butter, 324, **325**
amaranth, 90, 264
    Amaranth Cake with Caponata, 264, **265**
apples
    Black Chickpea Salad with Apple and Sunchoke, 124
    Bread and Fruit Cake, 327
    Honey-Quinoa Cake, 330
    Leek and Apple Quiche, 240
apricots
    Rice Pudding with Fruit Compote, 344
    Seeded Spice Cake, 328, **329**
artichokes
    Artichoke and Fennel Fritters, 41
    Artichoke and Zucchini Strudel, 247
    Artichoke Pie, 258, **259**
    Artichoke, Potato, and Rice Casserole, 301
    Buckwheat Crêpe Cake with Chard and Artichokes, 210, **211**
    Fennel and Artichoke Salad, 92, **93**
    Rice Salad with Artichokes and Fennel, 110
    Sauteed Spring Vegetables, 126, **127**
    Spring Ratatouille, 132, **133**
    Stuffed Artichokes with Quinoa and Mushrooms, 306, **307**
asparagus
    Asparagus and Herb Salad, 103
    Composed Vegetable Salad with Tarragon Vinaigrette, 95
    Cream of Asparagus Soup, 146
    Kamut Calzone with Asparagus and Egg, 82, **83**
    Rice Pilaf with Roasted Carrots and Asparagus, 278
    Rye Crostata with Peas and Asparagus, 234, **235**
    Spring Ratatouille, 132, **133**
    Warm Asparagus Salad, 136, **137**
aspics, 13
avocados, 182
    Avocado-Honey Parfait, 342, **343**
    Avocado Salad, 100, **101**
    Pasta Salad with Tomato and Avocado, 121
    Trio of Stuffed Vegetables with Avocado and Chickpeas, 308
    Whole Wheat Tagliatelle with Avocado Pesto, 182, **183**

B

bananas
    Banana-Pistachio Muffins, 338
    Orange Bundt Cake with Fruit Salad, 326
barley, 90
    Barley and Porcini Soup, 161
    Whole-Grain Olive Focaccia, 63
beans, 91, 233. *See also* chickpeas; fava (broad) beans; soybeans
    Bruschettas with Kale, Tomato, and White Beans, 23
    Buckwheat Pizza with Green Beans and Tomatoes, 72, **73**
    Cabbage Soup with Pasta and All the Beans, 169
    Cannellini and Black Bean Hummus, 20, **21**
    Composed Vegetable Salad with Tarragon Vinaigrette, 95
    cooking, 124
    Cornmeal and Vegetable Soup, 162, **163**
    Farmhouse Salad, 106
    Fresh Pasta and Beans in Tomato Broth, 168
    Genovese Minestrone, 164
    Green Beans with Tomato, 135
    Pasta Salad with Peas and Mint Pesto, 111
    Polenta with Kale and Beans, 304
    Pumpkin Stew with Adzuki Beans, 170, **171**
    Rice with Cabbage and Beans, 280, **281**
    Sautéed Vegetables with Sprouts and Seeds, 129
    for soups, 143
    Summer Vegetable Soup, 144, **145**
    Vegetable Fried Rice, 284, **285**
    White Beans and Tomato with Toast, 128
    Winter Salad with Mustard Dressing, 104, **105**
beets
    Beet and Fennel Gazpacho, 148, **149**
    Beet Torte, 260, **261**
    Composed Vegetable Salad with Tarragon Vinaigrette, 95

Fried Veggie Chips, 36, **37**
Millet Salad with Beets and Romanesco, 120
berries. *See also individual berries*
Berries with Granola and Almond Cream, 346, **347**
Frozen Berry Soufflés, 350, **351**
Blackberry Crostata, Peach-, 336
bok choy, 130
Vegetable Stir-Fry, 130, **131**
bread. *See also* focaccia; rolls
Basic Bread Dough, 74
Bread and Fruit Cake, 327
Bread and Potato Stew with Arugula, 160
Bread Dumplings in Broth, 204, **205**
Bread Gnocchi with Zucchini Salsa, 207
Bread Salad with Cucumbers and Tomatoes, 117
Bruschettas with Kale, Tomato, and White Beans, 23
Chickpea and Onion Flatbread, 266
Easter Cheese Bread, 68
Harvest Salad Sandwiches, 112, **113**
Hemp Sandwich Bread with Thyme and Pumpkin Seeds, 66, **67**
Herb-Stuffed Bread, 70, **71**
ingredients for, 52, 53
Kale-and-Potato Bread Soup, 158, **159**
nutrition and, 50, 181
Potato Flatbread with Salad, 54, **55**
Soda Bread with Seeds and Raisins, 58
Sourdough Farro Bread, 56, **57**
Tomato Strata, 302, **303**
Watercress Tartines, 24, **25**
breadsticks, 52
Ferrara Breadsticks, 64, **65**
broccoli
Broccoli, Kale, and Cauliflower Gratin, 296, **297**
Buckwheat Lasagna with Broccoli, 222, **223**
Cauliflower Custard with Broccoli and Walnuts, 42, **43**
Winter Salad with Mustard Dressing, 104, **105**
Winter Vegetable Soup, 156
bruschettas, 14
Bruschettas with Kale, Tomato, and White Beans, 23
Brussels Sprouts, Rice Gratin with Walnuts and, 291
buckwheat, 157, 210, 310
Millet and Buckwheat Soup, 157
Stuffed Cabbage with Buckwheat and Pumpkin, 310, **311**
buckwheat flour, 53, 178
Buckwheat Cannelloni with Eggplant, 201
Buckwheat Crêpe Cake with Chard and Artichokes, 210, **211**
Buckwheat Lasagna with Broccoli, 222, **223**
Buckwheat Pizza with Green Beans and Tomatoes, 72, **73**
Leek and Apple Quiche, 240
butter, 321

C
cabbage
Cabbage Soup with Pasta and All the Beans, 169
Genovese Minestrone, 164
Rice with Cabbage and Beans, 280, **281**
Stuffed Cabbage with Buckwheat and Pumpkin, 310, **311**
cakes, 322
Amaranth Cake with Caponata, 264, **265**
Bread and Fruit Cake, 327
Cashew-Milk Cheesecake, 340, **341**
Fruitcake, 334
Honey-Quinoa Cake, 330
Onion Bundt Cake, 46, **47**
Orange Bundt Cake with Fruit Salad, 326
Seeded Spice Cake, 328, **329**
Truffled Polenta Cake, 267
Whole-Grain Cake with Almond Butter, 324, **325**
calzones, 52
Kamut Calzone with Asparagus and Egg, 82, **83**
canapés, 14
Cannelloni, Buckwheat, with Eggplant, 201
cardoons, 305
Roasted Cardoons with Tomatoes and Pecorino, 305
carrots
Carrot and Paprika Soup, 152, **153**
Carrot Soup with Zucchini Salsa, 154
Fried Veggie Chips, 36, **37**
Rice Pilaf with Roasted Carrots and Asparagus, 278
Trio of Stuffed Vegetables with Avocado and Chickpeas, 308
Cashew-Milk Cheesecake, 340, **341**
cauliflower, 200
Baked Farro Gnocchi with Cauliflower, 200
Broccoli, Kale, and Cauliflower Gratin, 296, **297**
Cauliflower Custard with Broccoli and Walnuts, 42, **43**
Cauliflower Tart, 246
Composed Vegetable Salad with Tarragon Vinaigrette, 95
Pasta with Cauliflower and Pine Nuts, 186, **187**
Winter Salad with Mustard Dressing, 104, **105**
Winter Vegetable Soup, 156
celeriac
Rye Crêpe Noodles with Celeriac, 214, **215**
Winter Vegetable Soup, 156
cheese
Baked Fusilli with Tomato and Mozzarella, 225
Chestnut Crêpes with Sweet Peppers and Robiola Cheese, 220
Crêpes with Spinach and Ricotta, 217
Easter Cheese Bread, 68
Eggplant and Ricotta Lasagna, 224
Fava Bean Risotto with Pecorino, 286
Fried Turnovers with Tomato and Ricotta, 251
Oat, Spinach, and Ricotta Dumplings, 202, **203**
Ravioli with Ricotta, Spinach, and Marjoram, 212
ricotta, 181

Ricotta and Greens Dumplings, 206
Ricotta and Sweet Potato Tart, 263
Roasted Cardoons with Tomatoes and Pecorino,
    305
Spinach Quiche with Ricotta Salata, 237
Trio of Dips: Eggplant, Pea, and Robiola Cheese, 18
White Pizza, 78
Zucchini and Goat Cheese Frittata, 44
Zucchini and Halloumi Gratin, 314, **315**
Cherry Tart, Sour, 335
chestnut flour
    Chestnut Crêpes with Sweet Peppers and Robiola
        Cheese, 220
    Chestnut Lasagna with Squash and Kale, 226,
        227
chestnuts, 345
    Chestnut Pudding, 345
    Fava and Chestnut Pie, 257
chia seeds, 70
    Fava and Chia Pâté, 30
    Herb-Stuffed Bread, 70, **71**
chickpea flour
    Chickpea and Onion Flatbread, 266
    Mini Lentil and Chickpea Quiche, 236
chickpeas, 91, 233
    Black Chickpea Salad with Apple and Sunchoke,
        124
    Cabbage Soup with Pasta and All the Beans, 169
    Chard and Chickpea Soup with Tofu, 165
    Chickpea Ravioli with Tomato Sauce, 208, **209**
    Chickpea Soup with Tagliatelle, 155
    cooking, 124
    for soups, 143
    Sprouted Chickpea Hummus, 17
    Sprouted Lentil Salad with Three Dressings, 118,
        119
    Trio of Dips: Red Lentil, Fava Bean, and
        Chickpea, 22
    Trio of Stuffed Vegetables with Avocado and
        Chickpeas, 308
    Warm Couscous Salad with Tomatoes and
        Peppers, 107
chicories
    Quinoa Torte, 288, **289**
    Sautéed Chicories with Fava Purée, 125
chips (crisps), 15
    Fried Veggie Chips, 36, **37**
chocolate
    Chestnut Pudding, 345
    Chocolate Granola Bars, 332, **333**
    Fruitcake, 334
    Gnocchi with Cocoa and Raisins, 196
    raw, 332
cookies (biscuits), 322
    Almond-and-Honey Cookies, 331
coriander, 349
cornmeal, 53, 90
    Cornmeal and Vegetable Soup, 162, **163**
    Cornmeal-Millet Rolls, 59
    Polenta with Kale and Beans, 304

Truffled Polenta Cake, 267
corn pasta, 178
couscous
    Baked Farro Gnocchi with Cauliflower, 200
    Warm Couscous Salad with Tomatoes and
        Peppers, 107
crackers, 52
    Seeded Crackers with Shallots, 27
    Sunflower and Poppyseed Crackers, 26
crêpes
    Baked Crêpes with Tomato and Eggplant, 218,
        219
    Buckwheat Crêpe Cake with Chard and
        Artichokes, 210, **211**
    Chestnut Crêpes with Sweet Peppers and Robiola
        Cheese, 220
    Crêpes with Green Peas, 213
    Crêpes with Spinach and Ricotta, 217
    folding, 180
    ingredients for, 179, 180, 181
    Rye Crêpe Noodles with Celeriac, 214, **215**
croquettes, 272
crostatas
    Peach-Blackberry Crostata, 336, **337**
    Rye Crostata with Peas and Asparagus, 234, **235**
cucumbers
    Bread Salad with Cucumbers and Tomatoes, 117
    Harvest Salad Sandwiches, 112, **113**
custards
    Cauliflower Custard with Broccoli and Walnuts,
        42, **43**
    Mini Semolina Custards, 28, **29**

D
daikon, 130
    Fried Veggie Chips, 36, **37**
    Vegetable Stir-Fry, 130, **131**
desserts
    Almond-and-Honey Cookies, 331
    Avocado-Honey Parfait, 342, **343**
    Banana-Pistachio Muffins, 338
    Berries with Granola and Almond Cream, 346, **347**
    Bread and Fruit Cake, 327
    Cashew-Milk Cheesecake, 340, **341**
    Chestnut Pudding, 345
    Chocolate Granola Bars, 332, **333**
    Frozen Berry Soufflés, 350, **351**
    Fruitcake, 334
    Honey-Almond Nougat, 348
    Honey-Quinoa Cake, 330
    ingredients for, 323
    Mango-Papaya Tiramisu, 339
    nutrition and, 319–21
    Orange Bundt Cake with Fruit Salad, 326
    Rice Pudding with Fruit Compote, 344
    Seeded Spice Cake, 328, **329**
    Sour Cherry Tart, 335
    types of, 322
    Whole-Grain Cake with Almond Butter, 324, **325**
dips, 13

Cannellini and Black Bean Hummus, 20, **21**
Sprouted Chickpea Hummus, 17
Trio of Dips: Eggplant, Pea, and Robiola
   Cheese, 18
Trio of Dips: Red Lentil, Fava Bean, and
   Chickpea, 22
dumplings
   Bread Dumplings in Broth, 204, **205**
   Oat, Spinach, and Ricotta Dumplings, 202, **203**
   Ricotta and Greens Dumplings, 206

E
Easter Cheese Bread, 68
edamame, 15, 120, 276
   Millet Salad with Beets and Romanesco, 120
   Wild Rice Balls, 276, **277**
eggplants (aubergines)
   Amaranth Cake with Caponata, 264, **265**
   Baked Crêpes with Tomato and Eggplant, 218,
      219
   Buckwheat Cannelloni with Eggplant, 201
   Eggplant and Ricotta Lasagna, 224
   Eggplant-Tomato Strudel, 248, **249**
   Marinated Eggplant, 16, **17**
   Medley of Fried Snacks, 38, **39**
   Pasta Bundles with Ratatouille, 216
   Rice and Eggplant Casserole, 300
   Roasted Vegetable Salad, 96, **97**
   roasting, 201
   salting, 308
   Trio of Dips: Eggplant, Pea, and Robiola
      Cheese, 18
   Trio of Stuffed Vegetables with Avocado and
      Chickpeas, 308
   Vegetable Stew with Peppers and Tomatoes, 172
eggs, 181, 233
   Farro Salad with Poached Eggs, 108, **109**
   Kamut Calzone with Asparagus and Egg, 82, **83**
   Watercress Tartines, 24, **25**
   Zucchini and Goat Cheese Frittata, 44
elderberry syrup, 59
Escarole Stuffed with Olives and Capers, 312

Farmhouse Salad, 106
farro, 90
   Farro Salad with Olives and Tomatoes, 114, **115**
   Farro Salad with Poached Eggs, 108, **109**
farro (emmer) flour, 53
   Baked Farro Gnocchi with Cauliflower, 200
   Rye Crostata with Peas and Asparagus, 234, **235**
   Sourdough Farro Bread, 56, **57**
   Whole-Grain Olive Focaccia, 63
farro pasta, 178
   Farro Spaghetti with Vegetables and Fresh Herbs,
      184
   Whole Wheat Tagliatelle with Avocado Pesto, 182,
      183
fava (broad) beans, 91, 233
   Cabbage Soup with Pasta and All the Beans, 169

Fava and Chestnut Pie, 257
Fava and Chia Pâté, 30
Fava Bean Risotto with Pecorino, 286
Kamut Gnocchi with Fava Purée, 198, **199**
Pasta Salad with Peas and Mint Pesto, 111
Pasta with Favas and Peas, 190, **191**
Sautéed Chicories with Fava Purée, 125
Sauteed Spring Vegetables, 126, **127**
Spaghetti with Fava-Tomato Sauce, 189
Tomato Risotto with Spring Vegetables, 282
Trio of Dips: Red Lentil, Fava Bean, and Chickpea,
   22
fennel
   Artichoke and Fennel Fritters, 41
   Beet and Fennel Gazpacho, 148, **149**
   Fennel and Artichoke Salad, 92, **93**
   Fennel and Pink Grapefruit, 99
   Rice Salad with Artichokes and Fennel, 110
Ferrara Breadsticks, 64, **65**
figs
   Spiced Figs, 349
   Walnut, Fig, and Raisin Rolls, 60, **61**
flans, 14, 232
   Kale and Red Onion Flan, 31
flour, 50, 53, 320
focaccia, 52
   Onion Focaccia, 69
   Puglian Focaccia, 80, **81**
   Whole-Grain Olive Focaccia, 63
Frittata, Zucchini and Goat Cheese, 44
fritters
   Artichoke and Fennel Fritters, 41
   Tomato Rice Fritters, 35
fruits. *See also individual fruits*
   Bread and Fruit Cake, 327
   as dessert, 322, 323
   Fruitcake, 334
   Orange Bundt Cake with Fruit Salad, 326
   Rice Pudding with Fruit Compote, 344

G
Gazpacho, Beet and Fennel, 148, **149**
gnocchi, 179–80, 181
   Baked Farro Gnocchi with Cauliflower, 200
   Bread Gnocchi with Zucchini Salsa, 207
   Gnocchi with Cocoa and Raisins, 196
   Kamut Gnocchi with Fava Purée, 198, **199**
   Pumpkin Gnocchi with Almond-Sage Pesto, 194,
      195
   Saffron Gnocchi, 193
grains. *See also individual grains*
   nutrition and, 87
   for salads, 88, 90
   for savory pies, 233
   for soups, 142
granola
   Berries with Granola and Almond Cream, 346,
      347
   Chocolate Granola Bars, 332, **333**
Grapefruit, Pink, and Fennel, 99

gratins, 272
    Baked Wild Rice with Parsnip, 290
    Broccoli, Kale, and Cauliflower Gratin, 296, **297**
    Potato-Leek Gratin, 294
    Rice Gratin with Brussels Sprouts and Walnuts, 291
    Swiss Chard Gratin, 295
    Zucchini and Halloumi Gratin, 314, **315**
greens. *See also individual greens*
    Green Salad with Three Dressings, 94

H
Harvest Salad Sandwiches, 112, **113**
Hemp Sandwich Bread with Thyme and Pumpkin
    Seeds, 66, **67**
honey
    Honey-Almond Nougat, 348
    Honey-Quinoa Cake, 330
hummus
    Cannellini and Black Bean Hummus, 20, **21**
    Sprouted Chickpea Hummus, 17

K
kale
    Broccoli, Kale, and Cauliflower Gratin, 296, **297**
    Bruschettas with Kale, Tomato, and White
        Beans, 23
    Chestnut Lasagna with Squash and Kale, 226,
        227
    Cornmeal and Vegetable Soup, 162, **163**
    Kale-and-Potato Bread Soup, 158, **159**
    Kale and Red Onion Flan, 31
    Polenta with Kale and Beans, 304
Kamut flour, 53
    Kamut Calzone with Asparagus and Egg, 82, **83**
    Kamut Gnocchi with Fava Purée, 198, **199**
Kamut pasta, 178
    Pasta with Favas and Peas, 190, **191**

L
lasagna
    Buckwheat Lasagna with Broccoli, 222, **223**
    Chestnut Lasagna with Squash and Kale, 226, **227**
    Eggplant and Ricotta Lasagna, 224
leaveners, 321
leeks, 214
    Leek and Apple Quiche, 240
    Potato-Leek Gratin, 294
lentils, 91, 233
    Cabbage Soup with Pasta and All the Beans, 169
    Mini Lentil and Chickpea Quiche, 236
    for soups, 143
    Sprouted Lentil Salad with Three Dressings, 118,
        119
    Trio of Dips: Red Lentil, Fava Bean, and
        Chickpea, 22
Lettuce Soup, Pea and, 151

M
Mango-Papaya Tiramisu, 339

mayonnaise, vegan, 95
millet, 90, 157
    Cornmeal-Millet Rolls, 59
    Millet and Buckwheat Soup, 157
    Millet Salad with Beets and Romanesco, 120
    Millet-Stuffed Tomatoes and Zucchini, 313
minestrone, 141
Genovese Minestrone, 164
miso, 20
mousses, 13
muffins, 322
    Banana-Pistachio Muffins, 338
mushrooms
    Barley and Porcini Soup, 161
    Oat Flour Pizza with Mushroom-Stuffed Crusts,
        76, **77**
    Rice with Mushrooms and Tomatoes, 279
    Spinach and Mushroom Salad, 102
    Stuffed Artichokes with Quinoa and Mushrooms,
        306, **307**
    Tomato and Mushroom Stew, 173

N
nuts, 15. *See also individual nuts*

O
oats, 90
    Berries with Granola and Almond Cream, 346,
        347
    Oat Flour Pizza with Mushroom-Stuffed Crusts,
        76, **77**
    Oat, Spinach, and Ricotta Dumplings, 202. **203**
    Peach-Blackberry Crostata, 336, **337**
olives
    Escarole Stuffed with Olives and Capers, 312
    Farro Salad with Olives and Tomatoes, 114, **115**
    Flaky Onion and Tomato Roll, 252, **253**
    Fried Turnovers with Capers and Olives, 250
    oil, 321
    Rice Salad with Black Olives, 116
    Whole-Grain Olive Focaccia, 63
onions
    Chickpea and Onion Flatbread, 266
    Flaky Onion and Tomato Roll, 252, **253**
    Kale and Red Onion Flan, 31
    Onion and Potato Slab Pie, 256
    Onion Bundt Cake, 46, **47**
    Onion Focaccia, 69
oranges
    Orange Bundt Cake with Fruit Salad, 326
    Radicchio Risotto with Orange, 283

P
Papaya Tiramisu, Mango-, 339
Parfait, Avocado-Honey, 342, **343**
Parsnip, Baked Wild Rice with, 290
pasta and noodles. *See also* gnocchi
    au gratin, 177
    Baked Fusilli with Tomato and Mozzarella, 225

Baked Pasta with Sunchokes and Spinach, 221
Buckwheat Cannelloni with Eggplant, 201
Cabbage Soup with Pasta and All the Beans, 169
Chestnut Lasagna with Squash and Kale, 226, **227**
Chickpea Ravioli with Tomato Sauce, 208, **209**
Chickpea Soup with Tagliatelle, 155
cooking, 176
dried, 176
Eggplant and Ricotta Lasagna, 224
Farro Spaghetti with Vegetables and Fresh Herbs, 184
Fresh Pasta and Beans in Tomato Broth, 168
Genovese Minestrone, 164
homemade, 176
ingredients for, 178
Pappardelle with Walnuts, 188
Pasta Bundles with Ratatouille, 216
Pasta Salad with Peas and Mint Pesto, 111
Pasta Salad with Tomato and Avocado, 121
Pasta with Cauliflower and Pine Nuts, 186, **187**
Pasta with Favas and Peas, 190, **191**
Pasta with Parsley and Breadcrumbs, 192
Pici with Walnut Pesto, 185
Ravioli with Ricotta, Spinach, and Marjoram, 212
Rye Crêpe Noodles with Celeriac, 214, **215**
Spaghetti with Fava-Tomato Sauce, 189
Sweet Spiced Tortelli, 197
Whole Wheat Tagliatelle with Avocado Pesto, 182, **183**
Winter Vegetable Soup, 156
pâtés, 13
Fava and Chia Pâté, 30
peaches
Cashew-Milk Cheesecake, 340, **341**
Peach-Blackberry Crostata, 336, **337**
peas, 91, 213, 233
Crêpes with Green Peas, 213
Green Risotto with Peas, 287
Pasta Salad with Peas and Mint Pesto, 111
Pasta with Favas and Peas, 190, **191**
Pea and Lettuce Soup, 151
Rice Balls, 40
Rye Crostata with Peas and Asparagus, 234, **235**
Sauteed Spring Vegetables, 126, **127**
for soups, 143
Tomato Risotto with Spring Vegetables, 282
Trio of Dips: Eggplant, Pea, and Robiola Cheese, 18
Vegetable Fried Rice, 284, **285**
peppers
Chestnut Crêpes with Sweet Peppers and Robiola Cheese, 220
Farro Spaghetti with Vegetables and Fresh Herbs, 184
Pasta Bundles with Ratatouille, 216
Rice Timbale with Zucchini and Peppers, 298, **299**
Roasted Vegetable Salad, 96, **97**
Sweet-and-Sour Stuffed Peppers, 317
Tomato and Sweet Pepper Soup, 147
Upside-Down Pumpkin and Pepper Tart, 238, **239**

Vegetable Fried Rice, 284, **285**
Vegetable Stew with Peppers and Tomatoes, 172
Warm Couscous Salad with Tomatoes and Peppers, 107
pies, savory, 229–33
Artichoke Pie, 258, **259**
Fava and Chestnut Pie, 257
Onion and Potato Slab Pie, 256
Radicchio Pie, 254, **255**
Swiss Chard and Potato Pie, 262
pilafs, 272
Rice Pilaf with Roasted Carrots and Asparagus, 278
pine nuts
Fruitcake, 334
Pasta with Cauliflower and Pine Nuts, 186, **187**
Zucchini and Pine Nut Tart, 242, **243**
pistachios
Banana-Pistachio Muffins, 338
Rice Balls, 40
pizza, 52
Buckwheat Pizza with Green Beans and Tomatoes, 72, **73**
Oat Flour Pizza with Mushroom-Stuffed Crusts, 76, **77**
Potato Pizza, 79
Tomato Pizza, 75
White Pizza, 78
polenta. *See* cornmeal
potatoes, 181
Artichoke, Potato, and Rice Casserole, 301
Bread and Potato Stew with Arugula, 160
Farmhouse Salad, 106
Kale-and-Potato Bread Soup, 158, **159**
Medley of Fried Snacks, 38, **39**
Onion and Potato Slab Pie, 256
Potato Flatbread with Salad, 54, **55**
Potato-Leek Gratin, 294
Potato Pizza, 79
Spring Ratatouille, 132, **133**
Stuffed Squash Blossoms, 316
Summer Vegetable Soup, 144, **145**
Swiss Chard and Potato Pie, 262
Vegetable Stew with Peppers and Tomatoes, 172
Winter Salad with Mustard Dressing, 104, **105**
puddings
Chestnut Pudding, 345
Rice Pudding with Fruit Compote, 344
Puglian Focaccia, 80, **81**
pumpkin
Chestnut Lasagna with Squash and Kale, 226, **227**
Pumpkin Gnocchi with Almond-Sage Pesto, 194, **195**
Pumpkin Stew with Adzuki Beans, 170, **171**
Pumpkin Tart, 244, **245**
Stuffed Cabbage with Buckwheat and Pumpkin, 310, **311**
Upside-Down Pumpkin and Pepper Tart, 238, **239**
Winter Vegetable Soup, 156

Q

quiches, 232
    Leek and Apple Quiche, 240
    Mini Lentil and Chickpea Quiche, 236
    Spinach Quiche with Ricotta Salata, 237
quinoa, 45, 53
    Chocolate Granola Bars, 332, **333**
    Honey-Quinoa Cake, 330
    Quinoa Torte, 288, **289**
    Stuffed Artichokes with Quinoa and Mushrooms, 306, **307**
    Vegetable and Quinoa Tartare, 45

R

radicchio
    Black Chickpea Salad with Apple and Sunchoke, 124
    Potato Flatbread with Salad, 54, **55**
    Radicchio Pie, 254, **255**
    Radicchio Risotto with Orange, 283
    Winter Salad with Mustard Dressing, 104, **105**
raisins
    Baked Farro Gnocchi with Cauliflower, 200
    Berries with Granola and Almond Cream, 346, **347**
    Bread and Fruit Cake, 327
    Fruitcake, 334
    Gnocchi with Cocoa and Raisins, 196
    Pasta with Cauliflower and Pine Nuts, 186, **187**
    Raisin and Rosemary Rolls, 62
    Soda Bread with Seeds and Raisins, 58
    Sweet Spiced Tortelli, 197
    Walnut, Fig, and Raisin Rolls, 60, **61**
raspberries
    Frozen Berry Soufflés, 350, **351**
    Orange Bundt Cake with Fruit Salad, 326
ratatouille
    Pasta Bundles with Ratatouille, 216
    Spring Ratatouille, 132, **133**
ravioli
    Chickpea Ravioli with Tomato Sauce, 208, **209**
    Ravioli with Ricotta, Spinach, and Marjoram, 212
rice, 90
    Artichoke, Potato, and Rice Casserole, 301
    Chocolate Granola Bars, 332, **333**
    cooking methods for, 272
    cooking times for, 271
    Fava Bean Risotto with Pecorino, 286
    flour, 53
    Green Risotto with Peas, 287
    nutrition and, 270
    Radicchio Risotto with Orange, 283
    Rice and Eggplant Casserole, 300
    Rice Balls, 40
    Rice Gratin with Brussels Sprouts and Walnuts, 291
    Rice Pilaf with Roasted Carrots and Asparagus, 278
    Rice Pudding with Fruit Compote, 344
    Rice Salad with Artichokes and Fennel, 110
    Rice Salad with Black Olives, 116

    Rice Timbale with Zucchini and Peppers, 298, **299**
    Rice with Cabbage and Beans, 280, **281**
    Rice with Mushrooms and Tomatoes, 279
    Seedy Basmati Rice, 292, **293**
    Summer Vegetable Soup, 144, **145**
    Tomato Rice Fritters, 35
    Tomato Risotto with Spring Vegetables, 282
    types of, 275
    Vegetable Fried Rice, 284, **285**
    Warm Black Rice Salad with Tofu, 122, **123**
    Wild Rice Balls, 276, **277**
    Zucchini and Rice Galette, 241
risotto, 272
    Fava Bean Risotto with Pecorino, 286
    Green Risotto with Peas, 287
    Radicchio Risotto with Orange, 283
    Tomato Risotto with Spring Vegetables, 282
rolls
    Cornmeal-Millet Rolls, 59
    Flaky Onion and Tomato Roll, 252, **253**
    Raisin and Rosemary Rolls, 62
    Walnut, Fig, and Raisin Rolls, 60, **61**
Romanesco, Millet Salad with Beets and, 120
rye flour, 53
    Rye Crêpe Noodles with Celeriac, 214, **215**

S

Saffron Gnocchi, 193
sage, 194
salads
    as appetizers, 14
    Asparagus and Herb Salad, 103
    Avocado Salad, 100, **101**
    Baby Zucchini Salad, 98
    Black Chickpea Salad with Apple and Sunchoke, 124
    Bread Salad with Cucumbers and Tomatoes, 117
    Composed Vegetable Salad with Tarragon Vinaigrette, 95
    Farmhouse Salad, 106
    Farro Salad with Olives and Tomatoes, 114, **115**
    Farro Salad with Poached Eggs, 108, **109**
    Fennel and Artichoke Salad, 92, **93**
    Fennel and Pink Grapefruit, 99
    Green Salad with Three Dressings, 94
    Harvest Salad Sandwiches, 112, **113**
    ingredients for, 86, 88–89
    Millet Salad with Beets and Romanesco, 120
    Pasta Salad with Peas and Mint Pesto, 111
    Pasta Salad with Tomato and Avocado, 121
    Potato Flatbread with Salad, 54, **55**
    Rice Salad with Artichokes and Fennel, 110
    Rice Salad with Black Olives, 116
    Roasted Vegetable Salad, 96, **97**
    Spinach and Mushroom Salad, 102
    Sprouted Lentil Salad with Three Dressings, 118, **119**
    Warm Asparagus Salad, 136, **137**
    Warm Black Rice Salad with Tofu, 122, **123**
    Warm Couscous Salad with Tomatoes and Peppers, 107

Winter Salad with Mustard Dressing, 104, **105**
Sandwiches, Harvest Salad, 112, **113**
seaweed, 15
seeds, 323
    Sautéed Vegetables with Sprouts and Seeds, 129
    Seeded Crackers with Shallots, 27
    Seeded Spice Cake, 328, **329**
    Seedy Basmati Rice, 292, **293**
    Soda Bread with Seeds and Raisins, 58
    Sunflower and Poppyseed Crackers, 26
seitan, 230
    Rice Balls, 40
    Tomato and Mushroom Stew, 173
semolina, 193
Soda Bread with Seeds and Raisins, 58
Soufflés, Frozen Berry, 350, **351**
soups
    Barley and Porcini Soup, 161
    Beet and Fennel Gazpacho, 148, **149**
    boosting flavor of, 140
    Cabbage Soup with Pasta and All the Beans, 169
    Carrot and Paprika Soup, 152, **153**
    Carrot Soup with Zucchini Salsa, 154
    Chard and Chickpea Soup with Tofu, 165
    Chickpea Soup with Tagliatelle, 155
    Cornmeal and Vegetable Soup, 162, **163**
    Cream of Asparagus Soup, 146
    Fresh Pasta and Beans in Tomato Broth, 168
    Genovese Minestrone, 164
    Green Creamed Soup, 150
    ingredients for, 142–43
    Kale-and-Potato Bread Soup, 158, **159**
    Millet and Buckwheat Soup, 157
    nutrition and, 140
    Pea and Lettuce Soup, 151
    styles of, 141
    Summer Vegetable Soup, 144, **145**
    Tofu and Vegetable Soup, 166, **167**
    Tomato and Sweet Pepper Soup, 147
    Winter Vegetable Soup, 156
sourdough starter, 51, 56
    Sourdough Farro Bread, 56, **57**
soybeans, 91. *See also* edamame
spices, 323
spinach
    Baked Pasta with Sunchokes and Spinach, 221
    Crêpes with Spinach and Ricotta, 217
    Herb-Stuffed Bread, 70, **71**
    Oat, Spinach, and Ricotta Dumplings, 202, **203**
    Pasta Salad with Tomato and Avocado, 121
    Ravioli with Ricotta, Spinach, and Marjoram, 212
    Sautéed Vegetables with Sprouts and Seeds, 129
    Spinach and Mushroom Salad, 102
    Spinach Quiche with Ricotta Salata, 237
    Tofu and Vegetable Soup, 166, **167**
squash blossoms (courgette flowers)
    Fried Squash Blossoms with Tofu and Capers, 34
    Stuffed Squash Blossoms, 316
stock, vegetable, 142
Strata, Tomato, 302

strawberries
    Frozen Berry Soufflés, 350, **351**
strudels, 232
    Artichoke and Zucchini Strudel, 247
    Eggplant-Tomato Strudel, 248, **249**
sugar, alternatives to, 320
sunchokes (Jerusalem artichokes)
    Baked Pasta with Sunchokes and Spinach, 221
    Black Chickpea Salad with Apple and Sunchoke, 124
    Sweet Potato Tart, Ricotta and, 263
    Swiss chard
    Buckwheat Crêpe Cake with Chard and Artichokes, 210, **211**
    Chard and Chickpea Soup with Tofu, 165
    Genovese Minestrone, 164
    Kale-and-Potato Bread Soup, 158, **159**
    Ricotta and Greens Dumplings, 206
    Summer Vegetable Soup, 144, **145**
    Swiss Chard and Potato Pie, 262
    Swiss Chard Gratin, 295

T
tahini, 118
Tartines, Watercress, 24, **25**
tarts and tartlets, 232
    Cauliflower Tart, 246
    Pumpkin Tart, 244, **245**
    Ricotta and Sweet Potato Tart, 263
    Sour Cherry Tart, 335
    Tomato Tartlets, 32, **33**
    Upside-Down Pumpkin and Pepper Tart, 238, **239**
    Zucchini and Pine Nut Tart, 242, **243**
    Zucchini and Rice Galette, 241
tatins, 232
tempeh, 230, 256
    Onion and Potato Slab Pie, 256
terrines, 13
timbales, 272
    Rice and Eggplant Casserole, 300
    Rice Timbale with Zucchini and Peppers, 298, **299**
tofu, 15, 230
    Chard and Chickpea Soup with Tofu, 165
    Fava and Chia Pâté, 30
    Fried Squash Blossoms with Tofu and Capers, 34
    Kale and Red Onion Flan, 31
    Radicchio Risotto with Orange, 283
    Tofu and Vegetable Soup, 166, **167**
    Vegetable Stir-Fry, 130, **131**
    Warm Black Rice Salad with Tofu, 122, **123**
tomatoes
    Baked Crêpes with Tomato and Eggplant, 218, **219**
    Baked Fusilli with Tomato and Mozzarella, 225
    Bread Salad with Cucumbers and Tomatoes, 117
    Bruschettas with Kale, Tomato, and White Beans, 23
    Buckwheat Pizza with Green Beans and Tomatoes, 72, **73**
    Chickpea Ravioli with Tomato Sauce, 208, **209**

Chickpea Ravioli with Tomato Sauce, 208, **209**
Eggplant-Tomato Strudel, 248, **249**
Farro Salad with Olives and Tomatoes, 114, **115**
Flaky Onion and Tomato Roll, 252, **253**
Fresh Pasta and Beans in Tomato Broth, 168
Fried Turnovers with Tomato and Ricotta, 251
Green Beans with Tomato, 135
Harvest Salad Sandwiches, 112, **113**
Herby Stuffed Tomatoes, 309
Medley of Fried Snacks, 38, **39**
Millet-Stuffed Tomatoes and Zucchini, 313
Pasta Bundles with Ratatouille, 216
Pasta Salad with Tomato and Avocado, 121
Puglian Focaccia, 80, **81**
Rice with Mushrooms and Tomatoes, 279
Roasted Balsamic Tomatoes, 134
Roasted Cardoons with Tomatoes and Pecorino,
   305
Roasted Vegetable Salad, 96, **97**
Saffron Gnocchi, 193
Spaghetti with Fava-Tomato Sauce, 189
Spring Ratatouille, 132, **133**
Summer Vegetable Soup, 144, **145**
Tomato and Mushroom Stew, 173
Tomato and Sweet Pepper Soup, 147
Tomato Pizza, 75
Tomato Rice Fritters, 35
Tomato Risotto with Spring Vegetables, 282
Tomato Strata, 302, **303**
Tomato Tartlets, 32, **33**
Vegetable and Quinoa Tartare, 45
Vegetable Stew with Peppers and Tomatoes, 172
Warm Couscous Salad with Tomatoes and
   Peppers, 107
White Beans and Tomato with Toast, 128
Tortelli, Sweet Spiced, 197
tortes
   Beet Torte, 260, **261**
   Quinoa Torte, 288, **289**
truffles, 267
   Truffled Polenta Cake, 267
turnovers
   Fried Turnovers with Capers and Olives, 250
   Fried Turnovers with Tomato and Ricotta, 251

V
vegetables. *See also individual vegetables*
   Composed Vegetable Salad with Tarragon
   Vinaigrette, 95
   cooking methods for, 272–73
   Cornmeal and Vegetable Soup, 162, **163**
   Farro Spaghetti with Vegetables and Fresh Herbs,
      184
   Fried Veggie Chips, 36, **37**
   raw, 87
   Roasted Vegetable Salad, 96, **97**
   Sauteed Spring Vegetables, 126, **127**
   Sautéed Vegetables with Sprouts and Seeds, 129
   for savory pies, 233
   seasonal, 274
   for soups, 142
   steamed, 87, 270
   stuffed, 272
   Summer Vegetable Soup, 144, **145**
   Tofu and Vegetable Soup, 166, **167**
   Tomato Risotto with Spring Vegetables, 282
   Trio of Stuffed Vegetables with Avocado and
   Chickpeas, 308
   Vegetable and Quinoa Tartare, 45
   Vegetable Fried Rice, 284, **285**
   Vegetable Stew with Peppers and Tomatoes, 172
   Vegetable Stir-Fry, 130, **131**
   Winter Vegetable Soup, 156

W
walnuts, 42
   Cauliflower Custard with Broccoli and Walnuts,
      42, **43**
   Pappardelle with Walnuts, 188
   Pici with Walnut Pesto, 185
   Rice Gratin with Brussels Sprouts and Walnuts,
      291
   Walnut, Fig, and Raisin Rolls, 60, **61**
watercress
   Green Creamed Soup, 150
   Watercress Tartines, 24, **25**
wheat, 53, 90
wheat germ, 292
wild rice, 290
   Baked Wild Rice with Parsnip, 290

Z
zucchini (courgettes). *See also* squash blossoms
   (courgette flowers)
   Artichoke and Zucchini Strudel, 247
   Baby Zucchini Salad, 98
   Barley and Porcini Soup, 161
   Bread Gnocchi with Zucchini Salsa, 207
   Carrot Soup with Zucchini Salsa, 154
   Farro Spaghetti with Vegetables and Fresh Herbs,
      184
   Millet-Stuffed Tomatoes and Zucchini, 313
   Pasta Bundles with Ratatouille, 216
   Rice Timbale with Zucchini and Peppers, 298, **299**
   Sautéed Vegetables with Sprouts and Seeds, 129
   Spring Ratatouille, 132, **133**
   Tofu and Vegetable Soup, 166, **167**
   Tomato Risotto with Spring Vegetables, 282
   Trio of Stuffed Vegetables with Avocado and
      Chickpeas, 308
   Vegetable and Quinoa Tartare, 45
   Warm Asparagus Salad, 136, **137**
   Zucchini and Goat Cheese Frittata, 44
   Zucchini and Halloumi Gratin, 314, **315**
   Zucchini and Pine Nut Tart, 242, **243**
   Zucchini and Rice Galette, 241

Recipe Notes

Butter should always be unsalted.

Pepper is always freshly ground black pepper, unless otherwise specified.

Eggs, vegetables and fruits are assumed to be medium size, unless otherwise specified.

Milk is always whole, unless otherwise specified.

Garlic cloves are assumed to be large; use two if yours are small.

Cooking and preparation times are for guidance only, as individual ovens vary. If using a fan oven, follow the manufacturer's instructions concerning oven temperatures.

To test whether your deep-frying oil is hot enough, add a cube of stale bread. If it browns in thirty seconds, the temperature is 350–375°F (180–190°C), about right for most frying. Exercise caution when deep frying: add the food carefully to avoid splashing, wear long sleeves, and never leave the pan unattended.

Some recipes include raw or very lightly cooked eggs. These should be avoided particularly by the elderly, infants, pregnant women, convalescents, and anyone with an impaired immune system.

All spoon measurements are level. 1 teaspoon = 5 ml

1 tablespoon = 15 ml. Australian standard tablespoons are 20 ml, so Australian readers are advised to use 3 teaspoons in place of 1 tablespoon when measuring small quantities.

Phaidon Press Limited
Regent's Wharf
All Saints Street
London N1 9PA

Phaidon Press Inc.
65 Bleecker Street
New York, NY 10012

phaidon.com

First published 2020
© 2020 Phaidon Press Limited

ISBN 978 1 83866 058 1

A CIP catalogue record for this book is available from
the British Library and the Library of Congress.

The Vegetarian Silver Spoon originates from *Il
cucchiaio d'argento vegetariano*, first published in
2017, *Il cucchiaio d'argento: estate*, first published
in 2005, and *Il cucchiaio d'argento*, first published
in 1950, eighth edition (revised, expanded, and
updates in 1997) © Editoriale Domus S.p.a.

Commissioning Editor: Emilia Terragni
Project Editor: Anne Goldberg
Production Controller: Abigail Draycott
Design: Pentagram
Photography: Simon Bajada

Printed in Italy